SONIC SPACE IN
DJIBRIL DIOP MAMBETY'S FILMS

AFRICAN EXPRESSIVE CULTURES

Patrick McNaughton, *editor*

Associate editors
Catherine M. Cole
Barbara G. Hoffman
Eileen Julien
Kassim Koné
D. A. Masolo
Elisha Renne
Zoë Strother

SONIC SPACE IN DJIBRIL DIOP MAMBETY'S FILMS

Vlad Dima

Indiana University Press

Bloomington & Indianapolis

This book is a publication of

Indiana University Press
Office of Scholarly Publishing
Herman B Wells Library 350
1320 East 10th Street
Bloomington, Indiana 47405 USA

iupress.indiana.edu

© 2017 by Vlad Dima

All rights reserved

No part of this book may be reproduced or utilized in any form or by any means, electronic or mechanical, including photocopying and recording, or by any information storage and retrieval system, without permission in writing from the publisher. The Association of American University Presses' Resolution on Permissions constitutes the only exception to this prohibition.

The paper used in this publication meets the minimum requirements of the American National Standard for Information Sciences—Permanence of Paper for Printed Library Materials, ANSI Z39.48-1992.

Manufactured in the United States of America

Library of Congress Cataloging-in-Publication Data

Names: Dima, Vlad author.
Title: Sonic space in Djibril Diop Mambety's films / Vlad Dima.
Description: Bloomington : Indiana University
Press, 2017. | Series: African
    expressive cultures | In filmography. | Includes bibliographical references and index.
Identifiers: LCCN 2016025320 (print) | LCCN 2016044070 (ebook) | ISBN 9780253024213 (cloth : alk. paper) | ISBN 9780253024268 (pbk. : alk. paper) | ISBN 9780253024336 (ebook)
Subjects: LCSH: Diop Mambéty, Djibril, 1945-1998—Criticism and interpretation. | Sound in motion pictures.
Classification: LCC PN1998.3.D56 D56 2017
(print) | LCC PN1998.3.D56 (ebook)
    | DDC 791.4302/33092—dc23
LC record available at https://lccn.loc.gov/2016025320

1 2 3 4 5   21 20 19 18 17

To my American mothers,
Judy S. and Eileen S.

Contents

Acknowledgments — ix

Introduction: Aural Contexts — 1

1 Aural Space and the Sonic Rack Focus in *Touki Bouki* — 41

2 Flaneur, Geography, and *Caméra-Flâneur* in *Badou Boy* and *Contras' City* — 74

3 Trauma and Zombie Narratives in *Hyènes* — 106

4 Voice(s) in *Le franc* and *La petite vendeuse de soleil* — 144

Gallery of Film Stills — 180

Conclusion: Current Contexts and Legacies — 190

Notes — 201

Bibliography — 215

Filmography — 225

Index — 227

Acknowledgments

I MUST BEGIN THE acknowledgements with Charles Sugnet, in whose African cinema course I first began to think about sound and Mambety. Also, at the University of Minnesota–Twin Cities, I would like to thank Mária Brewer, Eileen Sivert, and Christophe Wall-Romana for their patience, scholarship contribution, and friendship. Eileen and Christophe were instrumental in the development of the early stages of this study; in particular, Christophe contributed his film expertise and knack for new terminology. A special thank you goes to Alan Smith, who first sparked my curiosity in all things cinema.

At the University of Wisconsin–Madison, I owe a huge debt to my colleague Richard Goodkin, who carefully read over different drafts of this study. I also want to acknowledge the contributions of Aliko Songolo and Steven Winspur. Even though Steven has tragically departed, he has remained a tremendous source of inspiration to me.

Infinite thanks go to my editor at the University of Indiana Press, Dee Mortensen, her team (Paige Rasmussen, Rachel Rosolina, Jim Cappio), and the anonymous readers who were extremely generous with their time and comments. This project is much better because of them.

I also want to acknowledge a series of people who have played important roles in my development as a scholar throughout my life: Dumitru Neagu, Valentin Sgarcea, Mirela Ghinea, Marina Nicolau, Judith Sarnecki, Eilene Hoft-March, Lifongo Vetinde, and Mark Dintenfass. Finally, I would like to thank my family for their constant, unwavering love and support, without which none of these words would have been written.

SONIC SPACE IN
DJIBRIL DIOP MAMBETY'S FILMS

Introduction
Aural Contexts

SEVERAL ICONIC IMAGES come to mind when one thinks about Djibril Diop Mambety's films: a boy and a kora, a motorcycle with the horns of an ox adorning the handlebars, hyenas, a young girl's face superimposed on the running printing press of a journal, a door with a winning lottery ticket. The last example comes from *Le franc* (1994),[1] a short from an unfinished trilogy about people at the margins of society. The film follows Marigo as he attempts to retrieve his beloved musical instrument from the possession of a landlady. In the process, he strikes it rich by winning the lottery. The character's journey is a suitable metaphor for Mambety's career. The value of his films certainly owes a debt to the visual, but what renders his work unique is an elusive element that goes beyond the image: sound. It is Mambety's prized instrument and the tool that allows him to introduce the audience to an entirely new scale of stories.

Mambety is a quintessential storyteller and that quality comes through most forcefully from an insistence on pushing sound to the narrative foreground. The way sound is constructed and manipulated in his work suggests the creation of new narrative planes—what I call aural narrative planes—that continue the oral tradition of layered African stories. The specificity of Mambety's cinema then lies in the tension created between the visual narrative and the aural narrative, which potentially leads to a fusion of Western and West African sociohistorical traditions. This study surveys the entirety of Mambety's body of fictional work by focusing on the role that sound plays in these films.[2] Once sound emerges as a primary narrative tool, it also takes on phantasmagoric qualities, and separately a corporeal quality. The latter is a physical presence of sorts that challenges traditional cinematic uses of sound and soundtrack. Ultimately, sound generates several types of space—phantasmagoric, diegetic (heard by both audience and actors), and one that both envelops and breaks the fourth wall, an extradiegetic kind (heard just by the audience)—that are in constant dialogue. The stories that

1

stem from these spaces and aural narrative planes bridge Western practices of cinema and the oral tradition of West African storytelling in order to create a new cinematic aesthetic that pushes Africa to the foreground of artistic creativity. Mambety addresses the reason he consciously sought to mesh the two in the following way: "It is good for the future of cinema that Africa exists. Cinema was born in Africa, because the image itself was born in Africa. The instruments, yes, are European, but the creative necessity and rationale exist in our oral tradition.... Oral tradition is a tradition of images.... Imagination creates the image and the image creates cinema, so we are in direct lineage as cinema's parents" (Ukadike 2002, 128–129). This is an incredible declaration that paves the way toward the materialization of phantasmagoric spaces, because in spite of the several references to images, the implication of Mambety's words is that sound (that of the oral stories) generates images. Furthermore, it is probably safe to assume that the word "instruments" refers equally to actual European tools of filmmaking and to European practices of cinema, which have a long history of engagement with the narrative role of sound at creative and critical levels.

For example, French theorist André Bazin believed that with the advent of the talkies, cinema became something new, something that would come closest to fulfilling the myth of a total cinema (1967, 23–26). The image changed because it had sound attached to it. Suddenly cinema was perceived differently. The relationship between image and sound has been a thorny subject in film theory, and only in the last couple of decades has sound claimed its rightful place as a crucial element in our understanding and analysis of cinema. This work has mostly been done in the context of Western cinema (Hollywood, experimental, auteur, etc.). However, an argument can be made that sound is considerably more important in Third Cinema—a militant and political type of cinema. More precisely, Mambety *revolutionizes* the use of sound in the sociocultural context of Senegal, a country indelibly marked by postcolonial political complications. Sound achieves enough narrative power that it often becomes the primary means for telling a story and the image can disappear behind it, as opposed to the traditional way of thinking about this dynamic (i.e., image first, sound second). As we shall see, the idea that sound holds power bespeaks an alternative to Michel Foucault's panopticon, the classic *visual* metaphor for disciplinary power and knowledge: the acousmatic panopticon. The point is that even though the image never relinquishes its narrative powers completely, its impact can be drastically reduced by the emergence of sound, which is able to mediate postcolonial relationships of power. By emphasizing the development of the aural narrative capabilities of sound in cinema, Mambety offers the postcolonial subject and the postcolonial spectator the possibility of reappropriating both a lost space and a complex identity through sound. In other words, from the exploration of Mambetian sound it will be established that the sonic component of Third Cinema is a key element in the construction of a fundamental postcolonial fantasy meant both to protect and to navigate through the delicate balance of postcolonial subjectivity.

Djibril Diop Mambety was born in 1945, during a period of great unrest in Senegal,[3] and he died in 1998 of lung cancer. There is sparse information regarding his early life, but a patchy biography can be put together, especially when one takes Mambety's few but candid interviews into consideration. Of particular importance in this endeavor are Sada Niang's illuminating book, *Djibril Diop Mambety: un cinéaste à contre-courant* (2002),[4] and Nwachukwu Frank Ukadike's interview published in 2002 (*Questioning African Cinema*, 121–132). To great narrative effect, Niang's book alternates evocative passages with keen observations on Mambety's films. While Niang's writing seems to marvel constantly at Mambety's prowess as a filmmaker, it also provides the reader with analytical insights that make the book an important starting point for any scholarly work on the director. The general consensus in the extant literature on the filmmaker is that he was supremely gifted, a precocious talent, mercurial, and more substantially, that he represents a revolutionary approach to the aesthetics of African cinema—an avant-garde director with a Marxist tinge.[5]

Niang traces Mambety's early trajectory toward becoming a revolutionary figure in film aesthetics: young Mambety grows up in an ethnically diverse neighborhood in Dakar called Colobane, spends a considerable part of his childhood in the Gueule Tapée neighborhood,[6] joins a theater group at age eleven, attends the Blaise Diagne high school, and without prior formal training in filmmaking makes *Contras' City* (1968) at the age of twenty-four (2002, 23–32). Mambety had already attempted to shoot *Badou Boy* two years prior (Pfaff 1988, 218; Murphy and Williams 2007, 91–92), but the result was unsatisfactory and soon discarded. The failure of this first try did not discourage the young filmmaker, but it may have contributed to his developing a reluctance of sorts, a constant questioning of his relationship with filmmaking. In fact, he goes as far as to tell Ukadike that he favors acting over directing (2002, 124). In an earlier book, *Black African Cinema* (1994), Ukadike's first reference to Mambety is actually as "a famous Senegalese actor" (84) who performed at the Daniel Sorano Theater in Dakar. This acting job did not last, as Mambety proved "undisciplined" (Ukadike 2002, 121) and was let go. Similarly, Niang suggests that young Mambety hated the discipline and rules of high school, and preferred learning about life in the streets of Dakar (2002, 33). Both elements—the indiscipline and the penchant for the life of the streets—will later play a crucial role in Mambety's actual filmmaking practices, the former as a form of revolt against cinematic rules and the latter as his preferred subject matter.

Nevertheless, perhaps "revolt" is not a sufficiently nuanced word, as Mambety expresses the hope that "Africans, in particular, must reinvent cinema" (Ukadike

2002, 123). Moreover, in speaking of *Hyènes* (1992), he declares, "I have a great desire to demystify cinema.... Africa is rich in cinema, in images. Hollywood could not have made this film" (Ukadike 2002, 125). The Western traditions Mambety particularly aims to avoid are in fact those of classical Hollywood cinema. As a component of First Cinema,[7] classical Hollywood cinema presents a set of fairly rigid conventions that can be juxtaposed to the aesthetics of Mambety to great effect. Furthermore, the fact that he starts making films during the late 1960s in Senegal, a country dealing with the political ripple effects of independence, pushes him toward Third Cinema. On the other hand, some of these rules and conventions are inescapably followed in Mambety's films as well. One could also argue that his filmmaking abilities entrench him solidly in the auteur category.

In truth, categorizing Mambety is not the goal of this book. Instead, I propose to treat his entire career as one long flash of genius that has altered cinema itself. It would not be wrong to situate Mambety within the realm of any of the cinema traditions mentioned above,[8] or to analyze him in contrast with Ousmane Sembène—the forefather of African cinema—or to look at some obvious technical similarities with Jean-Luc Godard and his montage, or to look even further back at Sergei Eisenstein's intellectual montage. Historically, Mambety must be placed in the context of the ongoing postcolonial discussion; one may even be tempted to throw in the overused "postmodern" label, although it is perhaps better to avoid this term, as theorist Clyde Taylor proposes.[9] In spite of the fact that there is no need for such categorization, one cannot consider Mambety's oeuvre in a vacuum, even if one thinks that he is a transcendental director. So inevitably, every category, label, and influence noted in this paragraph will be revisited in more depth. In particular, several references will be made to the cinema of the auteur, the New Wave, and Godard to facilitate the transition from theorizing Western sound to theorizing Senegalese sound. While this book proposes new ways of analyzing (and listening to) sound in cinema, an equally important goal is to excavate Mambety's entire filmmaking career to justify the claim that he is a vastly important figure not only in Senegalese or African cinema but also in all of cinema—a veritable enfant terrible. To that end, the next part of the introduction focuses on situating the director within the loose confines of the following geographical and aesthetic levels: Senegal and West Africa; world cinema as represented by Third, Second, and First Cinemas; and these traditions' respective aesthetics.

Third Cinema and Mambety

The flexibility that characterizes sound in Mambety's films is not unique. For example, the French New Wave directors, particularly Godard, also stressed the importance of sound. Like Godard's in the French context, Mambety's films prove to be original among his Senegalese peers and in the larger context of African cinema. Mambety's work is heavily stylized and characterized by pastiche and a collage of genres; as an oppositional cinema it turns to parody, favoring smaller-scale stories. Emerging from the particular and from marginality, these films share thematic trends such as locomotion, comings and goings, physical and mental exiles, sounds and voices. Unlike Godard and the rest of the New Wavers who were somewhat unified aesthetically (although Godard eventually broke away from that mold), Mambety did not make motion pictures amid a large community of filmmakers. This poses a problem when one tries to define an artistic movement or to find an aesthetic consistency among Senegalese directors, but it is also liberating; does the autonomy of Senegalese cinema not ultimately stem from the uniqueness of each individual director?

Mambety's work should be studied at the microlevel of each text in order to unveil a chameleonic approach to genre and to narrative. There are moments when his cinema is pastoral or contemplative; at other times it is political and satirical.[10] The director indeed has a sharp sense of satire—he constantly skewers inept government agencies, for example—which he combines with an inventive editing style at the level of the image and of sound. As a result, he simultaneously attacks sociopolitical forms (the police especially) and cinematic aesthetic forms (such as the presumed compatibility between image and sound). Mambety crafted his own style, his own language, and his own delivery, as Niang notes: "Mambety built a project of cinematic language starting with *Contras' City*. First, there was the exploration of cinematic space, of possibilities of combinations, juxtaposition, narration, and description through the mediation of image and sound" (2002, 197).[11] Given his experimentation with sound and image, his occasionally avant-garde style, and his persistent subversion of the existing conventions of cinema, perhaps the most obvious category for Mambety would be countercinema, but he ultimately escapes generalization. His editing is often disruptive and discontinuous, which leads to severe narrative fragmentation, but there are moments when his cinema is quite seamless and does not draw attention to the apparatus allowing the spectator to be stitched onto the narrative. In other words, it allows for suture.

In Hollywood-style cinema, editing—how the film is put together in postproduction—should remain invisible. The act of filming should avoid drawing attention to itself, so as to give the impression of seamless continuity both at a technical level between shots and within the narrative arc of the story. Therefore, as critic Kaja Silverman explains, the role of narration is to transform "cinematic space into dramatic place, thereby providing the viewer not just with a vantage but a subject position" (1983, 204). It is the narration that allows the audience to reach a subject position, but in doing so, the spectators are tricked and forget that they are part of the narration themselves: "Cinematic suture is thus largely synonymous with the operations of classic narrative, operations which include a wide variety of editing, lighting, compositional and other formal elements, but within which the values of absence and lack always play a central role. Those values not only activate the viewer's desire and transform one shot into a signifier for the next, but serve to deflect attention away from the level of enunciation to that of the fiction" (Silverman 1983, 204). According to Silverman, suture can be observed most clearly in the tension created by the opposition between the shot and the reverse shot, which Mambety occasionally ignores, as will be shown in the analysis of *Touki Bouki* (1973). Therefore, Mambety poses an interesting problem because he meshes several styles together and his films oscillate in and out of the countercinema mode. According to Paul Willemen, "one of the main differences between Third Cinema and the European notion of counter-cinema is this awareness of the historical variability of the necessary aesthetic strategies to be adopted . . . the notion of counter-cinema tends to conjure up a prescriptive aesthetics to do the opposite of what dominant cinema does" (1989, 7). But Mambety's films also come in and out of the Third Cinema mode and rely on a particular mixture of Russian formalism, French realism, and Hollywood panache. John D. H. Downing alludes to a similar mélange concerning Third Cinema in the afterword of his edited volume, *Film & Politics in the Third World*: "Cinematic movements in a series of nations of the South have addressed themselves to the problems of liberation in their own contexts, but often drawing as they did so on the experiences and precepts of a number of non-dogmatic socialist artists, whether the Soviet Dziga Vertov, the German Bertolt Brecht, the Italian Roberto Rossellini, or the Frenchman Jean-Luc Godard. To name only four. In this sense the topics and treatment may truly be said to be different from 'first' and 'second' cinemas" (1987, 315).[12] All these elements lead to the conclusion that Mambety presents himself as a master of hybridity.[13]

Hybridity is clearly at the heart of Mambety's cinematic methodology, his political views, and most relevantly his characters. The recurring ontological ambivalence of Mambety's films means, as Nar Sene says, that "his cinema is not classifiable in any drawer" (Sene 2001, 39).[14] It is partly because of this chameleonic quality that he deserves the epithet of "auteur," since every auteur has his or her own personal "*tiroir*" ("niche" would be a more accurate translation here than the literal "drawer"). Moreover, Sene suggests, "a cinephile is not in the same state of mind when he sees a film by Godard, Howard Hawks, Kurosawa, or Satiajit Ray because they are 'epithets' within their own genre. It is the same for Djibril" (2001, 61).[15] Yet the defining trait behind the concept of hybridity, which will be explained in further detail below, invalidates the idea that there could be a fixed genre for Mambety, even one that recognizes his essential idiosyncrasy. Kenneth Harrow's important contributions to the theory of African cinema, *Postcolonial African Cinema: From Political Engagement to Postmodernism* (2007) and especially *Trash: African Cinema From Below* (2013), systematically engage with the need to move away from "conventional cinema readings of dominant western forms of commercial or of auteur cinema" (2013, 3) and to embrace instead theories of hybridity as developed "from below" (i.e., in and about the global South). Harrow's rhetoric amps up considerably as it progresses from exploring the "erasable differences between western and African filmmaking" (2007, 105) and challenging the boundaries of mégotage[16] to "validating those people, those cultural artifacts, considered trash by dominant political and aesthetic discourses" (2013, 3) and to opening "the glance that falls on African cinema to the possibilities of reversals in conventional estimates of value" (2013, 282). While Harrow's position is valid, the crux of Mambety's use of sound is that it marries a well-defined perspective from below with conventional norms and auteurist tendencies. Moreover, this study seeks to validate a reversal similar to the one sought by Harrow; the revalorization of sound's narrative capabilities should offer the opportunity to express the vibrancy of African cinema in new terms.

Similar issues with boundaries arise when one scrutinizes Mambety's work against the backdrop of Third Cinema. The original 1968 manifesto by Octavio Solanas and Fernando Getino, *Towards a Third Cinema*, refused to offer a recipe, a common aesthetics, but it did classify (perhaps too loosely) most films adhering to Third Cinema as making an attempt to deliver political statements about the filmmakers' respective countries, through allegory or direct satire. In the case of Mambety, *Touki Bouki* is really his first political film, "the one where, for the first time, the images converge to illustrate a project on a seemingly nationalistic society" (Niang 2002, 106).[17] The political commentary in his last film, *La petite vendeuse de soleil* (1998), is equally strong. In it, Mambety's dream is that Africa should leave the "zone franc" and be able to survive on its own resources; indeed, financial autonomy (from the colonizing power) is one of the essential ideological goals for the Third Cinema directors.

The qualifier "Third Cinema" is applied mostly to films made in Third World countries, and it is mainly understood in opposition to Western cultures and Western forms. It is an oppositional type of cinema that stresses nonlinearity. However, "Third Cinema" and "Third World Cinema" are not interchangeable terms. The former suggests a more political cinema geared toward countering the ideology of First and Second Cinema, while the latter is much wider, covers more thematic elements, and has geographical parameters. In *Questions of Third Cinema*, Willemen thinks of Third Cinema as an ideological project, a body of films adhering to certain political and aesthetic programs whether or not they are produced by Third World filmmakers. This body of films fuses "a number of European, Soviet and Latin American ideas about cultural practice into a new, more powerful (in the sense that it was able to conceptualise the connections between more areas of socio-cultural life than contemporary European aesthetic ideologies) programme for the political practice of cinema" (Willemen 1989, 5). A perfect example is Gillo Pontecorvo's *The Battle of Algiers* (1966). Pontecorvo is Italian and thus not from the Third World, but the political aspect of the film focuses on postcolonial conflict, which tends to be associated with Third Cinema. But although one may occasionally set aside social and geographical limits when speaking of Third Cinema, it is a cinema that contains strong national and regional components, particularly in the case of Senegal. Another tendency exhibited by Third Cinema is the recurrence of certain themes; according to Mbye Cham, these include conflicts between cultures, challenges posed by postcolonial life, disillusionment with political independence, declining quality of life, political instability and corruption, rethinking gender and gender roles and expectations, and the need to rewrite African history from an African point of view (1996, 4).

The last theme implies that West African cinema needs to be examined outside of the European theoretical framework. In his article "The Theoretical Construction of African Cinema," Stephen Zacks quotes V. Y. Mudimbe on several movements that have influenced the creation and development of African discourse: Negritude, Sartrean existentialism, missionary writings, ethnophilosophy, anthropological structuralism, and Fanonian neo-Marxist nationalism. But in Zacks's opinion, there are only three main theoretical positions that emerge when one interprets African cinematic texts. First, neo-Marxism emphasizes opposition or resistance and tries to subvert "dominant forms, methods, genres, and institutions" (1995, 7). Second is neostructuralism, whose aim is to "describe or translate cultural products for different audiences rather than to prescribe or proscribe cinematic practices" (7). This theory distinguishes itself from neo-Marxism mainly in its less aggressive approach. While neo-Marxism aims to distinguish between African and European film, "to valorize and heighten the difference" (7) through opposition, neostructuralism is satisfied with merely exposing those differences. Finally, Zacks refers to modernism, which also lacks a clear polemical inclination but "emphasizes its own subjectivity in ascribing value to a text, attempting to relativize descriptions, level categorical differences, and move toward universalistic interpretation and critique by means of a more detailed, particular, contextualized discussion" (8). Following this reading, text and author are closely linked, with the product of the auteur being regarded as an "aesthetic event." As we shall see, this happens to be one of the crucial qualities of Mambety's works.

The aesthetic angle brings us to a longstanding debate over authenticity: is West African cinema an "authentic" cinema? Initially all of African film had to fight against demeaning representations of the continent by the West; has that tendency evolved into a particular, specific style that belongs only to Africans? It is difficult to say with certainty, even though renowned Africanist Manthia Diawara originally spoke with verve about narratives that "define their Africanness within dominant cinematic forms" (1992, 165). Diawara has since qualified his approach and moved away from the reductive term "Africanness": "I do not believe that there is such a thing as an authentic African film language . . . there are variations, and even contradictions, among film languages and ideologies, which are attributable to the prevailing political cultures in each region, the differences in the modes of production and distribution, and the particularities of regional cultures" (2000, 81). More compellingly, Harrow's *Postcolonial African Cinema* dismisses the notion of authenticity.[18] Harrow's point emerges most clearly in an inconspicuous endnote:

> The bullet that renders all arguments over authenticity pointless is that there is no site where one can stand from which to evaluate the authentic. If one is authentic, the only knowledge one could have of it would come from standing outside of oneself and reflexively observing one's authentic being. That model of the divided subject, fundamental to all poststructuralist thinking, deauthenticates any attempts to assert the presence of the authentic, what Derrida terms the "metaphysics of presence." Butler (1990) carries this argument further in her claims that subject identities are performed, that the metaphysics of presence or substance rests conventionally on patriarchal, or, in fact, phallocentric assumptions that function like ideology, i.e. that naturalize, or authenticate, what retains and sustains existing systems of power. (2007, 239)

Misrecognition and confusion about personal and ideological identities eliminate the possibility of a fruitful dialogue on authenticity.[19] Furthermore, such a discussion would prove unproductive because there are several ontological influences at work in African cinema, particularly in Mambety's films. For example, Teshome Gabriel, one of the first theorists of African cinema, picks up on an important detail that connects auteur cinema with African film: African film is not linear (a notable exception is Ousmane Sembène), does not follow a single path, and does not tell only one story. On the contrary, "stories tend to bend back upon themselves, to circle as they circulate, so that their fabric contains many interlocking stories and permutations of stories" (1982, 203).

Gabriel also attempts to establish an ideological connection between what he calls "Third World films" and the practices of Third Cinema by way of Frantz Fanon, while being mindful in his excavation of what might pass for a common aesthetic that links all Third Cinema films. This was an important attempt to establish a theory of Third Cinema, something that was sorely lacking in the early 1980s and that continued to be ignored during the following decades; for example, some twenty years later Anthony R. Guneratne still calls attention to influential film critics' "denying the grandeur to Third Cinema theory" (2003, 4). According to Gabriel there are three main tendencies that define this cinema, just as there are three genealogical stages of Third World culture in Fanon's work (Chanan 1997, 7). The first is called "unqualified assimilation," which is characterized by an attempt to imitate Hollywood film to such an extent that even the names of the production companies are Americanized (the example given by Gabriel is the Nigerian film company Calpenny—California, Pennsylvania, and New York; 1989a, 31). The second tendency is called the "remembrance phase," characterized by more aggressive attitudes that reject "the ways of the past." The third stage is liberation, the "combative phase," when film becomes an "ideological tool" that deals with themes of resistance (1989a, 31–35). According to Michael Chanan, this phase "is third cinema proper" (1997, 7), which may also be characterized by a "process of becoming" (Chanan 1997, 8). These three categories reveal that our understanding of Third Cinema must be negotiated at the intersection of memory, identity, and history—all fluid concepts that also happen to be key in postcolonial theory. Throughout this study, reference will be made to these concepts and to the theorists who have tackled them, particularly Edward Said, Frantz Fanon, and Homi Bhabha. The last one's treatment of hybridity fits well with Mambety's personal style of filmmaking.[20] Bhabha's other important term, the "third space," is tightly linked to hybridity, and is also originally a venue for challenging the established relationship between the colonizer and the colonized according to binary oppositions (e.g., civilized/savage). The word "challenge" may be too confrontational, though, since Bhabha's central argument calls for a cultural negotiation between the elements occupying the third space:

> It is significant that the productive capacities of this Third Space have a colonial and postcolonial provenance. For a willingness to descend into that alien territory . . . may reveal that the theoretical recognition of the split-space of enunciation may open the way to conceptualizing an *inter*national culture, based not on exoticism or multiculturalism of the *diversity* of cultures, but on the inscription and articulation of culture's *hybridity*. To that end we should remember that it is the "inter"—the cutting edge of translation and negotiation, the *inbetween* space—that carries the burden of the meaning of culture. (2010, 56)

Third Cinema is an appropriate site to explore the negotiation between colonial and postcolonial spaces as well as between the colonizers' spatial "reach" and the colonized space that remains stifled as a consequence of that reach.[21] These cultural negotiations, as seen and analyzed through the concept of space, make an extrapolation possible; in cinematic space the image has long stifled the narrative power of sound, but in Mambety's cinema sound emerges as a viable narrative alternative to the image. Rearranging the narrative space of film by elevating sound from mere complement to the visual to at least an equal producer of "images," partially approximates the classic colonial binary relation. In other words, African images and sounds are no longer mediated through a Western perspective.

Nevertheless, the ability to create permutations of stories in cinema should come equally from the visual and aural narratives. Sound can be separated from the main visual storyline, and when it is, it takes on a life of its own. What happens is that the film splits and begins telling different stories; sound tells its own story.[22] When sound is analyzed separately from image, its signified value changes, and while the aural stories are not necessarily opposed to what is offered visually, they do appear to function at a separate narrative level than the image, which in turn must change its meaning depending on the presence or absence of sound. However, sound does not completely negate the narrative impact of the visual. In fact, Mambety exhibits a keen visual sense. One of his main visual interests is his birth city, Dakar, depicted as always being in transition, always changing as it attempts to free itself of the colonial shadow. Yet traces of colonialism and neocolonialism still linger visibly, as historian James Genova remarks: "It's been more than fifty years since Senegal . . . achieved independence . . . but the scenes of contemporary Dakar, marked by coterminous signs of renewal and decline, belie the heritage of that half century" (2013, 1). Analysis of Mambety's films will reveal that postcolonial space is indeed organized so as to constantly remind people of their previous colonized state. Visual reminders abound in Mambety's depictions of Dakar because this city in particular has "more colonial structures than other major African urban centers" (Pfaff 2004, 92). It must not be forgotten, though, that similar traces persist audibly as well. Brian Larkin's groundbreaking book *Signal and Noise* (2008) documents how the media (especially radio) create "unique aural and perceptual environments, everyday urban arenas" (2–3) in postcolonial Nigeria. These environments lead to the construction of a "colonial sublime," which is "about Europeans' tactile and symbolic effort to make technology mean"[23] (42). Of course, the technology was first introduced through the operations of colonialism, and then (protected partially by the operations of neocolonialism) it continued to produce an audible materiality meant to function like an echo of colonialism. The control exercised over the colonized was perpetuated thanks to the visual form of the infrastructure (including the physical radio), and more insidiously through the dissemination of English broadcast radio: "Radio diffusion . . . continued the process of mediating urban space . . . creating new types of aural experience" (49).[24] Larkin's findings can be extrapolated to Senegal, where French-language broadcasts flourished during the Senghor years.[25] The final chapters of this volume will deal with Mambety's use of the radio as a kind of aural fetish.

Gabriel is quite open to the idea of hybridity when he dissects the tendencies of Third Cinema, an idea that Guneratne echoes and takes further, suggesting that there is hybridity not only within Third Cinema but also among the three cinemas: "Interactions between varying forms of cinema within national industries [are] diverse enough to sustain coexisting forms of First, Second and Third Cinema" (2003, 20).[26] Furthermore, in the essay "Beyond Third Cinema: The Aesthetics of Hybridity," Robert Stam considers hybridity to be a "constitutive" part of Third Cinema aesthetics because it is "deeply entangled with colonial violence" (2003, 32–33). Finally, according to Ima Ebong, hybridity is also the idiosyncratic element of Senegalese contemporary art: "In the case of Senegal, the most effective art today is open to multiple, hybrid context. It oscillates between the grey areas of cultural identity with a taunting sense of free play, reflexively deploying various meanings, sometimes exaggerated or conflicting, across many different lines of interest" (1999, 143).

Taken out of context, this description could be applied to Mambety's cinema too. Furthermore, Ebong's description resonates with parts of Elizabeth Harney's findings in her study of modern art in postindependence Senegal.[27] Harney meticulously explores the prolific avant-garde period in Senegal during the 1970s, defined by experimentation and eclectic artistic communities—such as the Laboratoire Agit-Art, led by Issa Samb, that sought to "reinvigorate artistic practice and to free it from its Senghorian jacket" (2004, 106). Mambety contributed to the building of the Laboratoire community (2004, 271), and this avant-garde period happens to coincide with the production of two of his first three films. Consequently, it can be said that the director fit well in the revolutionary artistic context of that time while remaining a de facto participant in Third Cinema.

To some extent Manthia Diawara's three trends in Third Cinema oppose themselves to the ideas of hybridity discussed above. Diawara looks at the history of African cinema in terms of cause and effect—specific regimes creating specific practices and products—not as a clear political opposition between the West and Africa (1996, 141–164). His categories are called "social realism," "colonial confrontation," and "return to the source," all of which resemble Gabriel's phases. Diawara's understanding of African cinema appears to be more rigid than Gabriel's, which is more in line with Willemen's internationalizing concept; there is not much dialogue between Diawara's categories.[28] But these categories cannot possibly be clear-cut, and there is a lot of common ground between the last two—"colonial confrontation" and "return to the source." The latter appears to be the most important and richest category; it is not as polemical as the first two, and it supports the creation of a distinctive African film language (1996, 160). In "Popular Culture and Oral Traditions in African Film," an article that appeared four years after the publication of the book project *African Cinema* (1992), Diawara also argues passionately that oral tradition is embedded in the fabric of African cinema (1996, 209–218); Olivier Barlet (1996, 157–199) and Frank Ukadike (1994, 201–222) make this argument too. In his influential book, *Black African Cinema* (1994), Ukadike specifically describes how the oral tradition percolates through the aesthetics of cinema, "The process of narration in black African films is an outgrowth of the oral tales and the epic poem narrative tradition. The African cinema . . . has antecedents in African oral literature. The most important element in oral literature (as in the novel and the cinema) is the story, which builds the structure, the climax, and the resolution. In order to establish how oral tradition operates in the aesthetic mode, it is essential to posit the structure of oral art . . . that enables the construction and creation of alternative cinematic forms" (203). Anthropologist Karin Barber strengthens the connection between the narrative structures of stories and films by filling in a major gap, oral tradition as performance art, in her essay "Text and Performance in Africa" (2005).[29] Barber expands the limited comprehension of "text" by hypothesizing that "performances within oral traditions entail some kind of textual dimension" (2005, 265). Moreover, "everywhere in African orature there is evidence of a will to fix speech, to give it the compact solidity and durability of a material object. Oral texts in Africa are often actually attached to or secreted in material objects" (Barber 2007, 75). In other words, a materiality of sounds makes its presence felt. What is interesting about cinema, then, is that it offers both a version of the text as a permanent artifact (the visual and the aural do not change every time one watches a film) and also a more nuanced dimension of orality through sound that is not necessarily stable, that escapes its connection to the visual and projects further narrative planes. Mambety has found a way, through cinema, to fix the fleeting sound of oral expression as song or voice while simultaneously conserving its phantasmagoric quality. But most common references that connect African cinema to orality are made at the level of film as text (e.g., mentions of hyenas, retelling of stories and myths, and construction of narrative) or through song and other music—what Charles Sugnet calls "primary orality," as opposed to a secondary type mediated by cinema (2006, 1229–1230). Through an elaboration of what one perceives as sound, though, it may be proved that African cinema and orality are inextricably linked at all film levels.

Diawara also notes particular technical trends in camera movement in African film that present a challenge to established Western forms by "deemphasizing the psychologically based shot / reverse shot and close-ups of Western cinema, and by valorizing long shots and long takes, which through their 'natural' feel are destined to describe the characters' relationships to each other and to time and space" (1996, 165). The argument has value in identifying a particular modus operandi in a few African films, but ultimately it amounts to an untenable essentialist argument that embraces global divisions. Perhaps Diawara's claim comes from Gabriel's earlier essentialist argument (1989a, 45); Gabriel proposes similar opposing conventions by pointing out, for example, the contrast between Western formal devices like eye-level perspective and the "deliberate choice" in the postcolonial world to use high and low angles in order to underline "dominance and power relations between the oppressed and the oppressing classes" (1989a, Table 2, 46). In a subsequent article, "Third Cinema as Guardian of Popular Memory: Towards a Third Aesthetics" (1989b), Gabriel moves from aesthetics to a less divisive discussion of the concepts of hero and story: "The aesthetic form of the narrative in Western film culture is the aesthetics of the hero—it starts with a hero, develops with a hero and ends with a hero. . . . If Third Cinema are said to have a central protagonist, it is the 'context' of the film. . . . Most Third Cinema films focus on the story as opposed to action" (1989b, 60).

While all of these observations are at least partially germane and Mambety's films contain several visual examples that support Diawara's and Gabriel's arguments, a more thorough analysis should also challenge absolute global divisions, particularly when it comes to the way Mambety controls the medium of sound in order to alter the viewing process. It remains to be determined if Mambety's use of sound represents an improvement or simply a subversive method capable of displacing the visual as the primary mode of storytelling in cinema. The key point is that Diawara's and Gabriel's categories should be viewed as flexible (Willemen finds that a "fundamental flexibility" leads to Third Cinema being "a cinema forever in need of adaptation to the shifting dynamics at work in social struggles," [Willemen 1989, 10]), inasmuch as the recurrent themes of African cinema crisscross both sets of categories and aesthetic questions are much more unpredictable than initially conceptualized.

The most frequent connections among Gabriel's and Diawara's six different categories are made through the common concern with the position of women in society, shown especially by Sembène and Mambety but also by other West African directors. The female subject appears to be the nexus that most unifies West African film thematically. Jean-Pierre Bekolo's *Quartier Mozart* (Cameroon, 1992) tells the story of a woman who becomes a man and finds herself in the position of a pursuer; in the same vein Adama Drabo's *Taafe Fanga* (*Skirt Power*) (Mali, 1996) portrays women in a village who, through magic, switch gender roles with the men. Sembène's last film, *Moolaadé* (2004), and before it, Cheick Oumar Sissoko's *Finzan* (Mali, 1990), both deal with the issue of female genital mutilation. In 1996, Safi Faye made *Mossane,* a movie focused entirely on the right of African women to own their bodies. The theme of return to the source ranges from ideology and traditional issues concerning African film to questions of aesthetics: Gaston Kaboré's *Wend Kuuni* (Burkina Faso, 1982), Souleymane Cissé's *Yeelen* (Mali, 1987), Idrissa Ouédraogo's *Tilai* (Burkina Faso, 1990), and Abderrahmane Sissako's *La vie sur terre* (Mali, 1998) are all good examples of directors concentrating on the beauty of the African landscape while subverting the anticolonial discourse from the perspective of the masses. The concern with the female subject not only unifies West African film but brings it closer to Hollywood-style cinema and that tradition's tenuous relationship with poststructuralist feminism. This is another term to which Clyde Taylor might object; even more forcefully, Oyèrónké Oyěwùmí argues in *The Invention of Women* (1997) that gendered categories are not universal (e.g., "The Yorùbá world is not dichotomized into male and female" [Oyěwùmí 1997, 106]) and therefore that "feminism" is exclusively Western (ix–xiii). However, importantly, Oyěwùmí critiques feminism as it stems from the legacy and *"visual* logic of Western thought" (15, my emphasis). Instead of following the "West's privileging of the visual over other senses," the author sets out to proclaim "the dominance of the auditory in Yorùbá-land" (15). A similar argument can be made northwest of Yorùbáland, in Senegal, and the nuanced focus on voice in feminist theory of the 1990s may prove more useful than image-based, classical feminism.

Following in the footsteps of Molly Haskell, Claire Johnston, Judith Mayne, and Laura Mulvey—who, among many others, brought feminism into film theory—feminist theorists fleshed out gender representation in cinema in the 1990s by addressing the issue of the female voice and including a necessary commentary on how women are portrayed aurally and not just visually. For example, Kaja Silverman proposes that the subjectivity of the infant is generated by an acoustic mirror, in which the child (mis)hears his or her voice fused together with that of the mother (1988, 72–86). Silverman also documents the ways in which the narrative primacy of the male voice constricts the female voice. Two other important theorists, Mary Ann Doane and Amy Lawrence, support and complement Silverman's work. Doane contributes the notions of disembodied voice and aural space (1985, 162–179), while Lawrence proposes that an authorial female voice that challenges the submission to patriarchal rules is possible, if rare (1991, 7, 169, 186).

Even more than the common concern with women as visual and aural subjects, another interest unites African directors: poignant commentaries on the political rift between Africa and Europe that occurred postindependence. This political split is one of the main theoretical preoccupations of postcolonial studies. The term "postcolonial" may be wrongly applied to contexts from which colonialism has never really disappeared, in which case the term "neocolonial" is more appropriate. Ella Shohat's seminal essay "Notes on the 'Post-Colonial'" supports the idea that the postcolonial can be understood as a continuation of colonialism: "The 'neocolonial,' like the 'postcolonial,' also suggests continuities and discontinuities, but its emphasis is on the new modes and forms of the old colonialist practices, not on a 'beyond'" (Shohat 2006, 241). In a pivotal essay, "When Was the 'Post-colonial'? Thinking at the Limit," Stuart Hall, drawing on studies by Shohat and Anne McClintock, acknowledges the sheer difficulty of making such distinctions. Hall also points out that there is always a slippage in the term's usage, so that it covers much more than just history since formal independence (Hall 1996, 242–253). The origins of the notion of postcolonialism could thus be located at various stages throughout the history of mankind, a history tilted profoundly in favor of Europe. Eurocentrism, in Shohat and Robert Stam's definition, "sanitizes Western history while patronizing and even demonizing the non-West; it thinks of itself in terms of its noblest achievements—science, progress, humanism—but of the non-West in terms of its deficiencies, real or imagined" (Shohat and Stam 2014, 3). When one looks at the two cinemas, it is common to encounter such dichotomies. In the introduction to *Questions of Third Cinema*, Paul Willemen demarcates two categories that lead to a series of binaries: ours and theirs. More precisely, he means *our* nations, religions, culture, and art, as opposed to *their* tribes, superstitions, folklore, and artifacts, respectively. Willemen opposes these demarcations, which would lead to an overly simplified understanding of African cinema (1989, 15–17), and while they are present in the films of Mambety they do not do justice to his films as cultural endeavors meant to blur rigid distinctions. Nevertheless, these differences certainly bespeak the breadth of many African films, which decry the dichotomy "ours and theirs" that constructs the non-West as a negative compound term. The dichotomous categorization continues with the term "Third Cinema," which opposes two representatives of the Western Hemisphere, classical Hollywood and Second Cinema, at least at first glance.[30]

More specifically, Third Cinema films address the effects of colonialism, for example in West Africa and that region's relation to France. From this perspective, one finds such themes as exclusion and oppression. Gabriel maps out the central themes of political African cinema: issues of class, race, culture, religion, sex, and national integrity. Class struggle occurs at the level of the conflict between rich and poor; West African cinema goes beyond the obvious opposition by exploring the parallels between the newly rich and the colonizers. West African films also commonly examine the conflict between the preservation of indigenous culture and the colonial presence suggested by technological advancements. Religion plays a large role in the colonial conflict; because women have been silenced by a deeply rooted religious tradition that has long placed them in a subservient status to men, their struggle for emancipation often emerges from it. For these reasons, West African cinema can be about voice, and furthermore surprisingly vociferous about the female voice. Yet the strongest voice that has to be heard is the one that belongs to the community of African filmmakers.

The concept of community plays a systematic role in African cinema, which manifests itself in the cases of Mambety and Sembène by filming in Wolof, because "to speak Wolof signifies belonging to the community, being traditional and in solidarity with other Moslems . . . it is a sign of belonging to a place" (Diawara 2010, 44).[31] More importantly, though, through the use of regional language and a self-conscious deployment of everyday oral forms as modality for artistic expressions, Mambety primarily reinforces the local cultural impact of his films: "In traditional African cultures the reason why oral tradition has had such an enormous impact on communication is its reliance on one of the most powerful elements of culture, the indigenous language, for its exposition" (Ukadike 1994, 215). So the director succeeds by way of orality and sound in making above all a local impact (followed in some cases by an international one) that establishes his cinema as an autonomous entity, a "reinvention." Not surprisingly then, his work is about beginnings, and tumultuous beginnings at that, as noted by Sene (2001, 89). In the beginning there was orality. Then there was cinema. And Mambety marries the two through sound.

The unique use of sound actually brings the filmmaker closer to auteur cinema. Second Cinema has long experimented with sound and voice. It is not necessarily important to situate Mambety within the loose confines of Second Cinema, but some mention should be made of obvious connections to the French New Wave and Godard in particular. As Harrow observes, "From the outset, Mambety constructed a distribution of the sensible that would fit more comfortably into a world of Godard films than those of Pontecorvo. Sembène took the direction that social realism had carved out, and Mambety inclined toward the edges of a New Wave surrealism that gave freedom a possibility for African cinema" (2013, 43). Therefore, it is also important to circle back occasionally to the French New Wave as a way of continuing the postcolonial dialogue through sound (i.e., does the France-Senegal relationship mirror the relationship between French New Wave and Senegalese cinemas?). There are references to emblematic New Wave films, directors, and techniques, including freeze frames, traffic noises, and voice-overs, not just in Mambety's films but in West African cinema in general. Sembène's freeze frames pay tribute to the ending of François Truffaut's *The 400 Blows* (1959), and every insistence on traffic noise echoes Godard's *Weekend* (1967).[32] Sissako's authorial voice-over in *La vie sur terre* is comparable to the technique employed by Godard in *Two or Three Things I Know About Her*

(1967). Mambety's tracking shots and jump cuts are also reminiscent of Godard, who appears to be a very broad source of inspiration. Last, in their search for identity Safi Faye's female characters could be viewed as displaced extensions of Agnès Varda's characters.

In spite of these examples, these connections are tangential in the end; they are homages to Cinema, but not necessarily to *French* cinema. Mambety's cinema is not an aftereffect of the New Wave aesthetic, but it is worth looking briefly at the French New Wave ideology, which is closely linked to that of Second Cinema, to better understand Mambety's place alongside Godard in the same fraternity of auteurs.

Through the Lens of the French New Wave: What is Second Cinema?

The French New Wave was born out of a cinephilic reflection on the work of Jean Renoir, Orson Welles, Alfred Hitchcock, Ingmar Bergman, film noir, and Italian Neorealism. These varied influences naturally led to a synthetic quality, best encompassed by Godard, who often broke away from the principles of the movement. In fact, the French New Wave was hardly a homogenous group. The intellectual inquiries and obsession with memory of the Left Bank/*Rive gauche* (Alain Resnais, Varda, Chris Marker), which is often lumped in with the New Wave, did not necessarily fit thematically or aesthetically with the core group (Truffaut, Godard, Eric Rohmer, Claude Chabrol, Jacques Rivette), itself diverse. Truffaut's fascination with Hitchcock and with Hollywood B movies led to homages such as *The Bride Wore Black* (1968). Godard's quintessential metafilm *Contempt* (1963) also had a Hollywood-worthy big budget, a star in Brigitte Bardot, and an extended acting role for director Fritz Lang.[33] However, the concept of the auteur is the common element to emerge from the movement that is crucial for an understanding of Mambety and other African directors.

The concept takes shape at the intersection of three theoretical stands: the writings of Bazin, Alexandre Astruc's notion of the *caméra-stylo*, and Truffaut's article "A Certain Tendency of the French Cinema" (1954). Bazin's writings are gathered in a volume entitled *What is Cinema?* (which inspires the title of this section), in which he argues for the necessity of mise-en-scène: the camera must tell the story through the careful arrangement of the visual elements in the shot and without much interference in the editing process. Astruc set forth the notion of the *caméra-stylo* in his seminal article, "Naissance d'une nouvelle avant-garde: la Caméra-stylo" (*L'écran français*, 1948). Astruc proposes that filmmaking is a means of expression akin to painting or writing a novel[34] and that the director controls and manipulates the film stock in the same way that a writer does pen and paper. The issue of writing is less applicable to Mambety's work, which foregrounds storytelling and performativity (to that end his camera not only writes—it also sings and dances),³⁵ but the idea of tampering with form is certainly pertinent.

Astruc's article is followed by Truffaut's "A Certain Tendency of the French Cinema," which virulently attacked the so-called *cinéma de papa* and ignited the discussion on the *politique des auteurs* in the famed theoretical magazine, *Cahiers du cinéma*. "*Cinéma de papa*" is a generic term referring to postwar script-led films in France, mostly unprestigious literary adaptations that stifled the characters' growth. Truffaut identified and developed the notion of the auteur, linking it directly to Bazin's concept of mise-en-scène and indirectly (i.e., without specification) to Astruc's controlling writer/director. Following the invasion by American cinema after the Second World War, the *Cahiers* critics identified style as the most important attribute in defining the concept of the auteur. The particular style of an auteur director would be easily recognizable by viewers because the films would reveal an ensemble of recurring traits unique to the filmmaker. These traits would create and define the personal universe of that auteur (the aforementioned "*tiroir*"/niche). Thus, "auteur" could refer to directors such as Alfred Hitchcock or John Ford because of their unique, recognizable styles. For example, Hitchcock relied on stylization, vertical structures, mise-en-scène oppositions between large and small or long and short, such as going from an extreme long shot to an extreme close-up in the same sequence.

Truffaut also proposes that the auteur's importance even surpasses the completed product. Thus, a failed film made by an auteur would be of more artistic value than a successful film by a non-auteur. However controversial, Truffaut's ideas about auteur cinema come from a positive impulse, from a need to "save" cinema. After all, he is a hopeless romantic: "The film of tomorrow will look like the man who filmed it and the number of people in the audience will be proportional to the number of friends the filmmaker has. The film of tomorrow will be an act of love" (1994, 19). The same can be said about Mambety's idealistic relationship with cinema when he declares, "The future belongs to images . . . making a film is a matter of love," and "It is very important to preserve the magic of cinema" (Ukadike 2002, 125, 128). Truffaut, the theorist who put his thought into practice, and Mambety, who achieved cinematic erudition *through* direct practice, both arrive at the conclusion that cinema is love, a highly subjective endeavor. This act of love, though, has the potential to evolve into an act of infatuation. The New Wave directors, Godard in particular, separate themselves from the larger community of filmmakers, and in doing so they isolate themselves in their own ivory tower. Geneviève Sellier makes this point when discussing the auteur aesthetic: "It is the figure of the auteur that has become the criterion of value in cinema, on the literary model inherited from romanticism, accompanied by a touch of formalism that establishes the connection with contemporary art.

This model valorizes the expression of a subjectivity isolated in an ivory tower and centered on itself—rather than that of an individual engaged with social and cultural determinisms—as well as a fantasy of absolute mastery that makes the filmmaker a demiurge rather than the motor of a collective project" (2008, 223). Sellier's tone is obviously not one of praise, but here Mambety separates himself from the auteur pack because he does stress the importance of community, and he sees West African cinema as an essential tool in the building of a collective project that is perhaps a larger manifestation of the same idealization of cinema. Mambety's work—a product of pluralism—renders that community visible and audible. For example, the music of renowned composer Wasis Diop (Mambety's brother) is featured in several films, and it definitely adds another creative and aesthetic layer to the visual stories.

Paulla Ebron's influential book, *Performing Africa* (2002), targets music in the context of live performance. Her groundbreaking study develops from the premise that "music is one of the dominant ways that Africa comes to the minds of many" (23), and is built around a comparison between the West and Africa that finds the two more connected than one would have thought: "Because Africa is the geopolitical ur-site of performance from the perspective of the West, 'African' performance and 'Western' conventions of representation of the continent are always intertwined" (2002, 16). To illustrate this point, the author looks at the transnational status of the *jali* (*griot* in French), Mandika praise-singers, in the world music scene: "Jali music—despite its sharp divergence from the 'primal beat' of Western fantasies of Africa—cannot escape European and North American evaluations within a discursive framework in which the spirit of Africa is music" (2002, 18). But Ebron does also differentiate sharply between African and European music: "Two key terms . . . illustrate how regional distinctions between Africa and Europe are configured. The first is *rhythmic repetition*, most often viewed as the salient feature of African music; it becomes a repeatedly told aspect of African music's difference. The second is *community feeling*: African music is said to create a communal experience" (2002, 33-34).[36] Momentarily sidestepping the loaded term "rhythm," I would point out that Ebron's last observation strengthens the importance of the concept of community in African arts, and that her successful comparative project substantiates my own resort to Western/French film criticism.

Alas, Truffaut's vision for the romanticized future of cinema has not yet come to fruition, although there are many contemporary directors who have followed in the self-centered footsteps of auteur theory. However, the New Wave aesthetic, including the auteur theory, should not be simply condemned for its elitist behavior. Instead, it should be applauded for valorizing plurality, hybridity, ambivalence, reflexivity, and intellectuality. Gilles Deleuze brings forth the last two characteristics in *Cinema 1* (1986), "by a reflexive or intellectual detour" (1986, 215), as a way of explaining how the New Wave breaks the mold and moves away from the contemporary framework of cinema. Mambety, too, takes a detour from the politicized Third Cinema of West Africa in order to establish postcolonial self-reflection and intellectuality as gateways toward an innovative and perhaps idealistic type of (aural) cinema.

Physical Sound, Sound Theories

The notion that sound has a material quality is not innovative by any means, but it has been somewhat overlooked in recent studies. By way of Freud, whose much-discussed footnote in *The Ego and the Id* refers to the ego as "ultimately derived from bodily sensations, chiefly from those springing from the surface of the body" (1952, 703), Jean-François Lyotard helps correct this overlooked aspect of sound in an interesting way: "We also tend to say that sound, matter itself, is analyzable into its parameters, amplitude, period, frequency, duration, resonance" (1988, 153). While Lyotard's argument centers around repetition and music, his use of the word "matter" in referring to sound is of particular importance: "musical matter—sound—subject to temporal (and spatial conditions)" (1988, 155). The imposed conditions probably occur because ontologically and historically speaking, film sound has been considered a sort of add-on to the image. This is Rick Altman's opinion (1992, 35), as well as John Belton's (1985, 64). It is because of this historical misperception that sound is relegated to secondary importance.

The materiality of sound mainly comes from the way it is produced, as Altman notes: "Three elements are required for the production of any sound. First, there must be *vibration*, such as the vocal cords or a violin string. Second, the vibration must take place in a medium whose molecules can be set in motion, such as air, water, or a railroad rail (sound cannot be transmitted through a vacuum). Third, the transmitting *medium* must absorb and transmit the original vibrations in the form of *changes in pressure*" (1992, 17).[37] In Altman's view, the processes that follow these three primary conditions lead one to conclude that the production of sound is in fact a "material event, taking place in space and time, and involving the disruption of surrounding matter" (1992, 18). Moreover, synthesizing studies by John Cage and Don Ihde, Ross Brown posits that sound has a shape—round (2010, 138–141).[38] The spatial nature of sound comes from the process of physical perception: sound comes to life only when heard, naturally, but it travels in all directions, unlike light.[39] That process can be delayed or, in the case of a theater, sound might reach different ears at different times, because it moves between the spectators, or rather among the listeners (Altman 1992, 20–21). Thus sound as perceived by the human ear is not linear, and it does not have the effect of immediacy generated by the visual. Altman calls each sound an event, or rather says that it begins an event (1992, 23). The basic idea here is that each sound is perceived in a different manner by multiple, simultaneous listeners depending on their spatial positioning or emotional investment. The claim he makes concerning the famous baseball example (a baseball breaks a window at his house) is that "each of us heard a different narrative of the same event" (1992, 24). These are all phenomena that Altman bunches under the term "spatial signature," which is another way of defining what makes a sound unique from spatial and temporal perspectives.

One of the most important documents concerning sound in cinema is Eisenstein's *Statement on Sound* (1928, written with two other Russian directors, V. I. Pudovkin, and G.V. Alexandrov), which—perhaps because of Eisenstein's background in silent film—does not argue strongly for sound in film, but does try to find the potential value way of integrating it into the medium that had achieved "one of the first places among arts" (1985, 83). The ability to add sound to film has affected the continuing development of cinema by undermining its basic hook on an audience—the image onscreen. Alfred Hitchcock has a similar view on sound in his interviews with Truffaut. Commenting on the transition from silent movies to talkies, Hitchcock claims that "the silent pictures were the purest form of cinema" and adds that the introduction of sound put that perfection at risk: "one might say that mediocrity came back into its own with the advent of sound" (Truffaut 1983, 61). To remedy this, the *Statement on Sound* directors thought about using sound as a montage technique because montage is what "brought the cinema to such a powerfully effective strength" (Eisenstein, Pudovkin, and Alexandrov 1985, 83). It is interesting to note that the three Russian directors admit not being technologically ready to use sound; since montage was one of the things they did best, one has to wonder how much of this theory has to do with trying to stay relevant in a very tough, fast-developing market.

Sound used in a naturalistic way, sound that perfectly matches the activity onscreen, will only create commercial movies, according to Eisenstein. Moreover, "every ADHESION of sound to a visual montage piece increases its inertia as a montage piece, and increases the independence of its meaning—and this will undoubtedly be to the detriment of montage, operating in the first place not on the montage pieces but on the JUXTAPOSITION" (1985, 84). What the group of directors proposes instead—a technique that Mambety often employs—is a "contrapuntal use" of sound, which allows for new ways of perfecting montage techniques: "The first experimental work with sound must be directed along the line of its distinct nonsynchronization with the visual images" (ibid.), and "only a contrapuntal use of sound in relation to the visual montage piece will afford a new potentiality of montage development and perfection" (ibid.). The three Russian filmmakers do not offer any examples, but their central argument is that sound has to be an independent part of the film process, something that adds to the art of film almost as a separate entity. Robert Stam agrees with Eisenstein's statement on sound and asserts that many directors interested in the question of reflexivity "have answered their [the Russian filmmakers'] call by exploiting sound to derealize rather than reinforce the image" (1985, 261).

While Bazin did not agree with Eisenstein's ideas on montage, he does use the word "counterpoint" himself when discussing sound: "Silent film was an art on its own. Sound could only play at best a subordinate and supplementary role: a counterpoint to the image" (1967, 26). Bazin's inquiries into sound refer to it mostly in terms of its realistic quality and do not provide the reader with much substance. According to Bazin, the advent of sound brought cinema closer to the myth of total cinema; in other words, sound, like Orson Welles's depth of focus, helps bring the spectator into a closer relation with the image than with reality (1967, 22, 24, 35). The chapter on sound in Siegfried Kracauer's most important work, *Theory of Film: The Redemption of Physical Reality* (1997), takes a similar position. For the most part, out of respect for the reality principle, Kracauer believes that sound communications "must originate with their pictures" (1997, 103). He places the origin of any meaning generated by sound (speech or sound proper, which is understood as "noise") in the visual. However, he claims that synchronism and asynchronism can be achieved not only through parallelism between image and sound but also through counterpoint, where speech and image carry different meanings (1997, 113). These meanings are not necessarily opposed, though, and his main argument that "genuine counterpoint on the screen is bound up with the predominance of the visuals" (1997, 120) remains valid. He revisits his thesis quite often: "Sound used contrapuntally must relate to the synchronized images in an understandable way to signify something comprehensible" (1997, 127). Kracauer makes a similar point concerning voice, sound proper, and music; these types of sound can work with the image (parallel), or against the image (counterpoint). For the latter he gives the example of a sleeping face over which nightmarish music is superimposed: "It is all but inevitable that the intriguing discrepancy between these sounds and so peaceful a picture should puzzle us" (1997, 141). Kracauer unwittingly stumbles on an analogy with the Kuleshov effect—the sound adds another layer to how the audience perceives a certain pair of shots.

Michel Chion, possibly the most influential sound theorist of the last thirty years, is more in line with Eisenstein, although he adds a few twists to the theory behind contrapuntal sound. In *Le son au cinéma*, Chion shows that music can create a specific emotion in relation to the visual story; it can contribute to the visual in the same narrative direction (empathetic music), or it can be indifferent to what happens on the screen (background music, or anempathetic music) (1985, 122–126; 1994, 8). In *Touki Bouki*, one song, Josephine Baker's "Paris, Paris, Paris" (1949), can be classified as either empathetic or anempathetic. In one of Chion's studies of sound, *The Voice in Cinema* (1999), in which he famously first declared that there was no soundtrack (13–14),[40] he describes audiovisual counterpoint as a rhetorical effect in which sound and image carry opposing ideas (1999, 87), which is a close approximation of Kracauer's theory. In *Audio-Vision: Sound on Screen* (1994), Chion expands on the same idea but warns against a linear interpretation of sound; the meaning of sound should not be reduced to an abstraction through a simple contrast with the image, one should not reduce the audio and visual elements to their abstractions (hear seagulls, think sea; see the subway, think urban): "It is not enough if the sound and the image differ in nature (the content of each, their spatial characteristics, etc.). Audiovisual counterpoint will be noticed only if it sets up an opposition between sound and image on a precise point of meaning" (1994, 38). In opposition to the meaning of the image, sound essentially splits off, as it searches to have meaning on its own; but because it cannot be physically separated from the visual, the aural component of the initial point of meaning referred to by Chion yields more than one meaning.

Chion tracks the split that occurs between the image and the sound; to him, there is no preexisting natural congruence between the two. In other words, they were not meant to coexist harmoniously. Sound and image influence one another and change one another; what the spectators see changes if they hear sound simultaneously, and vice versa. While the famous Kuleshov effect explores the relationship between images, if extended to include the use of sound, it also schematizes what Chion observes in the relationship between sound and image. The image changes with each sound added to it, as our perception of the successive images changed. So one's interpretation of the image is forcefully a production of one's brain; it is an invention. Or perhaps it is an intuition or an apprehension, like Kant's understanding of space, or Léopold Sédar Senghor's view of African art. Which returns us to the provocative declaration of the nonexistence of the soundtrack: "Film sound is that which is contained or not contained *in an image*; there is no place of the sounds, no auditory scene already preexisting in the soundtrack—and therefore, properly speaking, *there is no soundtrack*" (Chion 1994, 58). The result is that film is "audiovisual illusion" (1994, 5). The word "illusion" echoes and validates our interest in fantasy. The added value of a sound means that the sound may appear as unnecessary when in fact it "duplicates a meaning which in reality it brings about, either all on its own or by discrepancies between it and the image" (ibid.). According to Chion, because of the physical nature of sound,

> there is always something about sound that overwhelms and surprises us no matter what . . . and thus sound interferes with our perception, affects it . . . sound more than image has the ability to saturate and short-circuit our perception. The consequence for film is that sound, much more than the image, can become an insidious means of affective and semantic manipulation. On the one hand, sound works on us directly, physiologically (breathing noises in a film can directly affect our own respiration). On the other, sound has an influence on perception: through the phenomenon of added value, it interprets the meaning of the image, and makes us see in the image what we would not otherwise see, or would see differently. (1994, 33–34)

Sounds are classified through a judgment of the image or in relationship to the image, which changes constantly. So to Chion, cinema is a place of images plus sounds, but the sounds do not have a place of their own. I beg to differ with this latter assertion. Chion would even go beyond the idea that there is no soundtrack by claiming that there is no image track either, "but a *place* of images, plus sounds" (Chion 1994, 40). This connects us to Michel de Certeau and his view of lived space and place. If space is a practiced place where things "happen," the same definition may be applied to cinema, to images and sounds. Of course the question of space is tricky because people usually wonder where sound comes from, rather than where it is or where it is going, although the latter two are equally important.

(Just) Space

Gabriel argues eloquently, even if in essentialist terms, that African cinema is most concerned with space, as opposed to conventional Western cinema, which deals mostly with questions of time (1982, 44). He also points to the connections between orality and filmmaking: "Third World films grow from folk tradition where communication is a slow-paced phenomenon and time is not rushed but has its own pace" (1982, 44).[41] Moreover, "Third World Cinema is initiating a coexistence of film art with oral traditions. Non-linearity, repetition of images and graphic representation have very much in common with folk customs" (1982, 48). Gabriel continues his earlier argument about time and space by pointing out that what Westerners perceive as cinematic excess (when the action lags in the movie) is exactly the element that defines Third World cinema. He actually means excess of space, but the analyses of the films will show that time also expands alongside space; when "nothing" happens onscreen, both space and time expand. The natural conclusion is that there are multiple types of excess at work in the cinema of Mambety, as well as in that of other Senegalese filmmakers and those from other African francophone countries. Excesses also take the shape of exaggerated sound or sounds, as well as that of several narrative and sonic layers.

Mambety's films, particularly the first two—*Contras' City* and *Badou Boy*—challenge the spatial limits and limitations of the city through constant movement and engagement with the surroundings: space is reconstructed through and by the eye of the camera, as well as through an aural remapping of the Dakar neighborhoods. It would not be a stretch to consider Mambety's aural map of Dakar as tributary to the city symphony genre, particularly Walter Ruttmann's *Berlin: Symphony of a Great City* (1927), André Sauvage's *Etudes sur Paris* (1928), and Dziga Vertov's *Man With a Movie Camera* (1929). It is worth noting that the first two films offer a centripetal visual movement from the outskirts toward the center as they attempt to capture the spirit of the European city visually and aurally. On the contrary, Mambety's sound generally lingers over liminal spaces mostly on the outskirts and pushes out, expanding city space in a centrifugal progression. Both Ruttmann and Vertov rely on the visual to create a symphony of movement. Furthermore, Vertov uses the theory of intervals (distances between shots; in music it refers to the difference between two pitches) to organize film fragments into a coherent, cohesive visual narrative—in a word, montage. While Mambety also reorganizes the city visually, he makes a more concerted effort to add or even supplant the visual map with an aural one—a symphony of sounds, not just images.

At the center of this symphony of images and sounds, one finds the main character of *Badou Boy*, for example. Badou is a true flaneur of Dakar who helps transform and map a new city. The nineteenth-century flaneur—the epitome of modernity, as implied by Charles Baudelaire in "Le Peintre de la vie moderne" (1863)—shaped Paris sociologically and culturally. The character of Badou Boy morphs into the epitome of postcolonial subjectivity, because he engages with one of the great cities of the West African coast, Dakar, which has long endured the effects of colonialism and neocolonialism. Françoise Pfaff remarks that the nineteenth-century urban expansion of francophone sub-Saharan capitals was done to "serve the economic interests of European colonialism—that is, to funnel trade between African colonies and Europe—and not necessarily the interests of the native populations" (2004, 90). Badou's movement, on the contrary, expands the urban space of Dakar primarily for himself, and secondarily through him for other natives. *Contras' City* does not have any actual characters, which results in the camera being the main character—a veritable *caméra-flâneur*. In this instance, it is the camera itself that generates, expands, and controls space. However, a narrative shift from the visual to the aural is already at work in these two films, and it will come to fruition in *Touki Bouki*. As the characters and camera of Mambety's films transgress physical space, it would seem only natural that a similar event takes place at the level of sound. The noises and voices have a comparable capacity to generate new spaces, diegetically and extradiegetically, as the city and its characters (who are also the characters of the films) keep changing.

The Western ("our") understanding of space has gone through changes, too. In his *Principles of Philosophy*, Descartes argued for space as a corporeal substance, claiming that body, or matter, and space are interchangeable through the fundamental attribute of the former, extension. Extension is indelibly connected to the body: essentially, the body maintains its quality of a body no matter what changes might occur (losing hair, color, size, etc.). Space, like the body, has an extension. This is not the case for nothingness, which is inherently without property. So, there is no vacuum—there cannot be any empty space, and instead space is filled constantly.[42] Opposing Descartes, Leibniz asserted that it was body or matter that logically preceded the existence of space, and that bodies form an ideal system, an abstract structure of relations.

It is perhaps from this debate that Michel de Certeau drew his distinction between space (*espace*) and place (*lieu*), where the latter is "the order (of whatever kind) in accord with which elements are distributed in relationships of coexistence" (1998, 117). His definition of what constitutes space also relies on an established structure of relations, but these relations have a mobile quality: "Space is composed of intersections of mobile elements . . . *space is a practiced place*. Thus the street geometrically defined by urban planning is transformed into a space by walkers" (ibid.). The walkers are constantly moving, so naturally space should be changing along with their movement because "to walk is to lack a place" (de Certeau 1998, 103). It appears that de Certeau combines Descartes's and Leibniz's lines of thought, which eventually helps him explain the quotidian, the creation and expansion of the modern city, as well as the narrative dynamic of stories: "Stories thus carry out a labor that constantly transforms places into spaces or spaces into places" (118). Sound can function in a very similar manner. There are multiple sounds in/of a film that in theory are assembled by a set of relations. Their presence, their interaction as mobile elements should create space. This space may disappear, or become place, when the sound is completely taken away (although that rarely occurs), but ultimately there is no empty space even when there is complete silence. By the same token, Leibniz maintains that there is no empty space in the world, which this time is in line with Descartes's thought. Given that all objects are in a set of ideal relations, Leibniz posits that space is continuous, homogenous, and divisible; the last quality anticipates the argument that sonic space can split into different narrative levels. Leibniz clarifies that these properties of space are only possible once they are recognized to be ideal, or imaginary, which is exactly why diegetic sound produces space, ideal and imaginary (i.e., phantasmagoric). It should already be clear that sound challenges our original understandings of space.

Descartes does find a very important supporter who reshapes the rationalist and empiricist concepts of space in *The Critique of Pure Reason* (1781): Immanuel Kant. Kant argued that space is an *a priori* intuition (this usual translation of the German "*Anschauung*" is problematic; Kant may mean something closer to "apprehension"), and that humans require an idea of space: "Space is a necessary *a priori* representation that underlies all outer intuitions" (A25/B38–9). He also contends that people can imagine space as empty, with no objects filling it, but there is no absolute absence of space. It is "there": "One can never forge a representation of the absence of space, though one can quite well think that no things are to be met within it. It must therefore be regarded as the condition of the possibility of appearances, and not as a determination dependent upon them, and it is an *a priori* representation that necessarily underlies outer appearances" (A25/B38–9). Space is not a concept since it is "an infinite given magnitude," (A25/B39), and also because unlike concepts, the different spaces are not in a relation to a wider view of space as a unitary whole. Kant contrasts his view with previous notions established by Leibniz: "Now what are space and time? Are they actual entities? Are they only determinations or relations of things, yet ones that would pertain to them even if they were not intuited? Or are they such that they belong only to the form of intuition, and therefore to the subjective constitution of our mind?" (A23/B37–8) and "Space is not discursive . . . but a pure intuition" (A25/B39). Maurice Merleau-Ponty would later build on this notion of intuition/apprehension of space by focusing on perception as the only possible reality, one constructed by the intellect: "Thus space is no longer a medium of simultaneous objects capable of being apprehended by an absolute observer who is equally close to them all, a medium without point of view, without body and without spatial position—in sum, the medium of pure intellect" (Merleau-Ponty 2004, 41). The connection that brings together space, intuition, and intellect justifies the claim that sound can generate an imagined, sonic space.

There is another way to arrive at the same conclusion. Henri Lefebvre's *The Production of Space* (1991) demonstrates that space is not just a form of perceiving, "a mental place" (1991, 3),[43] but also a social form. Lefebvre's social space is a product; it is produced by social activities and relationships (73, 85). Furthermore, "*Social spaces interpenetrate one another and/or superimpose themselves upon one another*" (86, emphasis in original), which models my understanding of sonic spatial levels perfectly. In the essay "Space and the State" (2009), Lefebvre's social space is also linked with the idea of state: "The State binds itself to space through a complex and changing relation that has passed through certain critical points" (2009, 224). These critical points evolve from the physical space of the state to a social space (such as state institutions where laws are communicated through the national language of the state), and finally to a mental space that "includes the representations of the State that people construct" (2009, 225). The mental space constructed by the Senegalese concerning their own state connects with the cinematic phantasmagoric and aural space of Mambety's films. From the divergences and parallelisms between spaces of representation and representation of spaces, Lefebvre goes on to argue for the birth of many types of spaces: analogic, cosmological, symbolic, perspectival, and finally capitalistic. While the political aspect of his analysis of space is of less consequence, capitalistic space is described as being both homogeneous and fragmented (2009, 233). It is this absurd split that is fascinating in relation to the analysis of Mambety's sound space(s); there must be fragmented sonic spaces within the diegesis of his film. In other words, since space proves to be malleable in Lefebvre's analysis, one can reason that part of our collective space is not only social and ideological, but also phantasmagoric, imagined.[44] Subsequent chapters of this volume will reveal that the fluid quality of ideological space is well matched to the space created by sound in film, whether diegetic or nondiegetic. The phantasmagorical space is also unpredictable, so it has to be anchored in something concrete, like diegetic sonic space. The latter will necessarily be split from visual space in order to generate a new kind of space. Indeed, normally, "we accept seen space as real only when it contains sounds as well, for these give it the dimension of depth" (Balazs 1985, 119), and sound can be used to "elongate space" (Mintz 1985, 289) as it does in Orson Welles's films. In other words, sound makes the spectators aware of space, although it is a different space from the one enclosing the audience in the theater. This sonic space is an unlimited one, as opposed to our perception of the image, which is limited by its framing.

Hence, because phantasmagoric space is more or less a figment of the imagination that emerges from heard fantasies, there is a need to anchor it in some type of reality.[45] In other words, there must be a manifestation of it in "real," diegetic space. That anchor comes from Gilles Deleuze's gloss on Pascal Augé's term "any-space-whatsoever": "It is a perfectly singular space, which has merely lost its homogeneity, that is, the principle of its metric relations or the connections of its own parts" (1989, 109). These are spaces that confine us; they can be created through shadows (as in German Expressionist film), whites, or true-color images, but most importantly there is a movement from a physical space to a spiritual one: "The first space is cell-like and closed, but the second is no different, it is the same in so far as it has merely discovered the spiritual opening which overcomes all its formal obligations and material constraints by a theoretical and practical evasion" (1989, 117). The access to the second Deleuzian space is facilitated by sound, which challenges the homogeneity of the singular space of cinema.

So, what exactly is considered sound? I define sound as broadly as possible: sound as noise (diegetic or extradiegetic), synchronous and asynchronous;

sound as voice (diegetic and nondiegetic—voice-over); sound as music (diegetic, intradiegetic, and also, as pure soundtrack, nondiegetic).[46] These categories allow for gaps: the "fantastical gap" between diegetic and nondiegetic music, or the narrow line separating noise and voice, which is "elusive and uncertain" (Dolar 2006, 13). More formally, sound can be analyzed at three different levels: sound as a fantasy, or as it is perceived by the audience; sound in between audience and screen (sound occupying the space of the fourth wall); and finally, sound on-screen and within the diegetic space of the films, which also returns us to sound as fantasy. Thus, this study begins and ends with connections between sound and psychoanalysis, as a way to assert that sound can be understood as a fantasy projection. This is where the concept of space becomes critically important; in the films of Mambety, sound creates not only space but a space of fantasy meant to protect the postcolonial subject from the horrors of the Real. In other words, sound acts as a secondary, yet more powerful fantasy veil, and it helps postcolonial subjects negotiate their identity in the only space that belongs uniquely to them, sonic space.

The psychoanalytical conversation about sound turns to the corporeality of sound through an alignment with Freud's concept of the ego. Sound's physical quality entails a redefinition of Doane's acoustic space, and by using Gilles Deleuze's Baroque house metaphor (i.e., pleats of matter on the first floor, pleats of soul on the second) to explain the relationship between screen and audience we may eradicate the fourth wall through sound. Cultural differences between Western and Senegalese acoustic spaces will be essential to this eradication, because they present themselves as quite dissimilar; sound, like space, is conceptualized differently in the Hexagon, in Eastern Europe, in Africa. Finally, emerging from the conversation on Deleuze's pleats of matter, the argument returns to the screen, inside the films, in order to tease out the narrative planes generated by diegetic and extradiegetic sounds, and their effect on our construct of fantasy. According to Bela Balazs, "Just as the film can show visual landscapes, so it can show acoustic landscapes, a tonal milieu" (1985, 122). Again, within these landscapes, there are several avenues of analysis as one follows noises and sounds, voices, and music.

Music is particularly pertinent to the culturally specific conversation about sound. In other words, the final claim at stake here is that a typically Senegalese sound or music that creates a typically Senegalese space is possible, not unlike Fanon's view of specific blackness. That is to say that "blackness" has different connotations depending on the social context within which it is seen—"the black man possesses two dimensions: one with his fellow Blacks, the other with the Whites" (Fanon 2008, 1)—and blackness is understood in relationship to whiteness (93–97). Kaja Silverman observes that Fanon fights with his own image and is in perpetual conflict with it, which leads his body to fragment and have multiple points of spatial identity (1996, 28–19). In an important documentary, *Race: A Floating Signifier* (1997), Stuart Hall proposes a similar understanding of the construct of races, suggesting that race is an unfixed social construction that changes over time and space. If one transposes these thoughts to the relationship between image and sound (i.e., the latter has two dimensions, one evident through its relationship to the former, and one independent of it), and if one considers sound as having a floating signifier quality, then sound can begin to change its symbolic value depending on a culturally specific environment.

A quick example: most films by Mambety, and perhaps most incessantly *La petite vendeuse de soleil*, feature a mélange of Western music, like jazz, and traditional music, like that of a kora or the ever-present percussion instruments, the djembes. These categories might be in a binary opposition—ours versus theirs, as signaled by Willemen—but to Mambety, they are in dialogue and they create something new. Even the particular instruments suggest an innate narrative flexibility, as Ebron notes: "The kora does not produce a strong rhythmic dance beat . . . its rhythms are more subtle and layered" (2002, 57). Rhythm is associated with music and with subtle narrative layers. Fanon might not have protested against this association as strongly and acerbically as he did against Senghor's praise of rhythm in sculpture: "And this race staggered under the weight of one basic element. *Rhythm*! Listen to Senghor, our bard . . . Have I read it correctly? I give it an even closer reading. On the other side of the white world there lies a magical black culture. Negro sculpture!" (2008, 102).[47] To Senghor rhythm is indeed at the heart of African aesthetics. Undervalued in the European order, rhythm is emotion, the vital force that explains the imbalances or misperceived asymmetry of African sculpture.

In her study of Negritude, Ebong understands these values—intuition, emotion, rhythm, and vital force—or rather the "abstract characterization of the values it [Negritude] imagined as ancestral African art forms"—as the reasons why "Negritude was limited as an aesthetic" (1999, 132). Even though the influences of the cultural movement of Negritude—Senghor's lifelong fight—on Mambety's films are difficult to pinpoint, "Mambety's work often seems more in tune with certain aspects of Negritude thought" (Murphy and Williams 2007, 94).[48] Ebong does not mention Mambety explicitly in her essay, but she does discuss the cultural impact of the *École de Dakar* painters and the work of Negritude artists such as the aforementioned Issa Samb of the Agit-Art Laboratory (1999, 139–141), to whom Mambety was connected. The *laboratoire* artists, Mambety included, had an intense awareness of avant-garde French ideas that clearly influenced their aesthetic choices. Souleymane Diagne offers us a more direct link with Negritude and Senghor when he looks at the notion of rhythm in African poetry, which emphasizes parataxis—juxtaposition and coordination (2011, 93).[49] Extrapolated to cinema, parataxis anticipates a discussion of the aesthetic connections between Mambety and Sergei Eisenstein.

The layered rhythms of the kora are but one small component of a larger musical performance, but Ebron describes the latter in similar terms: "Jali performances are an exceptionally rich and multilayered site of cultural negotiation" (2002, 19). If one thinks of film as a performance act made up of several other performance components, then Bhabha's negotiation of and between spaces comes back into focus here. Two types of music, each multilayered, imply multiple separate spaces—multiple sonic spaces—within the same diegesis. Instead of explicating this binary relationship in terms of modernity and tradition (thereby implying that Senegalese culture is an anachronism), the focus will be on the delicate political and cultural negotiation between the colonizing and the colonized cultures, which align with the relationship between image and sound. This approach will further our analysis within the space created by culturally specific sounds and trace either their harmonious, emotional interactions or their contentious juxtapositions.

Classical Hollywood Cinema: Sonic Spaces

The introductory incursion into the aesthetic separation between the three types of cinema ends with the First Cinema, specifically with classical Hollywood cinema. For the most part the films in this category do not draw attention to the act of filming, making a sustained effort to conceal the cinematic apparatus. The plot is character-driven, and the editing gives the feeling of seamless continuity. Thanks to this illusion the spectators can identify more easily with the characters onscreen as they lose themselves in the diegesis (through suture). Hollywood-style cinema tends to close the oedipal cycle of its male characters (meaning that they search for stability, and following a period of distress or a crisis, they tend to conform to social norms such as marriage), and generally offers a positive denouement. Sound's role in Hollywood-style cinema has usually fallen under the same rules based on continuity. In other words, it has worked along with the image toward creating a nearly perfect impression of reality.

According to the rules of continuity, if a gun goes off, the spectators hear the sound of a gun; the sound matches perfectly with what they see onscreen, because that is what they expect to hear. In Second Cinema, directors experiment with sound, which occasionally goes against the image on screen. This is not necessarily an exact opposition, but rather a transgression; the spectators hear what they do not expect to hear following what their eyes register visually. For example, Godard's character Michel in *Breathless* (1960) picks up a gun from the glove compartment. The visual of the gun immediately suggests that something bad will happen. When he points the gun toward the sun and a loud gunshot is heard on the soundtrack at that very moment, it is an obvious extradiegetic addition because the gun does not actually go off. The loud sound of the gun (and its echolike follow-up) momentarily takes over the entire diegesis. Michel shoots at the sun metaphorically, and therefore, at visuality as a whole. If the sun dies, then obscurity (which is, interestingly, the *a priori* condition of cinema: being in the dark room, where the light of the cinema, of dreams, desires, fantasies, and fears, replaces that of the sun[50]), fantasy, and imagination will reign. So the audience is warned from the beginning that an often playful atmosphere will develop throughout the rest of the film. A split occurs here, where sound transgresses its limitations and begins to take on a life of its own. Sound tells us a story by itself, almost independent of the visual. The visual is still needed in order to situate the sound diegetically, but the slight echo heard following the sound of the gun continues to *live* on, independently of the image. Of course, the echo also becomes an editing tool, a sort of sound bridge between the visual shots, but within that space, the lack that occurs between shots, a new narrative plane is born.

The lingering echo of Michel's shot is the type of sound use that interests me even more in the context of Mambety's films, in which one finds several such instances (one might substitute the gun for the shrieking birds of *Touki Bouki*). Two immediate questions arise: what kind of spaces does sound create, and is there such a thing as a culturally specific sound? Concerning the latter question, the hope is to move past the reductive divisions between the West and Africa. The aim is to go beyond simply associating the sound of a drum, for example, with Senegalese culture. Instead, the hypothesis is that sound adorns African cinema, and Mambety's in particular, in ways that are congruent with regional cultural practices (just as certain conventional sounds inhabit Hollywood-style cinema), such as particular understandings of space or how stories are told.

Since Third Cinema and the cinema of Mambety do have a sociopolitical angle, another goal of this book is to unveil the role that sound plays socially for the Senegalese director. The intention is to connect this particular use of sound to orality, and to explore the unique type of cinema that develops from this alliance. This cinema is born out of a new type of space, a phantasmagoric sonic space that challenges existing notions of spatiality. Doane finds three different kinds of space in film: that of the diegesis, (i.e., where the action happens), that of the screen (as an actual rectangular space), and the acoustic space of the theater. In classical narrative film the last two spaces work in order to legitimize the existence of the first. In other words, the classic cinematic apparatus conceals the last two spaces, and "if a character looks at and speaks to the spectator, this constitutes an acknowledgement that the character is seen and heard in a radically different space and is therefore generally read as transgressive" (Doane

1985, 166–167). The first, diegetic space is also, significantly, a "virtual space." It is within that space that I will explore the creation of a unique aural space, one born out of fantasy, out of what is imagined when certain sounds are heard (or not heard).

Doane's acoustic space is an aural milieu in which the spectator is enveloped by the sound (Doane 1985, 170–171). This idea, and the study of the other theorists who have been concerned with subjectivity and voice, will take better shape in the discussion of singing voices in *La petite vendeuse de soleil*. This discussion reconstructs Doane's acoustic space to claim that it eradicates the fourth wall and thus unites diegetic characters and spectators in the common goal of reaching a stable postcolonial subjectivity. A director who does not follow the classic narrative constraints on image, sound, and continuity makes this reconstruction possible. The concept of fantasy will return numerous times throughout the book, and I am aware that using psychoanalysis, which is quintessentially Western, to explain African cinematic tendencies may be problematic to some. However, this line of thought follows in the footsteps of David Murphy and Laura Mulvey, whose work on Sembène has often benefited from the study of Freud and fetishism, and Kenneth Harrow, who uses heavy doses of Jacques Lacan and Slavoj Žižek in order to explore postmodernism in African cinema. Here is how Harrow explains his choice: "As the medium that brings us closest to the imaginary, to the mirror stage in which the specular is dominant, to the realm in which the viewing subject must relinquish a hold, if only temporarily, on the credibility of an authorized account of reality, film might best provide the site for us to understand how fantasy and desire are not simply distractions from truthful accounts, but inevitable factors in the ideological interpellation of any viewing audience" (2007, 15). The visual is the most developed human sense, and one tends to believe what one sees; this is a genetic predisposition from which cinema benefits greatly. Film is indeed Harrow's site of negotiating fantasy and desire, but a more nuanced dialogue concerning these two occurs at the level of sound.

The Acousmatic Panopticon

The troubled political negotiation between the colonizers and the colonized is thoroughly exposed in Mambety's work, and as a result it is the colonizer/colonized dichotomy that defines cinematic space and postcolonial space. The nineteenth-century French penal colonies, structures that relied on typical prison surveillance, must have covertly informed the ways in which control and power were maintained in other contexts, too. So how do control and power propagate in the postcolonial space, a space that is supposed to be independent, free of outside influences? The obvious answer is through vestiges, through architecture, through symbols, in other words through a constant visual presence. The colonizers are still present, even if that presence is not necessarily a physical one; it is no longer the flesh and bone but rather the idea of the colonizer that controls the space. Ultimately, it is the act of seeing that allows the colonizer to remain relevant, to continue existing in a space that was never a rightful possession. It is an interesting type of surveillance: a panopticon that lacks a physical structure in the traditional sense of a tower from which the observing, disciplining eye (of the colonizer) controls the space and the people. Mentally, though, the imaginary shadow of the tower still defines postcolonial space.

Mambety combats this visual presence in two steps: first, he exposes it, naturally through the camera; second, he offers an alternative, a focus on aural space. The postcolonial space sheds its attachment to the colonial predecessor through a refocalization, a departure from the restrictive rules of the visual. Sound—noises, music, voices, all unique and representative of Dakar, of Senegal, of Mambety's films—then, controls space and redirects power like Foucault's panopticon, but through the ear and not the eye. It works not through typical visual towers, but rather through *towering* sounds: among others, megaphones atop minarets, sirens, the radio, and especially the voices of several central characters, whether heard within the diegesis or outside of it, as voice-over. There is often a tension in play between the diegetic and the nondiegetic in African film that is strongest in Mambety's work, most obviously in the use of sound. The inside/outside dichotomy is one of the main points of interest to Diawara in his book on culture and aesthetics in African film, and it remains a point of discussion in his more recent work. He splits the two spaces aesthetically and narratively, with the outside representing danger and the negative while the inside embraces order and positivity (a typical example is outside/city, inside/village). Adding sound and image to this opposition (image/diegetic/inside versus sound/nondiegetic/outside) will complicate this current understanding of space and African film aesthetics.

There are several aural techniques that help construct this new version of power. The nondiegetic noises and music often provide the audience with an acousmatic effect: a new level of omniscient power is added through a sound technique that Chion calls the *acousmêtre*. The *acousmêtre* refers to a sound whose origin is not obvious; the disembodied voice seems to come from everywhere, and has four principal qualities: ubiquity, panopticism, omniscience, and omnipotence (1999, 23–24). Thus the *acousmêtre* has an intrinsically divine quality. Furthermore, in Chion's opinion, the greatest *acousmêtre* is in fact God, and "even farther back, for every one of us, the Mother" (1999, 27). The mother constitutes an *acousmêtre* because during gestation, the voice of the mother is all a child hears, and it is ever present like an umbilical web (1999, 61). In Mambety's last film, *La petite vendeuse*, the main character only has a grandmother. The grandmother happens to be blind, which reinforces the lack of narrative power of the visual in the film. She sings, and her songs carry through the entire neighborhood. The acousmatic and anchored voices of the grandmother dominate the soundtrack, and in their hovering, they become the primary narrative tool of the film. In fact, the voice and its song control and remap the space in the manner of the traditional visual panopticon. Because the audience can see the grandmother and hear her voice, the effect created is one of an "acousmatic panopticon," different from purely visual monitoring, different from the *acousmêtre* in that its location is actually known, and different from "panuralism," a term that has been used primarily by social scientist Michael Gallagher of the University of Edinburgh. In an article entitled "Are Schools Panoptic?" (2010) Gallagher conducts empirical research that establishes schools as panoptic spaces within which surveillance occurs equally at the level of hearing: "There is no reason to suppose that disciplinary surveillance must be limited to the realm of the visual" (2010, 268).

The acousmatic panopticon maintains all the qualities of the *acousmêtre*, while sometimes also revealing its position. Finding out the source of the grandmother's voice and song is not just a simple de-acousmatization, of which Chion says: "An inherent quality of the acousmêtre is that it can be instantly dispossessed of its mysterious powers (seeing all, omniscience, omnipotence, ubiquity) when it is *de-acousmatized*, when the film reveals the face that is the source of the voice" (Chion 1994, 130). Moreover, through the revelation of the face, and thus of the individual's singularity, de-acousmatization encloses the voice "in the circumscribed limits of a body—which tames the voice and drains it of its power" (Chion 1994, 131). At first, this process appears to dispel the acousmatic quality of the panopticon (i.e., that it maintains its acousmatic attributes regardless of the visibility of the source). However, even though the voice returns to the body and the audience can assign a source to the uncanny voice, that voice never *fully* returns, just as the disappearance of the physical tower does not erase the mental presence of the visual. Recent studies by Žižek, and particularly Mladen Dolar, to which I will return, also dismiss the process of de-acousmatization. The acousmatic panopticon allows for spatial coherence because it combines visual and aural powers (hears all, sees all). Because the characters (and the spectators) know where the voice and song are placed, they are suddenly under surveillance, under one voice. However, the acousmatic panopticon is not a structure for punishment, as described by Foucault and Bentham; on the contrary, it allows the postcolonial space to rearrange itself following the local perspective, local understanding of space, local *intuition*. That is to say that space (aural, cinematic, urban, etc.) is no longer perceived through the orientalist perspective, but rather is reclaimed via a most powerful African narrative tool—the voice, or fragments, fetishes of voice embodied by various noises. Of course, the narrative power of

Africans should not be reduced just to oral stories. African directors, and Mambety in particular, have mastered the apparatus of cinema, which is ontologically Western, and have altered the use of one element—sound—that is both a remnant of the oral tradition of storytelling and a way to shape cinema anew.

The relationship between the panopticon, an inherently visual device, and the *acousmêtre*, which belongs to the realm of sound, might help define the elusive postcolonial space. The concept of the panopticon is explained in Foucault's seminal work *Discipline and Punish*, which first recounts how punishments used to be publicly displayed, as a demonstration that underlined the power of the king (1995, 3–5). The public physical punishment is what Foucault calls an exercise of terror: "a policy of terror: to make everyone aware, through the body of the criminal, of the unrestrained presence of the sovereign. The public execution did not re-establish justice; it reactivated power" (49). These scenes of terror reach their potential because they are seen, observed. Without the visual element, the effect would be lost: "Not only must people know, they must see with their own eyes. Because they must be made to be afraid; but also because they must be the witnesses, the guarantors, of the punishment, and because they must to a certain extent take part in it" (58).

The spectators' involvement becomes particularly important in the postcolonial context, in which the subject reverses the witnessing. The practices of torture evolved, leading to "the disappearance of the spectacle and the elimination of pain" (Foucault 1995, 11), and "the body as the major target of penal repression disappeared" (8). Eventually, Foucault proposes, the panopticon becomes the most effective tool of punishment and discipline (197), a prison in which the slightest moves are observed and recorded, or might be, and in which "permanent visibility . . . assures the automatic functioning of power" (201). In the Foucauldian world, the panopticon produces "homogenous effects of power" (202), which in turn produce belief, even if sometimes that belief is misguided. The prisoners never know if they are being watched, but they must think that they could be watched at any moment. Permanent visibility, in fact "a single gaze to see everything constantly," ensures that the panopticon becomes the "perfect disciplinary apparatus" (173). The panopticon, like the *acousmêtre*, sees all. The ultimate goal of the punishment system is to discipline: "The perpetual penalty that traverses all points and supervises every instant in the disciplinary institutions compares, differentiates, hierarchizes, homogenizes, excludes. In short, it *normalizes*" (183).

In the preceding pages, the words "discipline" and "control" have been used, even though Foucault only hints at the latter. It is Deleuze who later exposes the transition from the nineteenth-century societies of punishment and discipline to the twentieth century and what he calls control societies, in which individuals cannot escape anything; they are always conditioned by a system. We may speculate that a variation is introduced in the postcolonial world: the control societies evolve from punishment societies but retain some of their features, which leads to the unification of space. So within the postcolonial world, the role of the acousmatic panopticon is ontologically similar to its two components; it seeks to normalize. It seeks to unify the postcolonial aural space through specificity: the specificity of regional sound, of the native voice, of traditional music, which are valuable and viable cultural alternatives to sounds from the colonizing space. Therefore, the acousmatic panopticon begins to compensate for the negative effects of the colonially centered visual and aural vestiges. In summary, the acousmatic panopticon seeks to normalize by limiting the influence of the West and by recharting and potentially homogenizing the space that rightfully belongs to the postcolonized.

It would appear unnecessary to discuss so-called normative attributes of punishment in the context of postcolonial space, although the idea of "normalizing" exists behind colonial endeavors. As already mentioned, it is through the buildings, vestiges, and even aural echoes of the colonial that the oppressing power maintains its control over the people. But that power exists also in other elements, even geographical ones, such as the island of Gorée, a slave hub off the coast of Dakar that stands as a remnant of colonization and a reminder of times past. This island plays a crucial role in almost all of Mambety's films. The way space is structured in the postcolonial world reinforces a spectral presence, the "shadow" of a tower. Foucault looks at punishment as having a social function and being a political tactic (1995, 23); colonization follows a similar pattern, and it is so effective that it allows the postcolonial to survive through an invisible punishment. The visual punishment in the postcolonial does not rely on the physical body; instead, it affects wider areas, concepts, and the construction of space itself. In the films of Mambety, though, in order to drive home the point of postcolonial punishment and to reveal the apparatus of the postcolonial, the bodies of the cinematic subjects do suffer obvious physical punishment; they degenerate from Anta's healthy, masculinized body, to Ramatou's artificial limbs, to Sili's atrophied legs, to characters with no legs at all.

Before we delineate the structure of the chapters, I shall set forth my central thesis. My overarching argument is that sound challenges the primacy of the image in the films of Mambety and that in doing so it remaps the narrative layers of the films. I propose that, directly stemming from this practice, the oral tradition of Senegal can coexist with and perhaps even supplant the medium of the moving image. After all, as Bazin declares, "the primacy of the image is both historically and technically accidental" (1967, 21). Mambety's reversal of the primacy of image and sound may have accidental roots, too. In an interview with June Givanni (1995), he relates that as a child he and his friends would go to an outdoor theater, but because they had no money, they just listened from the outside. Mambety credits his sustained interest in sound to how he first experienced cinema, as a listener (30). It would not be a stretch to imagine that the mature Mambety sought to recreate his original encounter with cinema for his viewers—not in a perverted, punishing way, but rather as an effort to maintain the magic of cinema as he first experienced it, through an overvalorization of sound.

The book begins with diegetic sonic space, within which several different narrative planes are explored—*sound as multiple narrative spaces*. Here the real and the fantastic overlap, inasmuch as diegetic sonic space, even though physically "heard," must also be imagined to a certain extent; this helps the transition to *sound as fantasy*—sound that produces a phantasmagoric space. Within that space, it is necessary to distinguish between voice (further categorized as diegetic voice and nondiegetic voice-over) and all other sounds that may generate an imagined space. Naturally, there are many links to psychoanalysis here, through Lacan's subjectivity, Silverman's acoustic mirror, fantasy (as understood by several theorists), and Freud's concept of the ego. In connection with this last aspect, sound will be shown to possess a physical, tangible quality, a sense of corporeality, and this venue will constitute the second level of critical inquiry: *sound is a physical presence*. Third, the reconsideration of Doane's acoustic space and its impact on spectatorship aligns that space with Deleuze's metaphor of the Baroque house. The acoustic breakdown of the fourth wall alters both spectatorship and screen space; sound carries both ways in a theater, as opposed to the tradition of one-way thinking, from the screen onto the audience.

Chapter Summaries

Chapter 1, "Aural Space and the Sonic Rack Focus in *Touki Bouki*," begins with an in-depth analysis of Mambety's most influential film, foregrounded because it is the best example of how sound works in his films. In order to reveal the various aural narrative planes, the chapter introduces a new term, the "sonic rack focus effect," which will also facilitate negotiating the inherent tension between diegetic and nondiegetic spaces. Chapter 2, "Flaneur, Geography, and *Caméra-Flâneur* in *Badou Boy* and *Contras' City*," turns to Mambety's first two films, which aurally map out the postcolonial city of Dakar; it is the aural maps, doubled by actual maps within the diegesis, that reconstruct the postcolonial space. These first chapters also constitute a move into a closer analysis of the dialogue between sound and orality. The next two chapters move toward fantasy, islands, and phantasmagoric space, necessarily suggested by the aural maps' imagined space. Chapter 3, "Trauma and Zombie Narratives in *Hyènes*," establishes connections between Mambety's *Hyènes* and Haitian zombie narratives to show how multiple cultures come together in the adaptation of a Swiss play set in contemporary

Senegal. Although sound plays a peripheral role in this film, the chapter is framed around the concept of "spectral sound," sound that cannot die, like a zombie. Chapters 1–3 will also provide us with enough evidence to link the first four films by Mambety into one cohesive narrative. The director takes his public from the cinéma vérité style of *Contras' City*, which reveals the postcolonial city of Dakar, to the creation of the African flaneur in *Badou Boy*, who roams the same city. This walker anticipates Mory from *Touki Bouki*, who in turn will become Draman in *Hyènes* and another type of walker—the dead kind. The last two films were meant to be part of a trilogy on power. According to Mambety himself, the character of Anta from *Touki Bouki* is reprised later on in *Hyènes*: "I began to make *Hyènes* when I realized I absolutely had to find one of the characters in *Touki Bouki*, which I had made twenty years before. This is Anta, the girl who had the courage to leave Africa and cross the Atlantic alone" (Ukadike 2002, 124). Thus this first block of related films comprises a series of stories, not unlike a collection of African fairy tales.

In the last chapter, the emphasis will be on Mambety's last two films, which begin another collection, a trilogy on money that is closely linked to African orality and storytelling. This final chapter, "Voice(s) in *Le franc* and *La petite vendeuse de soleil*," continues the discussion of orality, not only at the level of sound but also in the narrative construction of the films; this follows the typical structure of Western fairy tales, with a focus on the actantial model as well as several narrative elements associated with African folk stories. At the heart of the chapter will be a discussion of the role that the voice, particularly the female voice, plays within our larger consideration of sound. Finally, the conclusion looks to the legacy of Mambety, and speculates as to where his cinema might stand in history.

1 Aural Space and the Sonic Rack Focus in *Touki Bouki*

Since Djibril Diop Mambety's most influential film, *Touki Bouki*, acts as an aesthetic and thematic lynchpin that connects his entire oeuvre, it seems appropriate to begin this study with it. *Touki Bouki* is a movie about the particular but also about the universal and the community; it is a political satire, a lyrical work about love, a drama about exile. This drama accentuates the contradictions between outside and inside, even though "it is difficult to remember a shot filmed inside in a film by Djibril. Mambety likes transparency. He works in broad daylight and in front of everyone" (Sene 2001, 79).[1] A stark contrast arises nonetheless because the constant outdoor shooting is juxtaposed with the interior drama, the internal struggle of each character. Although *Touki Bouki* is poignant in its incisive sociopolitical commentary, it is slow and indirect when dealing with marginality, which informs the personal tragedy of the two main characters. However, the present analysis will focus on the internal conflict between image and sound. Reading the film at both visual and aural levels, quite as Michel Chion proposes to audio-view films (1994, 185–213), facilitates a better contextualization of current sound theories.

It has already been suggested that Mambety challenges the primacy of visual space by juxtaposing the various aural planes emerging from the plurality and plasticity of sound with the existing, more rigid two-dimensional visual planes. New, aural narrative planes are created by this juxtaposition. These narrative planes are revealed throughout the film, but most clearly in four separate sequences, which can be reduced to the following spatial and aural markers: the slaughterhouse, the neighborhood, the cliff, and the harbor. These markers, woven into the narrative fabric of the film, will reveal exactly what the aural narrative plane means.

The main characters of *Touki Bouki*, Anta and Mory, are a young couple dreaming of emigrating to France, but they have no money to travel. They become a Senegalese version of Godard's Patricia and Michel in *Breathless* (1960). The narrative arc of *Breathless* revolves around Michel, a small-time crook fascinated by the persona of Humphrey Bogart. Michel is on the run because he shot a policeman; he is also in love with an American girl, Patricia, who is a student at the Sorbonne and sells the *New York Herald Tribune* on the streets of Paris. The film moves slowly around Paris following the two characters as they attempt to figure out their relationship, each other, and the next step—all elements used by Mambety in the context of Dakar. In the end, Patricia decides to turn Michel in; he is subsequently shot by the police in the middle of the street. In the case of Mory and Anta, the woman, Anta, is fully an accomplice to her male counterpart.[2] Anta and Mory face the harsh economic and social realities of their country, while they also undergo constant changes. The two main characters of *Touki Bouki* thus oscillate between modernity and tradition. I disagree with Sada Niang's assessment that Mambety does not use that opposition to define his characters: "*Touki Bouki* makes us vibrate through this ambivalence: a fascination for elsewhere and an integration of the origin. Some have wanted to see an opposition between tradition and modernity. Mambety has always escaped this dichotomy. To him, modernity was in marginality, in challenging the power and indiscipline, in rebellion, in the force to say 'I' while integrating 'us,' not the 'us' of social constraints but the one of essential values brought on by the origin, transmitted by the story and the myth" (2002, 7).[3] On the contrary, the character of Mory encompasses both traditionalist elements (his very strong connection to the land) and modern ones (like his passion for the motorcycle). These elements help us define Mory as a postcolonial, hybrid subject; he has a split identity, with which he attempts to come to terms throughout the film—and really even beyond, because incarnations of Mory resurface in later films.

As a matter of fact, both characters are hybrids, and so is the film itself. It mixes conventional Western cinema practices, which cannot possibly be fully avoided, and the oral tradition of West African storytelling. Already from the title (frequently translated as "The Journey of the Hyena") it is possible to make a connection to the stories of Birago Diop, *Contes d'Amadou Koumba*, which locate the hyena as a central figure in West African animal tales. David Murphy notes another connection: he associates the film with the trickster narratives of *Leuk-le-lièvre* (2000, 244), although this link makes more sense when aligned with *La petite vendeuse*. However, there is an ongoing debate over the validity of the translation of *Touki Bouki* as "The Journey of the Hyena," which equates Mory with the hyena, "an animal accused of greed and mischievousness" who "symbolizes trickery and social marginality" (Pfaff 1988, 220). Furthermore, the hyena is always portrayed as dirty and lacking intelligence. Obviously few of these attributes apply to the protagonist of the film; even so, critics such as Dennis Essar have fully accepted the parallelism: "It is the main character who is the hyena: on the margins of a society convulsing with rapid, profound, and irreversible cultural change, he strives to achieve his fanciful goal at any cost" (Essar 1996, 78). Niang offers another translation. In his opinion the title remains enigmatic. He separates the two words, suggesting that they are in fact entire sentences and that the full, correct phrase should read "*Touki bu nu buki*, which should be translated as a voyage that has been 'hyenazied'" (Niang 2002, 129),[4] in which "hyenazied" refers to achieving one's goals and ambitions. Regardless of the outcome of this debate, Mambety's film exudes ambivalence starting with its very title. Mambety's dualism further separates him from other African directors. His films, and in particular *Touki Bouki*, are not mere attempts to appropriate an existing style (such as the French New Wave or Russian formalism) and to adjust it to an African context. Instead, they attempt to push further, to create new forms of cinema. Murphy also notes that Mambety creates something radically different from adaptation models of Western experimental films to Senegalese culture; the end result is that the film "can be read as an exploration of the cultural encounter between the West and Africa" (Murphy 2000, 243). There is definitely an auteurist aesthetic influence present at the level of film technique, most evident in the lack of narrative linearity, but in the end the main plotline is very simple, harking back to the stories told by griots.

This last term is radically important, because it will provide us with the necessary transition from storyteller to filmmaker. In fact, Murphy and Patrick Williams go as far as to propose the "hybrid *griauteur*, who is an appropriate figure for contemporary African filmic practices" (2007, 9). A griot is essentially a storyteller, and the name has various forms: Paulla Ebron's Mandinka "jali," "gewel" in Wolof, "gawlo" in Fulani, "djeli" in Bambara, and so on. Griots can be musicians or poets, and they range from money-chasing local griots who crash marriages and naming ceremonies in the hope of getting small sums from the celebrants, to griots who legitimize rulers by singing their deeds and advise heads of state on policies. Olivier Barlet describes the griot primarily as a storyteller but also as court jester, wandering minstrel, counselor, news bearer, and even therapist (2000, 162–165). Referring to Barlet's list, Murphy and Williams remark that it is the multiplicity of roles that unites griots and African filmmakers (2007, 9). Griots are a caste one must be born into, and there are both griots and griottes, though there usually are some gender rules about what functions women can perform. In general, griots do not tell stories like animal fables but sing the praises of their patrons and recite genealogies that preserve historical memory. And of course they sing and recite epics like the *Sundiata*.[5] Stories involving Bouki (Hyena), Golo (Monkey), and Leuk (Hare) are not at all confined to members of the griot caste and could well be told by mothers to their children.

It may be inferred that Mambety's film is quintessentially African in its form and more specifically Senegalese; but given that more than a hint of European cinema runs through it, *Touki Bouki* is an example of successful blending of African and European storytelling techniques. Mambety does not simply "Africanize" the European (auteur) cinema of the 1960s. Rather, he balances it with a revamped way of looking at West African oral tradition and storytelling. This modern-day griot has had to develop a new personal style to deliver the stories, to seize and maintain the attention of the audience, and he has taken the best of two often conflicting worlds.

Mambety's personal style is apparent from the composition of the film's first scene. The film begins with two shots of a herd of cows led by a young boy on an ox. These shots precede a series of images of cows being slain in a slaughterhouse, which represents our first spatial marker. From the beginning there is a movement from outside to inside, and this back-and-forth becomes a motif throughout the development of the movie. The outside-inside movement is cinematically doubled and therefore reinforced; the little boy and the herd are shown in long shots, while for the gory images in the slaughterhouse the camera moves in much closer, into medium shots and even close-ups. The length of the first two shots, which are essentially long takes, further emphasizes the sharp contrast between the two episodes. However, once the camera moves inside the editing drastically changes, offering eleven shots in rapid succession. Interestingly, the camera work and rapid editing suggest the killing of the animals; it is the montage technique that cuts, not just the actual knife. This is quite like Hitchcock's *Psycho* (1960); as Kaja Silverman observes, in the famous scene in the shower, the camera becomes an instrument of dissection because of the multiple cuts in the narration: "The cinematic machine is lethal; it too murders and dissects" (Silverman 1983, 202). One particularly graphic shot shows a man slitting a cow's throat open; the camera lingers as blood pours out. It is, however, the only shot in the sequence that is out of focus, as if the director could not show the full-blown violence and tried somehow to mask it. Here also, at the level of a single shot, one witnesses the director's and the film's ambivalence. Images of cattle being herded as a metaphor for the human condition are nothing new to cinema,[6] but in this case the counterpoint shots of people are missing. This sequence clearly echoes Eisenstein's *Strike* (1925) right down to specific details, such as shots of knives gouging open the throats of the cows. Alongside the French New Wave, Eisenstein and formalism are the other cinematic influences that will be compared to Mambety.[7] *Touki Bouki* is in fact an appropriate example of intellectual montage, as Eisenstein called his aesthetic approach to filmmaking. In short, the visual association of shots that normally have nothing in common should elicit a third, new meaning in the minds of the spectators. In *Strike* the shots of slaughtered animals are counterpointed with shots of people fleeing through the woods and being shot at by the military. The juxtaposition between running people and slaughtered cows creates a new meaning and suggests that people are subjugated and treated like animals.

Interestingly, Mambety adds a wrinkle to the intellectual editing: he waits to juxtapose the shots in the slaughterhouse. Thus, there is another subtext lurking at the beginning of the film, but it only comes to life when fellow students attack Mory. Senegalese men are slaughtering the cattle; the aggressors and the victims are both products of the same place. On an obvious interpretive level, this sequence is a negative commentary on halal beliefs and practices. On a more speculative level, it reminds us of Frantz Fanon's warnings about the colonized middle class taking the place of the colonizer and acting in the same abusive way (1968, 153–163). It remains to be determined if the juxtaposition of separated events can still be considered intellectual editing. I maintain that the temporal separation does not take away from generating meaning at the third level envisioned by Eisenstein. As a matter of fact, atemporality plays a large role in Mambety's film, as will become evident throughout this analysis. So Mambety utilizes an atemporal intellectual montage—a variation of the original theory that better suits a culture and society less keen on time, as Teshome Gabriel instructs us.

Time seems curiously absent from the very first scenes, a fact made even more obvious through the aesthetic use of noises and anachronous sound, which also provides the audience with another tension between inside and outside (in that anachronous sound remains on the outside of the diegesis, a literal add-on). It is appropriate, then, to return to the construction of the first sequence, which establishes the narrative rhythm of the entire film, particularly at the level of sound. In the first shot, the boy on the ox is framed in a very long shot. On the aural level, Mambety introduces cows' moos that are barely distinguishable, and most prominently, a flute playing. The music is very peaceful and understated, and the choice of the flute leads us to expect a bucolic story. The flute is also associated with shepherds in many oral traditions—it is a pastoral instrument. In the next shot, the boy is still far away. It is as if he could not quite approach the camera; there is a sense of distancing play in this opening sequence. The boy finally moves ahead of the herd a little, but importantly it is the sound that becomes louder; it is the sound that comes "closer" to the camera and thus to our point of "view" (hearing). The oxen and cows are heard more distinctly in the second shot, and as the boy disappears to the right of the frame the moos increase dramatically. At this juncture, Mambety cuts away to an ox being pulled by the horns into the slaughterhouse. Aurally, the moos have now intensified, and they are intercut with the yelling of the men working at the slaughterhouse. The action moves from the outside in the third shot to the inside. Thus far it seems that the audience can only relate to the story spatially, and not at all temporally. A similar shift occurs with the visual and aural dynamic. If the audience usually requires both spatial and temporal components to situate the story and image and sound to work together to create a fuller sense of reality, as André Bazin and Christian Metz would have it, then in the case of *Touki Bouki* the audience mostly relies on two components: space and sound. From here, it is only a small step to investigate the creation of space *through* sound.

Before the ox is hung up from a hook in the slaughterhouse, some focalization issues are noticeable. In a previous article (and above), I have claimed that this points to the director's reluctance to show us the full-blown violence (Dima 2012a, 44). To this I should add that the most important detail of the shot is that the sound stays clear throughout; it is never distorted. Throughout the film this will be established as a dominant trend: sound appears to be more coherent, more distinct than image. The visual fails us narratively in the sequence above. It fails to tell the appropriate story, but sound maintains the narrative course that reveals the entire story.

As the animals are being slaughtered, the sound works mostly with the image instead of against it. However, the horrible cries of animals dying are slowly muffled, to the point that they become inaudible; one gets the sense of having been thrust into a very chaotic world that is paralleled by a very chaotic noise mixture. As sound comes in and out of focus, a certain "sonic rack focus effect" is created.[8] Visually, when a shot comes in and out of focus, the effect is called "rack focus." On many occasions, Mambety applies the concept to sound. The horrible sounds of the oxen in the slaughterhouse appear to "assault" the image, not unlike the knife in *Psycho* in Silverman's view. Michel Chion tracks a similar process in his analysis of "a nearly invisible attack of birds that we hear but cannot see all around the house" in Hitchcock's *The Birds* (1963): "It is as though the sound were attacking the image. The sharp beaks that are picking through the door, associated with the terrible sound of the attackers, suggest the idea of sound seeking to leave its trace on the image, of piercing a hole in the canvas of the screen" (2009, 166). Of course, in the case of *Touki Bouki*, the animals do not pose the same kind of deadly threat. Nonetheless, even though the threat is directed toward the animals, the effect of the sound on the image remains. In fact, the blurriness of the shots from above could be construed now as a direct result of the aural attack.

The inside/outside dichotomy continues in this first sequence through one shot of several oxen waiting outside for their fate. The animals are filmed from inside the slaughterhouse. The visual narrative explores the outside first, and then in the next shot it moves completely outside, back to the young boy. This time he is riding alone and no cows follow him. It is a stark contrast that suggests that the entire herd has just been dropped off at the slaughterhouse. On the soundtrack the music of the flute returns triumphantly, but soon the sound of a motorcycle is heard, amplifying gradually. Visually, the film switches perspective from the little boy to Mory's back shoulder on the motorbike. Mory has attached the horns of an ox to the bike, and in the first shot over his shoulder only one of the two horns is visible. The transition from the boy to Mory occurs aurally through a sound bridge created by the flute music. This bridge aligns the little boy with Mory, which will prove problematic for the latter's persona: is he the leader of future Africa, or will take his people to the slaughter? Murphy contends that "time and location are fragmented" (2000, 243) during the transition from the rural scenes to the shots taken from the motorcycle; in other words, atemporal intellectual montage. In his study with Williams, Murphy returns to this fragmentation and lack of logical narration to propose that Mambety may be targeting Sembène's linearity (2007, 26). The fragmentation and the choice of shots push the audience into "a tale of modern Africa, complete with motorbikes, motorways, and machinery" (Murphy 2000, 243). This may be a modern Africa, but it is one deeply rooted in tradition, and the sound transition emphasizes the connection that still exists between times and locations. The camera returns to Mory, who is still driving through the neighborhood, with children following him on either side. When he finally clears the village and ends up on the highway, he is filmed from above, off a bridge. The engine of the motorbike is heard loudly on the soundtrack as Mory heads down the highway. As he moves away, the flute music begins to slowly die out, too. A shot from Mory's point of view while on the motorbike is interjected here. The spectators do not see the vehicle, but they hear it. In fact, other than the shot from the bridge, the motorbike is only present as sound—an aural signifier meant to bring past and present together.

The aural sensation generated by this opening and the meshing of animal sounds, flute music, human yelling, and the sound of the motorbike complicates the audience's comprehension of the events, which are no longer linear but rather convoluted like a helix. Everything seemingly spirals out of control; our senses are so overwhelmed that they are not to be trusted anymore. It is a very close approximation of a feeling of acute pain that suffuses the body to the point that the original source of pain is no longer clear. Hence the violence of the slaughter is transposed onto us, the audience, who experience it secondhand. It is a very powerful beginning that announces the complexity of this film and the difficulties one may have in understanding it; it is also an opening that will be echoed by a similar meshing of the senses at the very end. The gap between the noises at the beginning and the noises at the end does not prevent us from making a very similar connection to the one just made between the slaughters and Mory. We now make a temporal jump ourselves to the end of the film in order to illustrate this point.

On a visual level, Niang makes an astute connection between the shot of the oxen awaiting their fate and the shots showing the lines of young Senegalese waiting to embark on the boat leaving for France (2002, 113). This is, of course, a perfect example of atemporal intellectual montage. More importantly, as these young men prepare to walk onto the ship, the *Ancerville*, to head to Marseille, sounds of creaking metal are heard extradiegetically on the soundtrack. The ship is obviously large enough to hold everyone, but the message is that perhaps too many of those young men are setting off to France. The ominous sounds of the metal bring back images of overloaded slave ships. Immigration replaces slavery, as the West lures Africans away with the promise of a better life. Those awful sounds connect the ending of the film with its beginning, closing the narrative, shrinking the visual narrative as it were, which returns to actual images of the slaughtered cows, generating yet another narrative fold. Thus in this case, the atemporal intellectual montage (oxen await death + young men wait to embark = young men are waiting to embark to their death) is also supported aurally. The sounds of the beginning sequence (animals in agony) and the sounds at the end (the noises made by the overloaded ship and the repetition of mooing) collide, and a new, Eisensteinian third meaning is born: the imagined sight of people (slaves) being treated like cattle. This is how the diegetic sonic space is perceived, as it fills an imagined space. The delayed effect of the atemporal intellectual montage brings to mind the cultural negotiation of postcolonial subjectivity that suffers from a disparity between historical and economical reality and desire.

The beginning sequence of the film also establishes Mory as a biblical presence, almost akin to a messiah. The images and sounds reviewed above create a holistic effect that emerges out of chaos, something more than what meets the ear. Generally critics suggest that the little boy is literally young Mory; the cut to the older Mory represents a jump in time and space and supports that view. Mory too is physically followed; first by children, then by an angry mob. Moreover, in the long dream/fantasy sequence toward the end, the sorceress refers to him as the prodigal son and celebrates his return; his connection to the sorceress is revealed early in the film when it is said that he owes her money for rice. The debt represents the strong connection that Mory has with his native country; rice is the most common food in Senegal, something that people rarely lack. Mory is tied to the native soil through this debt. Mory's connections to the biblical are solidified by two shots posing him as a crucified Jesus. The first one has him tied to a jeep, standing, head hanging to the side, arms up. The American car thus becomes a modern-day version of the cross—the place where humanity goes to die. This shot also reminds us of Godard's political commentary on the connection between the jeep and napalm from *Pierrot le fou* (i.e., blaming the Americans for the Vietnam war atrocities). The second shot that mirrors the crucifixion finds Mory resting after being chased in the street by an angry mob; his arms are spread out wide and his head hangs to the side once again. The film is filled with instances in which Mory is tied down, whether literally or metaphorically: he owes money, he is tied to a jeep, or he himself lassoes his motorcycle and then ties it up to a baobab tree. All of these examples contribute to creating a prototypical character, one who cannot abandon Senegal because he is too strongly linked to it, foreshadowing his change of heart at the end of the film.

Even though Mory and Anta are a couple, they are quite opposite, which sets up Anta as an antiprototypical female character. The naturally antagonistic tendency of their relationship finds a parallel in the narrative and the camera movements. If the man appears to be more connected physically to Senegal, the woman enjoys more freedom. She can flee the country. After Mory fools around on his motorcycle, the director introduces Anta, but not before exploring her neighborhood in two long establishing shots, one slowly panning to the right and the other panning the opposite way. To the back and forth narrative movement (between past and present, or reality and imagination), Mambety adds now camera movement from left to right and right to left. These movements are sometimes coupled, which could lead to a stalemate, but often the movement of Mambety's camera goes from right to left. Culturally, this is the way things move in Senegal, even for something as trivial as counting people. Moving from right to left may also imitate the reading of the Qu'ran, an act often seen diegetically in the films perhaps because Senegal is "90 percent Muslim" (Pfaff 2004, 95). This social detail is important to the overall argument because if a culturally specific movement of the camera can be identified, it should be easier to entertain the possibility of culturally specific sounds and music and discuss them.[9]

In spite of the constant movement, the pace of the film slows down considerably right before the introduction of Anta; the film quiets down, as it were, to make room for the other main character. Aside from the aforementioned shots, there is a fixed camera shot of people coming down from a bridge, and the camera once again lingers on them. This is also the moment when the postman first appears, a figure who has been interpreted by some as a wink to Sembène's *Mandabi* (1968). Murphy reads the figure of the postman as another "sideswipe" at Sembène, whose character is "portrayed as someone who 'delivers' hope in the form of the film's political message of social solidarity" (2000, 244), probably the exact opposite of what the figure accomplishes in *Touki Bouki*, in which he mostly "wanders aimlessly" (Murphy 2000, 244). However, the notion that Sembène presents the postman earnestly rather than ironically ignores Sembène's general dislike for company men, for the ineffective representatives of government (the city cops from *Xala* are another good example) who cannot possibly be a true source of hope for the future. I will return shortly to Mambety's postman and his lack of purpose, but at this juncture of the film he is the montage counterpoint that suggests Anta is actually writing a letter in her initial shot. She could be doing homework, since she soon heads out to the university, but because of the cinematic proximity of the postman, providing another example of Eisenstein's intellectual editing, she is more likely to be writing a letter. It is an introspective moment that allows sound to take center stage, and one that will prove to be crucial to the overall structure of the film.

The Sonic Rack Focus

As Anta writes the letter, the neighborhood sequence that follows—the second spatial marker after the slaughterhouse—is potentially the most important one for the treatment of sound in this film. During the last establishing shot of the neighborhood, a plane is heard on the soundtrack that appears, judging from the attenuating sound, to be descending on Dakar. When the film finally cuts to Anta, the sound of the plane landing carries through to this shot, functioning as another sound bridge. The first shot of Anta is a long shot from a slightly high angle, almost as if the plane ended up having a point of view. It is a very intriguing perspective when aligned with the sound of the plane; it is as if the audience were descending, cinematically, onto Anta. The next shot of her is from the side; at this point the plane is no longer heard on the soundtrack, so the audience is now on the ground and on an equal footing with the main female character. The sound of the descending plane is a recurring one in Mambety. It appears in *La petite vendeuse*, too; in both situations, it establishes a contrast. In this instance there is a vertical and horizontal split and an advanced modern technology contrasting heavily with the poor, rural setting of Anta's home. The shot of Anta is fixed, and one immediately noticeable detail is the bottle of water on the table in front of her. It is a French bottle of water, the Vittel brand. Normally, such a prop would not elicit a long commentary, but it is impossible to ignore the similarities with Sembène's *Xala*, which came out two years after *Touki Bouki*. The character in Sembène's film, El Hadji, has a postcolonial fetishistic relationship with Evian water; he tells his daughter he drinks two liters of it every day, a declaration underlined by a close-up of him with a bottle of Evian water next to him and nothing else in the background; he has his driver wash the Mercedes with the same brand of water, and he even uses it for the carburetor. It is interesting that the grandfather of all African cinema (and therefore Mambety's senior) makes use of this very similar metaphor; the French water suggests that the presence of the French and French culture is still strong in Senegal. As for Anta, she is the one who follows through with the plan to leave the country and emigrate to France.

Aural Space and the Sonic Rack Focus in Touki Bouki | 51

From the first time she becomes visible, then, she is ready, as she has already embraced elements of French culture.

The aural story that begins to develop during this scene may further support that claim. As the shot remains fixed on Anta, four sounds are heard in the following order: an Islamic prayer, a baby crying, a dog barking, and a police or ambulance siren.[10] These sounds overtake each other at certain moments: for example, the baby's cries predominate while the dog's barking takes a backseat and turns softer. Mambety thus provides another example of a sonic rack focus effect—a parallel oscillation to the image moving from outside to inside. While the visual and aural effects are similar, it is worth noting that visually the rack focus effect can only occur between two planes, usually foreground and background (and more clearly, between two characters carrying on a dialogue, which in effect represents a shot / reverse shot formation without the need to cut—suture without absence). On the contrary, the sonic rack focus allows movement between several narrative layers. The audience is introduced to an entirely new scape, a soundscape created by these noises through which we better understand the characters of Mory and Anta because it provides us with an aural background of their surroundings. Their lives are constructed through the noises of their neighborhood; we are hearing, not seeing, and yet we get an equally powerful picture. But it is not a simple picture of the neighborhood—it is in fact a map. The aural interjections help create a mental map of the neighborhood; the different sounds are ostensibly coming from separate locations, but they appear unified in this scene because they are mixed together in one location, the soundtrack. This technique is akin to that of the map that brings various locations together in one diagram; in both cases the locations are mentally accessible. Even though this is a map of a small region, it is nonetheless important to acknowledge the emergence of sound as a geographical tool and to continue delving deeper into the meaning of these particular aural choices.

First of all, it is worth remarking that while the visual story lags and remains focused on Anta, an entirely new, aural narrative takes shape on the soundtrack (see figure 1). Visually, the story eventually moves away from Anta, but there is a sense that the camera is trapped within the confines of the neighborhood. Furthermore, by dwelling on Anta with a fixed camera and allowing sound to come in at different levels, the director exposes the visual as somewhat lacking narrative power. If the camera does not move—and there is very little movement within the frame as well—the shot essentially becomes one frame, a photograph. Within the space of the photograph, the bottle and Anta emerge as the two possible puncta (Roland Barthes's point that establishes a direct, personal relationship between the photo and its viewer). The two visual puncta can create multiple stories or interpretations, as does, for example, the bottle that, as a fetish, links up to other Senegalese films. Nevertheless, it quickly becomes apparent that there are a multitude of aural puncta that surpass the importance of those belonging to the visual realm. And it is from their cohesion (or conflict) that the studium—the interest that the image generates, or, specific to this instance, the cultural interpretation of the "photo" of Anta drinking Evian water and writing—is created. The "photo" finds life in unseen, heard puncta. At the same time, the sounds of the neighborhood continue to tell a story parallel to the one witnessed visually. From Anta, Mambety shifts to the postman who delivers letters to various people in the neighborhood. As this shift occurs, the only sound remaining is that of the Islamic chant, and the word "Allah" becomes the aural focus of the soundtrack. There is such an emphasis placed upon this particular word that suddenly it feels unavoidable. It is a neat trick, because Allah should be everywhere, in everything and everyone, but it is through constant aural repetition that his presence is (physically) felt. It is also one of the first manifestations of the acousmatic panopticon. From the postman, the visual switches to Anta's mother, who perhaps is awaiting a letter, and the same chant is predominant. After another hard cut to the mother, the siren is finally heard loudly and ominously. Therefore, the aural intellectual montage should yield a third meaning: that she would not receive any letters.

Mambety returns the audience to Anta, framed in a shot from above that constitutes the third angle, while the siren is still very loud on the soundscape. The sound bridge connects the mother, postman, and Anta, who are now all under the aural umbrella of this particular sound. The baby starts crying again, almost annoyingly. The camera tilts up and away from Anta as it reveals the neighborhood and a large building in the far background. The camera finally catches up with the sound. In spite of several camera movements and the changing of angle on every occasion that Anta appears, the visual is limited spatially. It is contained by the neighborhood and by Anta's immediate surroundings. Sound appears to travel further, but it too might be limited to the space of the city. Chion observes that acoustically the city can be a "container," in which sounds bounce between different urban surfaces (2009, 242). Still, it is clear that sound in this particular instance moves further than the image.

While *Contras' City* and *Badou Boy* disregard the spatial limits of the city, *Touki Bouki* extends (both visually and acoustically) the very definition of aesthetic freedom. It is sound that most often transcends its usual limitations. That is not to say that the characters do not transgress spatial limitations (they do move between places, neighborhoods, cities, and so on); rather, as in the example above, the camera can appear to be trapped within physical boundaries, which allows sound to conquer further spaces. Sound offers what Roland Barthes calls "meanings that are not to be found in the image itself" (2007, 41). The imagined map of the neighborhood that one could build in one's head thanks to the noises only comes to life visually on occasion. The spatial limitation of the camera extends to the spectators and to what they are able to control visually. Niang claims that the narrative construction of this film liberates the spectators and forces them to rebuild the story from fragments (2002, 117). Niang is only partially right in his claim. While the film does splinter (and the visual and the aural do constitute separate entities), the spectator should feel more of an entrapment than a liberation. We as spectators are trapped with the camera in Anta's neighborhood, and we can only reconstruct the story from fragments—mostly aural fragments. Moreover, these aural fragments are broken off from the particular kind of sound emitted by the city.

Ben Singer's study of melodrama tackles the fragmentation of the city. The city and its dynamics constantly change, and Singer draws the following conclusion from the writings of Siegfried Kracauer and Walter Benjamin: "The urban environment of modern capitalism brought about some kind of fundamental change in the human 'sensorium,' creating a pervasive new 'mode of perception' which ultimately had a significant impact on the development of cinema, encouraging cinema to take shape in ways that mirrored the fragmentation and abruptness of urban experience" (2001, 7).

In addition to this, Singer later quotes Ludwig Weber, saying: "Noise is a problem, particularly to the metropolis, because sounds constantly vary so that there is no chance to adapt to them. . . . The difference with urban noise is the constant change, the sudden and unpredictable startling effect of always-different sounds" (2001, 117). The spectators of *Touki Bouki* are trapped in an aural labyrinth, from which they attempt to escape by adapting to the noises of the city. In the opening of the film, these noises are specifically the crying baby, the barking dog, the prayer, and the siren. It is debatable whether all these sounds are heard by Anta, too, which would make them into examples of point-of-audition sound as discussed in Rick Altman's article "Sound Space" (1992). We identify with Anta who hears for us, and we are stuck in a very specific, visual place. "Point-of-audition sound thus constitutes the perfect interpellation, for it inserts us into the narrative at the very intersection of two spaces which the image alone is incapable of linking, thus giving us the sensation of controlling the relationship between those spaces" (Altman 1992, 60–61). However, because the visual perspective changes and the sound does not, this physical source is ambiguous at best, and therefore the audience can move about the aural space of the film freely.

There are many ways in which one could understand these particular four sounds and their narrative power. A quick tangent here is warranted to explain finally what is meant by "narrative." I understand "narrative" according to Gérard Genette's structuralist definition, which I extrapolate from the literary world to sound in cinema. The four different sounds heard in these scenes are instances of narration, which in turn generate stories, or a series of events "told" to us by an omniscient narrator (because every narrative must have a narrator). Finally, the combination of sounds, or rather the (Altmanian) succession of sound events, elicits a narrative. In Genette's terms (1980, 189–194), the role of sound as described in this sequence carries an external focalization attribute (i.e., the "narrator" is heterodiegetic, removed from the action, an outside observer) that leads to a split from the zero focalization I would associate with the visual narrative. In this sequence, there is no cohesive narrative, the visual and the aural do not have congruent narrations, and therefore what is being narrated splits. A completely new technique at the level of sound emerges: first, sound as a counterpoint to the image, and second, sound as a counterpoint to itself. This is the opposite of literary embedding, which happens in film within the visual narrative (i.e., different stories are told from other perspectives that may complicate the narrative flow). In this crucial sequence at Anta's home, two types of narrative manifest themselves through two pairings: image and sound, and then sound and sounds.

The fixed shot of Anta lasts twenty-seven seconds, which is rather long considering that nothing really happens visually. Slavoj Žižek, with help from filmmaker and writer Sean Martin, notices that the audience must move from being initially bored with a long take to being curious (2008a, xix). The natural advantage of the long take is that we are given time to explore the shot more attentively, but in this case it is more about being given time to notice the four sounds and explore their meanings. The different reads of the shot that come as each sound dominates generate a great sonic Kuleshov effect. The original Kuleshov effect is based on visual counterpoints; the same image of a man juxtaposed with various objects or people, such as food, a coffin, or a beautiful woman should elicit different reads from the audience—"hunger," "sadness," "sexual interest" respectively. Similarly, the four sounds change the meaning of our visual shot, which can also be understood via Chion's rhetorical effect of counterpoint. The combination of Anta and the prayer indicates she is a religious person; the clash between Anta and the baby crying insinuates that she is not yet fit to be a mother; Anta and the dog barking at her could mean that she is an intruder in that space; finally, Anta and the siren points to a warning that she might be in danger. These four counterpoints to the image represent the first audiovisual level.

However, and most interestingly, at a secondary level it is possible to understand these sounds *in opposition* to one another, not as the kind of meshing of sounds that occurs in the first relevant sonic sequence. These sounds can be analyzed on their own initially, and then as counterpoints to one another for a more precise meaning. Through this reading, the visual disappears completely. In my opinion, the noise of the crying baby refers to a new beginning, one perhaps suggested in the opening sequence of the film as well. The other three sounds are more complex, and rather ominous. The barking dog functions as a warning—dogs usually bark when something is amiss. Similarly, there is the obvious threat of a siren going off. The prayer seems to engulf the neighborhood, but it is unclear yet if it is a welcome presence or a worrisome one. The recitation of the fatiha is part of the five prayers required daily under Muslim law; it focuses on asking Allah for refuge by his side and protection against the devil. Taken at its literal value, the prayer has positive connotations. Yet when juxtaposed with the two previous sounds, the Islamic chant can certainly be construed as a critique of Islamic values. The chant is the most constant sound in this scene, and the abrupt interruption caused by the siren functions as a warning about the dominance of religion (in this case, the dominance manifests itself aurally). Therefore, any new beginning (a new birth, for example, if one were to match up the baby crying with the prayer) is subjected to an established set of religious rules.

There is a heavy Islamic presence in Mambety's films, "All his films swim in this context [of Islam] and affirm its importance in the everyday life of the characters" (Niang 2002, 120).[11] Sometimes this presence is perceived as having a positive influence on the quotidian; the best example is Sili's grandmother from *La petite vendeuse*, whose Islamic singing serves as a wonderful aural decoration of the neighborhood. On other occasions, the Islamic presence has a negative connotation, as in the scene where Mory is tied up to a jeep, or in the scene above, which is aurally marked by the menacing sound of the siren. More explicitly, one of the voice-overs in *Contras' City* critiques the construction of several distilleries in the Dakar area in response to the question of whether or not he (the narrative voice, but it can certainly be deduced to mean the director) was Muslim, "Since then, so many preachers' sons gave up the Qur'an for the liquar'an!" If one contrasts these irreligious moments with the acoustic beauty of the Islamic singing in *La petite vendeuse*, then Mambety proves to be ambivalent in his treatment of religious practices. In fact, he usually turns to parody when dealing with Islamic discourse as a way to avoid more direct commentary.

The Islamic chant—the prayer—provides us with a rare moment that has a temporal quality. One cannot be sure if it is the morning or the noon prayer (or perhaps even the afternoon one), but it is certain that the prayer gives the film a sense of time for once. According to Chion, sound can have a temporalization effect on the image, particularly if that image is static, as is the case with Anta's. Sound provides the visual shots with a time continuum, a sense of succession, and of direction (Chion 1994, 13–16); it gives the static image a sense of moving. The passage of time is marked aurally (every "Allah" occurs at a sequentially later moment, not simultaneously), and thus the spectators perceive the passage of time in spite of the passivity of the visual shot. Of course, Chion's temporalization of sound can be applied to a variety of sounds, and it is not limited to sounds actually referring to time, such as a grandfather clock marking a specific hour through the necessary number of gongs. In Anta's shot, sounds mark the passage of time, but only one of them points to an exact time. By contrast with the temporalizing quality of the prayer, the siren, taken on its own, is more of an illustration of urban space. Still according to Chion, "no other noise is as symbolically and dramatically effective in marking territory as a vehicle horn or siren" (2009, 242–243), and "the sound of a horn or siren in a movie doesn't just evoke its source—police car, fire engine, taxi—but instantly allows our ear to get the feel of the urban landscape" (2009, 242). Thus the primacy of space over time reemerges quickly.

A film cannot be entirely atemporal, although *Touki Bouki* appears to try to be. This crucial shot of Anta and the sounds of the environs ultimately is not about temporalization, in spite of the obvious reference to the time of day. If anything, the prayer that is performed five times, each and every day, suggests a monotony of time, a repetition ad nauseam. This is not the case with the construction of space. Henri Lefebvre also places time within the realm of space; that is to say that time is "apprehended within space" (1991, 95), which would mean, again, that the sound—the prayer—creates space. It has already been claimed that the neighborhood and by extension the city are reconstructed via the sound and not the visual. Michel de Certeau's distinction between space and place is relevant again here. A place ("*un lieu*") is an order according to which several elements coexist. It can be inferred from this statement that the four sounds in the shot create a place because they coexist and have yielded relationships between them. These elements are rather mobile—there is a progression in time—and they help us map out the neighborhood, albeit in a fragmented map. Chion remarks that "In urban films, especially, sounds may very well not be translating any particular sensation but serving instead to express, through a series of audible points and lines that might include car horns, rumbles, and noises of subway doors, multiple combined rhythms that sonically constitute the life of the city" (2009, 239). Spectators imagine the visuals that normally would accompany these shots, and they "see" the city. The mobility of these sounds leads to interactions between them, and we have analyzed what meanings may result from their juxtapositions. The mobility and interactions metamorphose place into space ("*un espace*"). According to de Certeau, it is stories that have the capacity to transform places into spaces and vice versa. He refers here to literary stories, but one can generalize to the aural stories of this one shot as creators of space. The discovered map and space are indeed fragmented, as sound takes turns creating individual, mental images.

Fragmentation is at the heart of Mambety's aesthetic and characterizes his visual editing. It is analogous in some ways to the fragmentation that plagues the modern city, as observed by Singer. Fragmentation prevents Mambety's characters from appropriating the space of the city or the city itself. In short, they are essentially modern characters in the same vein as Baudelaire's flaneur. Their frenetic movement, particularly Mory's, sketches a different version of the city—a metaphorical city and space that coexist alongside the "real" one. Fragmentation also comes from the splintered space of a postcolonial country still at odds with the colonizing powers. The characters cannot appropriate this new space visually, but they may be able to do so aurally. The sounds that accompany the two characters in their quests do create another version of the city, an imagined, aural space that remains unattainable in practical terms.

It is perhaps from a sense of frustration—she realizes the impossible task in front of her—that the scene ends with Anta's voice saying *"merde"* ("shit"); the word functions as both a conclusion and a synopsis of the squalid neighborhood. Perhaps the swear word is justified by her being late (for school or for meeting Mory), but she does not hurry anywhere. Or perhaps she is just fed up with the constant noise of the neighborhood, which prevents her from concentrating. This one spoken word punctuates the aural space of the neighborhood violently. She does not move her lips, but logically it must be coming from her since she was last seen in the visual shot before the camera tilted up. On her way out, she stops to see her mother, who sells vegetables in the market. Anta's mother and her neighbor engage in a conversation about Anta's brother who is in France and has not communicated in a while. This is also a juncture when the postman appears more frequently; there are a few long takes of him, slowly walking around. But other than in the first scene, he does not put letters in any mailboxes. He is a mailman who brings no letters. The lack of correspondence from absent ones means that indeed, as the neighbor says, "those kids never come back from France." She adds scornfully, "or they bring back white women with their diseases." It is a reversal of the stereotypes that so heavily burden Africa and Africans; it is the French who are "dirty." The neighbor further blasts France, saying "France? Nothing good comes of it," suggesting another reversal, in this instance toward local values.

Anta rudely interrupts a dialogue between her mother and their neighbor who had just bought on credit, as is often the case in the markets of Dakar. Anta's reaction to this transaction is that the neighbor should pay upfront, and she aggressively takes away the vegetables. She goes against tradition on several levels, showing a more practical side because she does not trust the neighbor and being aggressive and rude with an elderly woman. The character of Anta is physically and morally constructed in opposition to the usual Senegalese representation of women: "[Anta] does not want to be a wife or a mother, submissive to a husband who would not allow her to access the desired comfort" (Niang 2002, 112).[12] She is in complete charge of her life, especially her body.

A few minutes later, Anta is walking toward the university. The fact that she is a student, unlike Mory, underlines her emancipation and makes her the precursor of a character from Sembène's *Xala*; the daughter of El Hadji, Rama (played by the same actress) attends *Université de Dakar* and exhibits a strong nationalistic streak. Anta passes several women who are washing clothes, marking another level of separation between her and the traditional women of Senegal. Soon after this episode, the camera gets distracted and the film moves outside of its main diegesis, showing several young girls getting water and carrying buckets of water away on their heads. It is a rather strange sequence, in which the eye of the camera, without clearly taking the point of view of any actual character, persists in exposing the voluptuousness of the young girls. In one instance the camera starts out on a shot of a girl's buttocks, and then lingers as she moves away, focusing on the undulation of her hips. The vague point of view adds an element of documentary aesthetic to this scene, and it certainly situates the audience as the main viewing subject. There is a strong contrast between these very feminine women, on display only for the delectation of the viewer in a conventional voyeuristic fashion (akin to the classical Hollywood narrative), and Anta, the main female character of the film. The shots of the beautiful young girls carrying buckets of water are stereotypical African images, something the new generation of African filmmakers might call "calabash cinema,"—misrepresentations of the indigenous population reminiscent of stereotypical and demeaning Western images of Africa and Africans. On the other hand, Anta is definitely not stereotypical, and she is masculinized through opposition with other girls seen in the film. Furthermore, she wears short hair, no braids, and dresses in a masculine way—pants and a shirt. Between Anta and Mory, it is she who takes on the traditional masculine role of setting a course for herself, for her life. The shift toward a less male-dominated society is further marked by the ending of the sequence, when two women who had been fighting one another engage in a separate quarrel with a man, whom they literally take down. During the fight, the soundtrack is inundated with loud shrieks from the women in the market; women dominate the physical space of the market and the aural space of the film.

The sequences that follow represent the turning point of the film, and this moment also anticipates its hidden ending. The episode begins with Mory being hazed by a few male students, and triple crosscuts with shots of a goat being sacrificed and Anta running downhill toward the sea. The mood is deeply ominous, a feeling the director further underlines by shooting Anta in Dutch angles and altering low and high angles. The same running sequence comes back a moment later, shot in a normal angle, but the repetition calls everything that happens here into question, because it seems that the director is taking us out of the diegesis again. Mambety plays with the editing and doubles the shots of the slain goat with shots of Anta looking down, as if she were witnessing the sacrifice. In this instance the director employs a sort of fake shot / reverse shot because, as it soon becomes clear, she is looking down at Mory. The fact that we are forced to suture the images of the sacrificed goat (now point-of-view shots) with those of a missing Mory in our minds explains the interlaced shots of Anta; she becomes the imam who is sacrificing an animal, and she thereby challenges the male-dominated religious system. Since she lowers herself toward Mory, a gesture that foreshadows her departure at the end of the movie, he is her sacrificial gift. She will leave him behind and sacrifice her love.

Her upper body is shot from a low angle, which reinforces the fact that she dominates both this scene and Mory. That image of her undressing and lowering herself out of the frame to be with Mory is also atemporal, since it has not happened yet.[13] Not only does the film physically move back and forth between two separate courses of action, but it also moves back and forth in time. The feeling that the witnessed events are not yet happening is further reinforced by another shot of Anta taking off her shirt; it is very similar to the initial shot but she is not quite in the same position, so it is not a mere duplicate. Mambety's sense of time is on display in this scene, and for him chronology is not sacrosanct. Nar Sene, perhaps invoking Senghor, says that time is more of a "rhythm" (2001, 61) for Mambety, but he does not expand on his affirmation. If one follows Ebron's definition of African music, then that cinematic rhythm may come primarily from the rhythm of sound and music. Aurally, the scene begins with soft, ominous jazz music. When Mory is tied to the jeep, the music becomes more penetrating, relying on the repetition of one sound, analogous to the insistence on the word "Allah" from the neighborhood scene. This is a percussive sound—it could be a cymbal, or a cowbell—and it rises in intensity as the scene progresses. The music goes along with the image in this instance, underscoring the stressful moment of Mory's capture. The music disappears completely when the imam sacrifices the goat and the fake reverse shot sequence alternates between Anta and the bloodied goat. The soundtrack goes quiet as if to suggest complete silence, or death.

But the soundtrack does not stay quiet for long. Just as in the initial scene with Anta at home, the following scene has multiple, overlapping sounds and proves critical in the treatment of sound. Aunt Oumi is the sorceress character to whom Mory is indebted. When Anta goes by her place, she reminds Oumi of that debt. As Anta leaves, the sorceress begins to laugh hysterically. A couple of quick visual interjections occur here, with shots of the sacrificed goat. Oumi is framed in a medium shot, and she continues to laugh loudly. Mambety chooses to jump cut this sequence and break the 30-degree rule (i.e., the camera should move at least 30 degrees between shots of the same subject)—it is an unnecessary cut, but it is also important because it emphasizes the laughter on the soundtrack, which now has an echoic quality to it like Michel's gun in *Breathless*. This is yet another repetition, an aural one, as the laughter of the sorceress is superimposed on itself. It is common practice in music to return to the same sound or theme, but in this case the overlapping of the same sound presages the complete mixing of all sounds that is about to take place. The laughter, the sound of the waves, crows cawing, and nondiegetic synthesizer music take turns being the dominant sound of the scene, while producing another sonic rack focus effect. As Anta runs down the hill toward the meeting place, first of all the waves take over the soundtrack and cover up all other sounds. It is a beautiful transference from the actual shots of waves covering up the land. After a transition to a shot of the sky, the cawing of the birds becomes audible; their noises are distorted through a synthesizer, and they soon metamorphose into the sorceress's shrieks. Nondiegetic sound becomes diegetic. Consequently, sound shrinks the visual space, everything the audience has just witnessed, and the normal diegetic distance between the two moments.

The lovemaking scene between the two main characters, the third important aural sequence, is preceded by shots of Anta facing and leaning against a rock while arching her back, arms up, and sticking out her buttocks. It is an unnatural position to say the least, and it is coupled with a high-angle shot of foamy seawater entering a shallow, closed space. The sequence obviously prefigures the lovemaking scene, and it also establishes the connection to water. Water may be considered a feminine symbol; if one were to separate the two characters according to cardinal symbols, Anta's would be water (this complicates her character even more given that she is also portrayed as masculine) and Mory's would be earth. Thus Mambety proposes a gender role reversal, as Anta is the one "entering" Mory and not the other way around. In a later scene on the beach, Mory, although covered in sand, even on his face, is comfortable, while farther from him Anta unsuccessfully tries to maintain her balance, as if she were not in her element. The power and fluidity of the water opposes the stability of the land, of the earth, and during the sex scene there is a constant movement between water and land. Not surprisingly, the final decision of the film also separates the two according to their respective elements: Mory stays put while Anta gets on the boat for France.

The sex scene between Anta and Mory is very lyrical, and it is also revealing for the treatment of contrapuntal sound. On the soundtrack, Anta's element, water, erases all other sounds once again. Slowly a hint of moaning gathers audible strength, and then suddenly the horn of a ship pierces the soundscape. This aural marker marks off the lovemaking on the cliff (the third spatial marker) between the two main characters. Along with the horn, the image of a half-naked Anta opposed by a Dogon symbol on the right of the frame jumpstarts a very poetic scene. The director is primarily concerned with creating reactions within the viewer, and the use of sound and noises grants him the necessary access to the audience's emotions. Alberto Cavalcanti's (1985) study of sound in film is concerned exactly with this connection between noises and feelings, because noise "speaks directly to the emotions.... Pictures speak to the intelligence. Noises seem to bypass the intelligence and speak to something very deep and inborn" (1985, 109). In other words, the image produces a literal meaning, but the sound suggests the nonliteral. According to Cavalcanti, sound reaches an affective potential and it begins to speak directly to the emotions of the spectator. More exactly, it is noises that accomplish this through their inherent quality of being "vague" and because sound is "the medium of suggestion" (Cavalcanti 1985, 109).

There is yet another strong hint of Russian formalist influence in this scene in the way Mambety uses the ocean waves and their sound, like Eisenstein's continuous exchange between land and sea in *Battleship Potemkin* (1925). Mambety's movement between sea and land is bracketed by two long takes of the water crashing against the shore, or against the rocks sticking out of the water close to shore, while the soundtrack is soon flooded with Anta's moans. Her moans and the sounds of the ocean coalesce. The camera moves into an extreme close-up of her hand on the Dogon symbol, and a visual rack focus effect occurs as the camera alternates focus between the foreground and the background. The camera moves back a little, creating another rack focus effect between the hand grasping the Dogon symbol and the sea in the background. The sense of repetition generated through the rhythmic sound of the waves (as well as the visual), the echoes lingering from the laughter and the crows, every element prepares us for the love scene. Anta's moans begin to sound like crying, which is very interesting when seen in correlation with the presence of water. The sex act is emulated cinematically without us actually ever seeing the two lovers: it is simply intimated through the in-and-out movement of the camera focus—another textual incarnation of the inside/outside dichotomy. Thanks to that and the soundtrack, we are able to reconstruct the scene in our minds. As Anta's hand firmly grabs the Dogon symbol, a shot of a big wave splattering against a rock punctuates the climax of the scene, figuratively providing an explosion. A climax is reached when a shot of foam produced by the waves spills very suggestively over rocks close to the shore, and then the sound goes back to the simple, soothing sound of the ocean. This type of repetitive narrative gives the film a sense of circularity and another narrative fold emerges. The denouement of the film returns the spectators to a high-angle shot of Anta and Mory, who are still on the cliff (see figure 2) as if they had never left, as if perhaps nothing had ever happened and they had never done anything. The possibility remains that it is all a dream. Like all fantasies, the ultimate fantasy, to leave Senegal, is not meant to ever come to fruition, to reality.

What is also noteworthy about this scene is the conspicuous lack of shots of Mory, the man, who is visible only at the very end of the scene when the camera finally moves back. The high-angle establishing shot of the place where the two had just made love is yet another example of the director avoiding the norm; in a conventional mainstream narrative, the establishing shot would occur before any of the action takes place in order to situate the spectator. In some ways this shot is unnecessary at the end of the scene. The power of the masculine is further subverted by the camera's dwelling on Anta, before all but her hand disappears from the frame. An argument could be made that the scene follows a conventional voyeuristic dynamic; the woman is made hypervisible, while the man is quasi-invisible. However, Anta is the one *looking*, so she controls the gaze.

The moments that follow are filled with silence. For the first time the two mention their desire to go to France, while two separate long, fixed shots follow boats coming in on the right of the frame and exiting left. Life passes by. Usually boats in Mambety's films are moving about; one exception occurs when the couple is on the beach, Mory looks at an abandoned ship, and an offscreen boat horn goes off on the soundtrack. Generally, these sounds all come from offscreen. According to Bordwell and Thompson, "off-screen sound can suggest space extending in various directions beyond the visible action" (1985, 193), which is relevant to the analysis of all four important sound sequences. The connection between the abandoned ship, stuck in shallow water, and Mory's condition, stuck in the sand of his country, is evident. This kind of shot, tracking movement from a fixed stance, is typical not only for Senegalese filmmakers like Sembène but for West African cinema as a whole, with Sissako's *La vie sur terre* being the most obvious example. The fixed camera, the long shot, and the act of having to "wait" for an object or person to move from all the way on the right of the frame out of sight on the left slow down the pace of the movie drastically. *Touki Bouki* often recreates the rhythm of life mentioned above through alternating fast-paced editing with slower-moving shots.

The same rhythm is displayed in the sequence during which Anta and Mory ride his motorcycle together, which ends with them disappearing behind a clump of baobab trees. The camera follows them until their vanishing act only to stop its movement and proceed to linger once again for about ten seconds. This is a shot that will be later reprised by Ousmane Sembène in *Guelwaar* (1992) when an entire Jeep hides behind a baobab tree. The message is similar; the grandeur of the baobab tree, a national treasure emblematic of the country of Senegal itself, swallows and covers up the insignificance of a symbol of the West (the Jeep and the motorcycle) and the problems of the young couple. This is also the first of several moments in the film when the song "Paris, Paris, Paris" comes forth on the soundtrack, generating an even stronger contrast—a perfect example of contrapuntal music, contrasting with the pastoral shot of the trees. The result is a subversion of the idyllic scenery of Senegal, as Josephine Baker proclaims that Paris "is paradise on earth."[14] There is a strong contrast between the lyrics of the song that hinge on a fantasy and the actual paradise—the beautiful, barren reality that the viewers see. Akin Adesokan proposes that this type of shot "against the wide expanse of Sahelian earth" (2011, 60) should not be dismissed as ethnographic, and that it reinvents social practices of folk culture. That may be true, but to me the visual choice here is simply a counterpoint to the aural, especially because the shot is from a fixed stance. Moreover, Baker's song about fantasy is empathetic music; it matches Mory and Anta's fantasy to leave. Fantasy is brought into focus not only by the lyrics but also by Baker's voice, a decision that cannot be haphazard.

Josephine Baker was born in 1906 in the United States, and she became a cultural icon in France in the mid-to-late twenties. However, the singer was a severely stereotyped icon—one cannot dissociate her image from the bananas she often wore around her waist on stage. Baker represented the exotic, orientalist view of the African/Black woman. In the conclusion to her study on ethnographic cinema, *The Third Eye: Race, Cinema, and Ethnographic Spectacle* (1996), Fatimah Tobing Rony uses Baker as an example to illustrate the difficulty of reaching a subject position among indigenous people when the prevailing stereotype is that of the ethnographic primitive: "When Baker debuted in Paris, she was portrayed as monstrous" (1996, 199). In other words, Baker is an ethnographic spectacle (199–200). As Adesokan proposes, the visual shots of the desert around Anta and Mory in *Touki Bouki* are not necessarily ethnographic, but ethnographic stereotyping certainly creeps in at the aural level through the voice of Baker, and further complicates the fantasy of departure—the voice and the singer are as trapped as Anta and Mory.[15]

Mambety carefully orchestrates the moments when Baker's voice features in the film. The first instance begins right as Aunt Oumi yells threats at Mory while whipping a knife through the air. This is an important moment in the plot because it follows the characters' lovemaking scene and represents the beginning of their adventure—the moment they act on their plan to leave Senegal. The aural transition (and the intellectual montage that ensues) from the ominous warnings about the debt Mory owes Oumi to the soothing voice of Baker acts as a reminder of the complications that come with the introduction of Baker's voice. As the song takes over the soundtrack, the camera frames Mory and Anta in a medium shot, which limits our view of the surroundings and takes the focus further away from the ethnographic value of the shot, in line with Adesokan's view. Instead, the scene continues to negotiate the character's relationship with space (on the bike, on the road, and behind the baobabs) and with fantasy through the song. As the song continues, through a series of disorienting reverse shots Mambety gives us the impression that Mory is attemping to lasso an ox, when actually he ends up lassoing the motorcycle for unknown reasons. So the characters' fantasy is fueled first aurally and then visually.

The song plays a second time at another key moment, just as Mory leaves the stadium with a chest strapped on his bike. The soundtrack alternates between Mory's interior voice, which mentions Paris and touristic destinations such as the Eiffel Tower or the Arc de Triomphe, and Baker's song. As Mory's voice grows quiet, the song takes over the soundtrack; they alternate two more times, but the song never fades out completely. It just cedes aural primacy and remains underneath Mory's voice, creating another sonic rack focus effect. Moreover, this alternation (Mory/Baker three times) is the aural surrogate for cross rhyming in poetry, which (unlike the inauspicious aural counterpoint between Aunt Oumi and Baker) underscores the success of the mission: they are much closer to their goal.

The third occasion on which Baker returns follows the quick visit to the travel agency where the characters get tickets for the boat. In this situation, too, the song comes back three separate times within the same episode. The element that interrupts the song this time is the bizarre Margot character who attempts to enter the harbor and avoid creditors. Margot raises a problem because his defining mise-en-scène trait is a very noticeable pipe, a fetish object most famously associated with Sembène. But Margot is clearly an idiot and a swindler according to Anta, and no animosity between the two directors has ever been documented to my knowledge. There is perhaps some value in analyzing the juxtaposition of the song with a debtor (i.e., does Baker owe Paris, or vice versa?), but the narrative role of the song likely has more to do with highlighting the return to Mory and Anta, who are together again, and to their fantasy.

Finally, the song's last occurrence comes after Mory makes the decision to stay. As the visual narrative hovers over the boat, Anta is shown alone on the upper deck. The pairing of the song with a solitary Anta completes the quartet of musical interruptions in yet another tight structure: together, Mory, together, Anta. The meaning of "Paris, Paris, Paris" changes in each instance in another approximation of the sonic Kuleshov effect, and offers a downward trajectory from hopeful to a very low note because Anta seems saddened and disturbed by Mory's change of heart. Baker's "Paris, Paris, Paris" thus punctuates four crucial moments in the plot of the film—the beginning, the theft, entering the harbor, and the ending—and adds tremendous narrative value to the visual.

Given the iconic status of Baker, the audience might be pushed out of the diegesis in these instances in yet another in/out movement, because inevitably Baker's voice brings her body to mind. The exoticism of the black female body in France can prove fatal, as evidenced by Sembène's Diouana, dead in a bathtub.

Diouana is quiet and quieted, but Mambety offers Josephine Baker the opportunity to come to life, to reign over the soundtrack, and practically to rule the latter portion of the film. Her song and voice offer aural and musical counterpoints, but also a *seductive* sound—anempathetic music—unusual for the aural space with which we have grown accustomed.

Turning back now to the progression of the plot, the juxtaposition between Western and Senegalese cultural values continues in the next segment, where Anta and Mory try to steal the aforementioned chest, which they think contains money. They go to a traditional Senegalese wrestling event, announced in the background to be a fundraiser. The event is aurally accompanied by drum music. The music on the soundtrack comes from djembes. However, when the arena is first shown, the camera tilts up to reveal a set of djembes that lacks any drummers. This is another interesting aural choice that does not allow nondiegetic music to become intradiegetic. The source of the music is shown, but the visual is incomplete. The result is that the nondiegetic music almost has a magical quality to it: it is heard in spite of the fact that no one is playing the drums.

The announcer of the games says that the top wrestlers of the country are putting their titles on the line in order to raise money for a Charles de Gaulle memorial. Soon afterward the same words are heard again on the soundtrack. In this instance Mambety proves to be very Godardian in his approach again; he makes sure that everyone heard the announcer, and leaves nothing to subtlety. Like his French contemporary, he hits the spectators with meaning over and over again. A few minutes later, when the couple absconds with the box, Mory angrily says, "De Gaulle can wait!" cementing the director's point that such a fundraiser is ludicrous. At the level of sound, it is worth noting that the soundtrack is filled with stadium-like noises, cheers, and shrieks whose source is not specifically displayed. The stands are full, and the camera slowly pans to show everyone in the crowd, revealing that many of the spectators are probably rich (judging by their lavish outfits). They obviously represent the upper class and conspicuously remain subdued and removed from the action of the wrestling match.

After leaving the stadium, another important aural shift occurs. Mambety introduces an internal voice-over, first by Mory as already mentioned, and then by the taxi driver who helps Anta move the stolen chest. The driver speaks to Anta over several different shots of the traffic without ever hearing her response. Eventually the camera moves inside the car and discloses whose voice it is, which attenuates the feeling of disorientation. When they arrive at the destination, the driver helps carry out the chest, and as he puts it on his shoulders a very loud extradiegetic noise disturbs the soundscape. It cannot be assigned to any visual source, nor is it really decipherable. Mambety finally reveals the taxi driver's face and he is heard again on the soundtrack, although it is clear that his lips are not moving. On the soundtrack cawing suddenly accompanies the driver's voice—vultures, which materialize visually a few shots later. When the driver carries the chest down the stairs of an abandoned building, the same loud noise from before is heard again, but now he does drop the trunk. The question is whether he drops the cargo because he is startled by the noise or whether the noise is that of the trunk, added postsynchronously and not matched perfectly with the image. In either case, the noise takes center stage narratively. The driver finally opens the trunk and finds a skull in it (which means that they stole the wrong trunk). The same noise explodes a third time, accompanied by thunder and rain. As the driver stumbles away, his scared yells are matched by the caws of vultures in the same way that the sorceress's laughter was superimposed on the seagulls' shrieks.

During this scene a subtle visual detail also takes on a relevant meaning, and in doing so it completes the construction of the acousmatic panopticon. When the driver fumbles around with the trunk, we can see the contours of Gorée Island (see figure 3) on the horizon, and the loud noises we just heard could originate from this spectral presence. The literary version of *La noire de . . .* by Sembène hints at the same contours, with similar melancholy traces. During one telling moment, Diouana, still in Dakar, looks out the window and is suddenly lost ("*transportée*") in thought and in the beauty of the view (Sembène 1971, 168). Sembène quite brilliantly connects the figurative meaning of the term "lost" (or "transported") with a subtle image of Gorée Island, which, according to the text, is barely visible at the horizon (1971, 168). Gorée Island is a fetish memory for the Senegalese, and features in Mambety's *Hyènes*, too. One of the main characters of this film, Ramatou, has returned to Senegal after traveling the world and accumulating riches beyond belief. She points to the island and refers to it as a possession. This is a sort of repossession, a way of finally appropriating a difficult past. It is, of course, a fantasy. In this film, the island is seen more clearly in an establishing shot at sunset. The beautiful light cast on the island, a light reminiscent of sepia-toned prints, brings forth a visual melancholia. The reason behind this visual insistence on the island is that Gorée is one of the archetypal symbols of slavery. It is an island off the coast of Dakar from which thousands of slaves were sent to the Caribbean (so it also becomes Žižek's third type of *objet petit a*, the large, oppressive, physical presence that is intrinsic to the construction of the postcolonial fantasy[16]). In *Touki Bouki*, the reference takes us back to the connection between the horrible moos of the animals in the slaughterhouse and those of the people getting on the *Ancerville*. Visual and aural mesh atemporally to produce the acousmatic panopticon; the island and the noise are always there, physically, visually, and aurally imposing themselves on the city of Dakar and in the Senegalese consciousness.

The island can also function as a sort of collective melancholia trigger for an entire nation, and in the case of the two main characters as a warning about their desire to immigrate to France. The reference to the island is reminiscent of Aimé Césaire's *Cahier d'un retour au pays natal*, the quintessential melancholy postcolonial text. Césaire dreams of returning to the island of Martinique, following the ancient trail of slaves from Gorée.[17] The melancholy in the *Cahier* comes from the loss of the original space, the original home, and from the futile attempt to retrieve it. Along with the physical space of the island, Subjectivity, too, appears lost: "The terrible futility of our reason to be" (Césaire 1983, 8).[18] There are other references to the island in Senegalese cinema. In Sembène's *Faat Kiné* (2001) the main character, Kiné, reacts with surprise to her son's desire to explore Senegal: "I haven't even made it past Gorée Island." Given the geographical position of Dakar on the shores of the Atlantic, her declaration does not make much sense; the son refers to traveling east, inside the country, but "past" the island means moving further west. The fetishistic importance of the island, which becomes a spatial identity marker, is obvious once again. Furthermore, it is also possible to understand her declaration as an acknowledgment that she is stuck and that she has not made it past the island emotionally and psychologically. Kiné, like Mory and Anta, and by extension all Senegalese, is still trapped in and by her colonial past—the real kernel/traumatic event at the core of the Lacanian symbolic order.

The characters' journey hits an unforeseen obstacle as they discover that the stolen box is not full of money. In response to the new crisis, Mory has the idea of robbing one of his acquaintances, Charlie, whose name reminds us of De Gaulle's, and who happens to be gay. His sexual preference subtly subverts the conventional masculine primacy (Sembène's use of impotence in *Xala* is a more direct variation).[19] As a matter of fact, Charlie may be the strongest masculine character in *Touki Bouki*—he is wealthy and wields power over men and women—which would seem paradoxical given that he represents a sexual minority. The power behind the minority is reinforced cinematically by the presence of several beautiful women, lying by the pool and framed in close-ups. Mambety rarely uses close-ups. He prefers to tell the story from a slight distance, so his insistence on the faces of these women is all the more intriguing. As opposed to Anta with her masculine features and haircut, these women almost seem to be on display. They lie motionless on beach chairs and look lifeless, statue-like. Mambety uses this series of close-ups to further deconstruct African stereotypes about gender and sexual minorities. It is a revolt against objectification, as Niang calls it (2002, 111). The stereotypical image of the African woman in paintings or statuettes is countered by this aesthetically pleasing parade of feminine beauty, women who seem to enjoy being free and being themselves in the private (outdoor pool) space of a powerful gay man. Furthermore, it is at Charlie's house that another Baker song,

"Plaisirs d'amour," features. The lyrics go, "I abandoned everything for the fair Sylvie, yet she abandoned me and found another." The audience hears this song while observing the statue-like women by the poolside and as the action of the film transitions into the house. The song prefigures the breakup between Mory and Anta, but more importantly it juxtaposes the stereotyped fantasy image of Josephine Baker with these African goddesses.[20]

As Mory and Anta flee Charlie's house in the latter's American car, Mory begins to undress in the stolen convertible. At this point another ambiguous sequence begins, in which Mory and then Anta are welcomed into the streets of Dakar by hundreds of people, who act as if they are witnessing the inauguration of a new president. Mory stands up in the car and waves at the cheering crowd that is suddenly out of sight. The vanishing crowd points to another phantasmagoric instance, and yet this represents the moment Mory is freed. Completely naked, he is exposed, vulnerable, and honest, so that is the way in which he offers himself to the people. Dozens of children are running along his side, like the crowds of children that followed him in the beginning of the film. He is transformed into the figure of a leader. All of the signs pointing to his status as a religious symbol rather than a mere troubled local lead to this climax: the Son of Senegal is reborn.

Naturally, the perception that this sequence is also a fantasy created to suggest a delusion of grandeur complicates the analysis. Soon after the car ride / fantasy begins, the camera descends to a low angle and tightens on Mory, this time next to Anta; they wave to the crowd. Mambety comes back to this shot on seven separate occasions; he persists in order to assure himself that everyone is aware that this is a projection and not reality. The alternation between reality and the imagined sequences does not affect the sound, which remains constant: a mixture of drums, applause, and cheers, covering up both the real and the fake visual narratives. The essence of the scene is that Mory is at his most sincere in a fantasy, in an imagined space—the phantasmagoric space—that will never become reality, like the ultimate fantasy of leaving the country. Murphy and Williams explain that Mambety shot *Touki Bouki* after spending several months in Marseille: "It was his first trip abroad and his experiences there shattered his long-held illusions about the mythical world of the former colonial power" (2007, 92). It is easy, then, to connect Mory's decision to stay with Mambety's shattered illusions. In the special features of the *La petite vendeuse* DVD, Mambety describes filmmaking as follows: "The cinema, it's simple, you have to close your eyes, and there's the story."[21] So he too is at his most sincere in a fantasy, in the world of film that is born with the eyes closed (and the ears open).

The narrative counterpoint to this sequence is the parallel action of Charlie calling the police to file a complaint about being robbed. Charlie's description of Mory as hungry and loving money (in a word, poor) contrasts with the projection of the lavish parade. The name that Charlie asks for on the phone is Djibril Diop, and once on the phone, he refers to the interlocutor as Mambety. Thus the director marks his presence with a very strange reference, a sort of acoustic cameo but without our ever hearing his actual voice. The visual shot is fixed on Charlie. Besides his voice, the soundtrack also features a return to "Plaisirs d'amour," presumably coming from inside the house, and toward the end of the conversation the sound of a helicopter (obviously from outside) emerges. This last sound hovers ominously over the rest of the conversation, just as a visualized helicopter would over the space below. Before judging this in-out clash as another example of aural intellectual montage (i.e., gays are discriminated and under "surveillance" in Senegal), there is another possibility worth exploring. Charlie's character may be problematic given that Senegal is not necessarily progressive when it comes to LGBTQ rights.[22] However, Mambety clearly adds Charlie to the gallery of marginalized people whom he defends and renders more visible. For example, Mory is not necessarily uneasy while in Charlie's house. When the latter speaks to him from the shower, there is a feeling that Mory has already been there. Niang observes, "He is in turn gambler, burglar, prostitute, macho man, frequenter of clandestine bistros, small-time politician before finding again his shepherd's soul" (2002, 106).[23] The only possible explanation for considering Mory a prostitute is to associate him potentially with Charlie in previous, unseen episodes. However, if this connection holds, Mambety might see himself as a prostitute. Of course this is not to be taken literally, but there is something to be said about the difficulties of finding the financial backing to make a film in Senegal. The director's project depends on external contributions, on rich "Charlies," a.k.a. producers, a.k.a. hyenas, and on the director's willingness to sell out.

As the conclusion of the film approaches, the action is restricted to the harbor—the fourth essential scene for the treatment of sound and fourth spatial marker—while the couple prepares to embark on the *Ancerville*. Before the two arrive at the harbor, Mory pays his debt to the sorceress, who proceeds to dance and sing with a group of others next to the American car. He is treated like a folk hero, and Oumi calls him the prodigal son. She also announces that vultures and hyenas will not get to him, and that he is the chosen one, the "son of the savannah." All these declarations remind us of the beginning of the film and align Mory again with the shepherd boy. He is meant to be a leader; perhaps he is the future of Africa, which would explain his sudden decision not to leave with Anta.

The last scenes of the film are also an aural culmination in which everything seems to blend together in a sort of a mind-numbing collage. Additionally, there are elements that remind us again of two French New Wave classics, Godard's *Breathless* and Truffaut's *The 400 Blows*. As already explained, Anta and Mory resemble Patricia and Michel because they have a dangerous lifestyle, except that Anta is much more than a simple accomplice. A radical difference between the two couples is the lack of affection between Anta and Mory; there is not much physical contact actually shown onscreen, and declarations of love are completely missing. However, the similarity between the two films lies outside of the main characters' respective relationships. On the one hand, Françoise Pfaff notices a connection to Godard through deconstruction, because in her opinion *Touki Bouki* requires the viewers to actively and constantly reconstruct a deconstructed reality (Pfaff 1988, 222). The viewers have to put together the bits and pieces of the story and fight their way through the lack of temporal linearity. A more obvious parallel is the conversation that Patricia conducts at the airport with a certain writer named Barbulescu (played by Jean-Pierre Melville), mirrored in Mambety's film by a conversation with an unnamed white character—a professor by all indications. The few things he says are as incongruent as the comments made by Godard's Barbulescu, but they are equally poignant and derogatory. Mambety's "professor" first talks about a need to kick all neocolonialists (whom, ironically, he represents) out of the country. The irony is that everyone including the neocolonialists themselves is aware that a change is needed, except the most important component of the equation, the colonized, the Senegalese people. The professor continues by attacking Senegal: "There is nothing in Senegal. Barren. Intellectually as well," and "African art is a joke made up by journalists." The film in which he utters these words is indisputable proof to the contrary.

There is another subtle connection to Godard's Michel, who fancies himself a gangster even though he is a small-time crook. There are two black automobiles that appear in Mambety's film without any diegetic explanation for their presence. They look like gangster vehicles from the film noir of the 1940s, cars that Michel would covet. The first time they appear, they head toward the camera frontally while a siren that does not come from them goes off on the soundtrack. Following a cut to Mory and Anta crossing the street, the siren picks up again, but the automobiles moving past the crosswalk are all white. The siren is comparable to the sound heard early on while Anta writes a letter. The black cars appear twice. The first time, they come down the street and they split off in opposite directions at the first intersection. The second time, they enter the port, and it looks as if they are supposed to be lifted onto the *Ancerville* for transportation to France, which could be a return to their place of origin.

The connection to France and French film also materializes in a sequence that mirrors the ending of Truffaut's *The 400 Blows* occurring after the young men of Senegal embark on the creaking metal of the *Ancerville*. The return to the beginning of the film is obvious, but it also means returning to a younger Mory, perhaps the little boy on the ox. Adult Mory hesitates; he is at a crossroad. Will he be the leader the film projects in the initial sequence, or a follower who will abandon Senegal? The boat horn goes off three times, announcing departure. After a few seconds of hesitation and a visual interjection that takes us back to the ox in the slaughterhouse from the beginning, Mory takes off running in the opposite direction, to the left. The horn of the boat pierces the soundtrack again, and it is matched to the agonizing noise of the dying ox. Then, all the noises from the beginning of the film resurface. The act of running left is the natural direction for Mory, the "correct" direction. The conflict between cultures, France and Senegal, is further underlined by Mory's running. It partially imitates the ending of *The 400 Blows*, which is basically a single long tracking shot of the main character, Antoine Doinel. He, too, runs, but to the right. Truffaut's shot is an uninterrupted long traveling shot, but Mambety makes use of both the tracking shot and rapid editing. If the act of filming the hero's run in a long take slows down *The 400 Blows* as it comes to its conclusion, in *Touki Bouki* the fast montage style and the alternation between low and high angles increase the tension of the action. The camera ends up moving very fast, circling, and not focusing on anything in particular, while the shots are all point of view, suggesting that Mory is getting tired and dizzy from running. Aside from the heavy visual stimulation, the soundtrack becomes inundated with a mixture of cow moos, men's yelling, creaking boat noises, boat horns, and very eclectic, multiple-instrument jazz band music. The decision to stay is charged with emotions, and the film cinematically supports that tension at both visual and sound levels, which overtake our senses.

In the denouement, Mory tries to reclaim his motorcycle and the ox skull attached to it, which seems to be another connection he has with the land. Unfortunately, the new owner of the motorcycle—a white man dressed like a savage—crashes it in the middle of the street. The image of the white savage, which appeared once before after the couple fled Charlie's house, is another stereotypical reversal by the director; he subverts the classical, orientalist presence of Tarzan, the "white superman in Africa" that has known close to fifty different movie versions (Gugler 2003, 2). In the same way that the neighbor declares that French women are "dirty," the perennial stereotype of the African savage is reversed using whites. The accident takes place in the middle of the street, creating a traffic jam, and it is impossible not to think once again about Michel's mishap at a crossroads in Godard's *Breathless*. Since intersections facilitate connections, both cases suggest a breakdown in communication. Moreover, Mory finds the ox skull broken. An ambulance comes to get the savage white man—the first time one can actually associate the sound of a siren to the visual image of a car. Following the reading offered earlier about the siren, Mory's decision to stay back does not appear to be off to a positive start.

From this point on there are only a few shots left in the film, mostly revisiting and paralleling earlier shots. Both Anta and Mory are shown to be alone, she on the boat that is suddenly unpopulated, he in the street holding one of the two horns that used to sit atop his motorbike. The corpulent postman reappears. In a long following shot he goes down some stairs, passes Mory, and eventually disappears to the left of the frame. He still has no letters to deliver. The film slows down considerably and everyone else seems to disappear. The disappearance of the public is rather bizarre, pointing to the possibility that the two main characters are part of a dream sequence. The *Ancerville* sets off, shown in two separate shots, one moving from right to left, the other one from left to right; there are no more possibilities, no actual progress—another stalemate. One of the last three shots of the film goes back to the high-angle establishing shot of Mory and Anta lying on top of a rock after having just had sex. They are in a privileged position, with a vantage on the ocean; they control the space visually, much as Ramatou will do years later in *Hyènes* (1992). It is exactly the same shot as before; it could be just a memory of the moment that the two had, but it could also mean a return to the moment when the they first discussed the possibility of leaving. During this last sequence, there are no more aural tricks. The shots are accompanied by neutral, nondiegetic music, so aurally the film steps "outside" completely. Given the allegorical ending, it is quite possible that nothing witnessed since the first twenty minutes of the film is real, that it is all a fantasy belonging to the characters, that their position of superiority allows them to invent the cinematic space of the entire film. In short, they imagine the space. The film continues to bend further back on itself until it reaches the original shot of the little boy riding the ox. When he moves completely out of sight, to the right of the screen, the film ends in a freeze-frame, again reminding the audience of *The 400 Blows* and the famous freeze-frame of Antoine Doinel by the sea.

As a concluding observation, it is worth mentioning that the fragmented character of Mory offers the perfect transition to a discussion of the flaneur. Mory and other Mambety characters can easily be seen as flaneurs in the African context, and Mambety's "lazy," lingering camera provides us with many examples of *flânerie*. Niang notices the following about Mory: "Mory, the first character meticulously constructed by Djibril-Diop Mambety, expresses himself equally through movement, gestures, and words, moves constantly, doesn't have a family or friends, and will attempt up to the very end to leave the country" (Niang 2002, 195).[24] Mory's most important attribute is that he is constantly on the move, but perhaps he is never really in danger of leaving his country. The country and the city both construct him as much as he constructs them. He is a different breed of flaneur. For the most part he moves around on his motorcycle, not on foot, which prevents him from being an apt observer. However, the motorcycle allows him to cover more ground faster and gain a better geographical knowledge of the city. His ability to move so swiftly inside and outside the city puts him in a separate category from that of most other Mambety characters. Like Mory with his ability to move in and around various spaces, the sound of *Touki Bouki* moves inside, outside, and around the image. In the process, Mambety's sound forces us to rethink its narrative role.

2 Flaneur, Geography, and *Caméra-Flâneur* in *Badou Boy* and *Contras' City*

C*ontras' City* (1968) and *Badou Boy* (1970), produced only two years apart, constitute Mambety's assertive introduction to the world of cinema. As a reference point, Sembène's seminal *La noire de . . .* came out in 1966, and given Sembène's subsequent mythic status in African and world cinema, it is very likely that Mambety was not only aware of this film, but was influenced by it. The powerful story that pitted a young Senegalese woman against a white French family (really, in the end she faced France in its entirety, not just one family, or one "madame") showcased the deplorable social status of the freshly postindependence Senegalese people. Without going into further detail, as *La noire de . . .* has already been discussed (chapter 1, note 9), it is worth adding that Sembène's main character, Diouana, undergoes a drastic change in terms of spatiality from the scenes in Dakar to those in France. If in Dakar Diouana is often shown in the streets, moving around as a veritable flaneuse, even hopping across the Veterans' Monument, her movement is severely limited in France (which in fact is a displacement); the character is completely trapped in the apartment of the French family and eventually in the white porcelain bathtub in which she commits suicide. The spatial limitations that Sembène imposes on his character are strongly connected with Diouana's fatal trajectory; the postcolonial subject is physically, and by extension socially, stifled.

An even more extreme case of spatial limitations in spite of apparent freedom is Sembène's *Borom Sarret* (1963). The main character, the cart driver, faces spatial (and social) restrictions as he goes from the poor neighborhoods to the plateau of Dakar. He may seem to be moving around freely, but urban divisions (in this case, essentially a segregated spatial system that forced the locals away from the European-style residences) certainly hamper his *flânerie*. Sembène's influences on Mambety's early career are undoubtedly thematic ones, from which one might glean the following questions: How does the postcolonial subject fit into his or her environment? Do the environment and the subject affect each other reciprocally? In the case of Mambety, that subject is still bound to the stifling historical context but also exhibits flashes of an unexpected freedom that grants him or her the luxury of a personal interaction with the space he or she occupies. If space bounds the characters in Sembène's early films, it is rather the opposite for Mambety—characters produce, alter, and control space. In fact, they exercise a basic right to the space, an expression drawn from Lefebvre's "right to the city." Along with the characters, the camera and the sound accompanying the film generate, change, and manipulate space, as well.

The result is that Mambety's films recreate and redefine postcolonial space. His first two short films represent the director's sociocultural project to map the city of Dakar through the movement of the characters as well as the movement of the camera and microphone. In fact, multiple, flexible maps come to light if one takes the aural imprint of the films into consideration. This is not unlike Deleuze and Guattari's famous definition of the map, which they associate with the rhizome (1987, 12), a concept they use mostly in connection with nomadic displacement. Connected to these ideas, the Deleuzian concepts of deterritorialization and reterritorialization are close approximations to what this study attempts to trace in the relationship between sound and image; we go from breaking regular habits (sound and image no longer work together necessarily) to forming new habits (sound exhibits a stronger narrative role). To put it another way, sound deterritorializes the space traditionally occupied by just the image or the combination of image plus sound, and reterritorializes the space according to the order sound plus image, the reverse of Chion's sound as an add-on.[1] After all, "ultimately, we hear things because we cannot see everything" (Žižek 1996, 93). The maps yielded by these processes, like all maps, are open products with multiple entry points, and therefore do not imply closeness. Graham Huggan states: "The benefit of Deleuze and Guattari's model is that it provides a viable alternative to those implicitly hegemonic (and historically colonialist) forms of cartographic discourse which use the duplicating procedures of mimetic representation and structuralist reconstitution as a strategic means of stabilizing the foundations of Western culture and of 'fixing' the position (thereby maintaining the power) of the West in relation to cultures other than its own" (2008, 29).

Mambety's characters are creators of space, too. This quality associates them with the nineteenth-century Baudelairean formulation, the flaneur, but in a radically different context. Like the original flaneur—one of the key symbols of Western modernity—Mambety's characters help define space and possibly reappropriate it for its rightful owners, shifting it from colonizers to the postcolonized. As paradigmatic flaneurs, Mambety's characters and the camera explore the postcolonial space of Dakar to unearth multiple unique maps while recontouring the limits of the city.[2]

Contras' City is in fact a film without a plot in the traditional sense. The camera moves around Dakar, working tirelessly to generate a contrast between the city's Beaux-Arts and baroque architecture—a vestige of colonial times—and the reality of everyday life for the more modest and poorer Senegalese people. Because of the director's mixing of cinéma vérité with pure documentary aesthetics, the film provides us with several instances of a unique use of sound that ultimately translates into a vociferous commentary on the postcolonial situation. Mambety's second cinematic effort, *Badou Boy*, continues the aesthetic trend established in the first, but it also begins to show signs of an actual narrative; a young rascal is chased through the city by a policeman (although it is never clear why, other than the officer calling him a "bandit"). The cat-and-mouse chase gives the camera ample time to observe the city and urban culture through a *caméra-flâneur* effect, and it validates the poignant antistate, anticolonial commentary initiated in the first film.

Visual, Mental, Aural Maps

The visual mapping of Dakar is most evident in *Contras' City* because the film lacks a clear point of view. It does not have an actual narrative or narrative characters, which leads to the city being portrayed as a fragmented entity and ultimately as a character itself. This result is emblematic of the Senegalese cinematic and postcolonial subject, who naturally takes on the qualities and defects of his or her city or space of birth. According to Frantz Fanon, "The colonial world is a world cut in two. The dividing line, the frontiers, are shown by barracks and police stations. In the colonies it is the policeman and the soldier who are the official, instituted go-betweens, the spokesmen of the settler and his rule of oppression" (1968, 38). The complicated relationship between the postcolonial subject and the cop/soldier will come more clearly into focus in the films that follow *Contras' City*. However, the separation between spaces clearly starts with this first film. For example, the Dakar of contrasts challenges Fanon's distinction between the city of the colonized and that of the colonizer: "The settlers' town is a strongly built town, all made of stone and steel. It is a brightly lit town; the streets are covered with asphalt.... The town belonging to the colonized people ... is a place of ill fame, peopled by men of evil repute. They are born there, it matters not where or how; they die there, it matters not where, nor how" (1968, 39).[3] We do not see this negative vision of the colonized city in Mambety's Dakar; we see only hints and warnings that the director wants eradicated.

Just as he challenges spatial limits and limitations, the director also blurs the lines between genres with his first film. The closest genre to *Contras' City* is the documentary, but in some ways the film also pays tribute to Jean Rouch's cinéma vérité, as already suggested, in spite of the lack of typical testimonials. Unlike the aesthetic of the cinéma vérité that favors as little editing as possible, including that of sound, Mambety's first two films contain an unusual number of aural departures from the norm. If the eye of the camera creates a visual map of the city, then the unorthodox aural interventions on the soundtrack create a sonic map of the same yet different city. This suggestion returns us to the main idea of this volume: sound subverts the narrative primacy of the visual and takes its place as the primary narrative venue. Sound closely matches the physical movement of the flaneur and the camera, but seems to enjoy much more freedom. It acquires a panoptic and omniscient quality that transcends the visual limitations of the camera and generates a type of unlimited sonic freedom, an acousmatic panopticon that redefines the space of the city and challenges the fragmentation observed by Fanon. The sound seeks to unify the postcolonial space as opposed to breaking it into fragments or opposing entities. This aural freedom parallels the conferred freedom of the postcolonial subject, and it must necessarily transgress the normative limits of the map.

The maps created by the camera and sound of *Contras' City* are not necessarily obvious. According to Tom Conley's *Cartographic Cinema* (2007), unearthing such maps may not be all that important, since every film should be considered a map in itself with several elements that can be construed as having a cartographic dimension: "Even if a film does not display a map as such, by nature it bears an implicit relationship with cartography" (2007, 1). Conley establishes that the beginning of a film promotes a geography of sorts that helps spectators situate themselves (2007, 2). The beginning of *Contras' City* purposely disorients the spectator, because while the film is a map of Dakar, it aims to be a "correct" or "corrected" map. However, there is one clear, diegetic example of a map that retroactively validates this discussion. Toward the end of this short film, the "Marseillaise" can be heard on the soundtrack, aurally superimposed on images of a ruined tower. The camera then returns to the slums, as if to underline the vestiges of the colonial period, and centers on a poster of a Gaulish warrior that bears the words "French taste" ("*Goût français*").[4] An excited female voice-over exclaims, "But it's Paris!" as the film hovers over two key shots: the first is of a subway map of the Hotel de Ville-Clichy station (see figure 4), and the second of a student metro ticket. A male voice-over offers an ominous answer: "But no, it's your father!" Like the beginning of the film, analyzed in detail below, there is misdirection in this sequence; Dakar does not have a metro system, so the shot of the subway map depicts the Paris metro. Conley's work helps us in this case, too, because it discusses the problem of place at length: the map "tells us that we are not where it says it is taking place. The story that is said to be there is nowhere"

(2007, 3–4). The author refers here to the fact that the reader of a map is never in the same physical spot that the map projects: "The effect of reading on a map under a plexiglass panel, 'You are here,' . . . bears witness to the same sense of exclusion. We are no more on the map than we may be in the space indicated by its geographical signs" (Conley 2007, 15). But in the case of the map of the subway, we are doubly removed: once thanks to Conley's argument and second because we are not in Paris but Dakar.[5] The aural reinforcement of the shot, the "Marseillaise," functions as yet another signifier of the film's message: in this particular moment the colonial, "fatherly" force of France is felt both visually and aurally. Conley advances the theory that the use of the national anthem in French film is "a sound cue for an absent map of France" (2007, 95). Most relevantly, the association between the shot of the map and the reference to the father (and even to the student representing the social position of the Senegalese as a learner who needs to be taught by the father figure—ostensibly France) bolsters the relevance of the map. Conley summarizes its importance as follows: "Broadly then, when a map appears in a movie a swarm of nagging questions arises about being, identity, space, and location. As a general rule a map in a movie can unsettle or displace the inferred contracts tendered at the beginning of every film about the conditions of viewing that follow" (2007, 208).

Only a few years later, in 1975's *Xala*, Sembène would expose the semiotic power of the map more forcefully. In this film Rama, playing the role of the traditional daughter, visits her father, the main character, neobourgeois El Hadji, at his work place. While Rama speaks, we notice a map of unified Africa behind her, with no borders between countries. As Françoise Pfaff notes in a general comment about the character, the daughter "serves as a metaphor for a future Africa, united and powerful, having erased the boundaries imposed by nineteenth-century Western colonialism" (1984, 159). This general observation works perfectly in the context of the map with no boundaries. To the left of El Hadji, a political map is visible. The maps underline the separation between the characters because they represent divergent mentalities, and by extension the sociohistorical split between France and its colonies. During the characters' dialogue, in a medium close-up of El-Hadji a two-liter bottle of Evian water appears in the foreground, another significant Western symbol that also plays a significant role in *Touki Bouki*. He had offered some to his daughter, but she refuses: "I don't drink imported water." This is the one major difference between Rama and Anta, characters from two contemporary directors representing the modern Senegalese woman: Anta drinks from the Vittel bottle and she does leave the country; Rama refuses all things French. In contrast, El-Hadji not only drinks Evian water but also uses it to have his car washed. Eventually, the father erupts and asks Rama why she does not use the French language. She stands up and heads to the door; she does not answer the question directly, but speaks several last words, still in Wolof. The insistence of the young, educated woman on using Wolof is in line with Sembène's overall preference, and it is not necessarily just a reactionary gesture. But it does exemplify Sembène's anti-Senghor, anti-Negritude agenda, as well as colonial confrontation as defined by Teshome Gabriel and Manthia Diawara. Rama's use of Wolof also honors the national language and continues a criticism begun by Mambety's playfulness concerning accents and differences between the pure French and the Senegalese French, a distinction to be revisited on several occasions.

As Rama exits, the map of unified Africa is now to her left, and once the girl is no longer in the frame the camera lingers a little before the next transition, just in case the audience had missed the detail. Rama's clothes are the same color as the map (a vivid purple that is strongly in contrast with the insipid colors on El Hadji's side and map), and thus when she speaks she basically blends into the background. The young girl is metaphorically pushed onto the map on the wall, which turns her into a symbol. The unified, public space of Africa mixes with Rama's private space and yields a new dimension; the map functions like a mirror in which Rama projects and imagines her subjectivity; in direct opposition to Conley's spatial separations, she is "here" in the map—she is the map.

This is something of a parallel case to the map from *Contras' City*. To the female voice-over it meant "Paris," but what it actually evokes is Conley's "controlling tool" (2007, 5)—it is the projection of colonial power and not an individual, emancipated subjectivity. Other maps constructed in Mambety's first film are not as literal, but they all find their ontological source in this one shot. They do not exist in reality; instead the spectator, who follows the director's vision, imagines them and their infinite possibilities like Deleuze and Guattari's rhizome/map. In other words, they could be called mental maps. The classic study of mental maps is Kevin Lynch's *The Image of the City* (1960), which postulates that like literature, cities can be "read" or recognized because of a coherent, unique pattern of buildings and surroundings. That recognition is imprinted in the observer's memory: "Nothing is experienced by itself, but always in relation to its surroundings, the sequences of events leading up to it, the memory of past experiences. . . . Every citizen has had long association with some part of his city, and his image is soaked in memories and meanings" (Lynch 1960, 1). So the city is constructed mentally through personal experience—the experience of walking through it and being physically in touch with it, which is a fascinating mixture of empiricist and idealist philosophies.

The mental aspect becomes even more important once the walker is no longer in direct touch with the city, because the latter remains "drawn" in the former's mind. In the modern city, this connection has become increasingly more difficult. Giovanni Maciocco (2009) attributes that difficulty to the sprawling malls in *The Territorial Future of the City*: "Urban cosmetics, urbanistic *make-up*, indeed hide the essential, disguising the city with large shopping malls and recreation centers, which constitute the sign of our incapacity to 'touch' the city" (2009, 2). In Mambety's first two films, the human presence trumps the shots of buildings and underlines the emotional and physical connection of the people with their city. Denis Wood declares, "Maps do not so much record locations as connect them to a living" (1992, 24). And Lynch adds, notably, "Most often, our perception of the city is not sustained, but rather partial, fragmentary, mixed with other concerns. Nearly every sense is in operation, and the image is the composite of them all" (Lynch 1960, 2). However, this study emphasizes hearing: how does the city come to life aurally? Cinematic sound facilitates the birth of mental maps because of sound's boundless quality: "The image is bounded in space, but sound is not" (Chion 1999, 144). The mental map of the city that ensues must be fragmentary and in constant flux, in spite of the film's apparent continuity, which actually comes across as fragmented even at the visual level in the case of Mambety. Like the city, film constantly changes though breaks and montage; therefore the mental maps that are created must also be in flux: "Maps in whatever form they appear are in a continual process of being reformed and read" (Howard 2010, 145).

Peter Gould and Rodney White apply a more experimental approach to mental mapping in their book *Mental Maps* (1974). They start from a simple question we have all asked ourselves: "Suppose you were suddenly given the chance to choose where you would like to live—an entirely free choice that you could make quite independently of the usual constraints of income or job availability. Where would you choose to go?" (Gould and White 1974, 15). The authors then investigate people's spatial desires, leading to a remapping of various areas of the world according to their environmental preferences and regional biases. Maps certainly carry a degree of subjectivity within themselves: "That is, maps, all maps, inevitably, unavoidably, necessarily embody their author's prejudices, biases and partialities" (Wood 1992, 24). But emerging from the subjective view of maps, a sense of reality is also achieved because maps "embody space" (Wood 1992, 126). If Chion's boundless sound leads to maps, and maps embody space, it follows that sound embodies space. Thus it is the biases, the subjective views that generate a false sense of space, that best explain what maps mean to the postcolonial world.

Maps and mapping are an essential aspect of colonial and postcolonial practices and cultures. They are linked to the idea of discovery, of extending the search into lands never before tapped (i.e., controlled). Maps textualize the spatial reality of colonization—once a land was "acquired" it morphed into something else, replaced by a different language, new names were given, and so on. In short, maps were tools for exploitation that clearly highlighted the mapmaker's partiality. Graham Huggan's important work on maps, "Decolonizing the Map: Postcolonialism, Poststructuralism and the Cartographic Connection" (2008), claims that the connections between cartography and colonial discourse have long enforced colonial power because of cartography's relationship to mimesis: "Mimesis, besides providing a theoretical basis for cartographic practice . . . has proved through the ages to be a cornerstone of Western culture" (2008, 21). Moreover, mimesis also reinforces "the representation of a particular kind of reality: that of the West" (Huggan 2008, 22). This reality is still very much present in postcolonial Dakar; Mambety's films attempt to alter it, even though it is an uphill battle. Finally, and more pertinently, Huggan indicates the links between cartography and postcolonialism: "The role of cartography . . . in postcolonial writing . . . cannot be solely envisaged as the reworking of a particular spatial paradigm, but consists rather in the implementation of a series of creative revisions which register the transition from a colonial framework within which the writer is compelled to recreate and reflect upon the restrictions of colonial space to a postcolonial one within which he or she acquires the freedom to engage in a series of 'territorial disputes' that implicitly or explicitly acknowledge the relativity of modes of spatial (and, by extension, cultural) perception" (2008, 30).[6] In one such territorial dispute, Mambety's camera breaks the confinement of a colonial map. Suddenly, borders can be crossed, and static representation becomes a flowing movement between different visual and aural spaces.

The intimate relation between maps and the reinforcement of colonial power brings Edward Said's notion of imaginative geography to mind. Imaginative geography has arbitrary limits that are created by only one group of people, the "us," reminiscent of Willemen's binary construction ours/theirs (1989, 15–17), who use their prerogative to split space into familiar and unfamiliar (Said 1979, 54). Once that unilateral decision is made, the opinion of those in the unfamiliar territory is rendered irrelevant, and imaginative geography dramatizes "the distance and difference between what is close to it [the mind] and what is far away" (Said 1979, 55). A few years later, Said revisits the role of geography in the postcolonial world and concludes: "Just as none of us is outside or beyond geography, none of us is completely free from the struggle over geography. That struggle is complex and interesting because it is not only about soldiers and cannons but also about ideas, about forms, about images and imaginings" (1993, 7). In this way the orientalist process is initiated as a means to expand control of places and people. This process is not unlike the initial depictions of the African as a savage in early colonial cinema that firmly established the African subject as Other. The people with means, the "us," reinvent meanings about the space they want to occupy and control, leading to the place's actually being reinvented, recreated from the controller's perspective. As Said claims, "It is Europe that articulates the Orient; this articulation is the prerogative, not of a puppet master, but of a genuine creator, whose life-giving power represents, animates, constitutes the otherwise silent and dangerous space beyond familiar boundaries" (1979, 57). Said reworks his argument once again in *Culture and Imperialism*, and it is worth considering a long citation on the link between imperialism, land, and geography:

> Underlying social space are territories, lands, geographical domains, the actual geographical underpinnings of the imperial, and also the cultural context. To think about distant places, to colonize them, to populate or depopulate them: all of this occurs on, about, or because of land. The actual geographical possession of land is what empire in the final analysis is all about. At the moment when a coincidence occurs between real control and power, the idea of what a given place was (could be, might become), and an actual place—at that moment the struggle for empire is launched. This coincidence is the logic both for Westerners taking possession of the land and, during decolonization, for resisting narratives reclaiming it. Imperialism and the culture associated with it affirm both the primacy of geography and an ideology about control of territory. The geographical sense makes projections—imaginative, cartographic, military, economic, historical, or in a general sense cultural. It also makes possible the construction of various kinds of knowledge, all of them in one way or another dependent upon the perceived character and destiny of a particular geography. (1993, 78)

At a first, visual level, Mambety already begins to challenge these familiar boundaries; *Contras' City* and *Badou Boy* "transgress the black-and-white spatial limits of the city, embrace and expose the cultural diversity of Dakar" (Niang 2002, 48).[7] However, it is at a second, aural level, that the director comes closer to a complete rearticulation of postcolonial space. Mambety's practice of relying on the aural as a counterpoint to the image and to itself reinvents or redefines the map of Dakar from the perspective of this "dangerous space," a "perverted urban space indelibly marked by the colonial experience" (Genova 2013, 123). The director is no longer a silent entity, and the loud noise he makes literally and figuratively with his first two films confirms him as a revolutionary figure.

Mambety circumvents the general tendency of Hollywood-style cinema—that sound should be in line with the visual and reinforce its validity and realism—by expanding the ways sound can be used, perhaps to extremes. While it is fairly clear how Mambety differs from the practices of classical Hollywood, his differences from Second Cinema, and Godard in particular, are less obvious. The fact that Godard still represents the Western world, in spite of his iconoclastic style, poses a further problem for our discussion. Godard has become increasingly engaged in political discourse throughout his career, particularly since

Weekend (1967). He opposes most institutions, most popular cinematic practices; in short he simply "opposes." In *Contempt* (1963), he gives us one of his more radical and controversial thoughts about the state of cinema: "cinema is dead" (seen on a diegetic poster in Italian; Godard reiterates this idea in the last title of *Weekend*—"*fin*," to which he adds "*de cinéma*"). This, of course, is not true; however, cinema as one knew it in 1963 was indeed dead because Godard and a few others were reshaping filmmaking. Thus, the nonconformist way Godard uses sound speaks more to his grand scheme to "kill" conventional cinema than to a larger social issue.

This, then, is the defining difference between Godard and Mambety: aural counterpoint for Godard means the reinvention of cinema, not following norms, experimenting with storytelling and representation; aural counterpoint for Mambety does not recreate cinema (although he does offer alternative narratives), but it speaks to the larger issue of postcolonial narrative space, a space of conflict. Furthermore, for Godard the use of sound does not seem to surpass what it actually is—an artifice, a playful montage effect employed to stretch the limits and limitations of the visual and of cinema. The use of sound and music in the cinema of Mambety goes beyond artifice and becomes an emblem of sociocultural struggles. That is not to say that sound cannot be a mere artifice for Mambety, too, as there is an inherent pleasure of play in his work.[8] The point is that Mambety's aural counterpoint, the disunion between visual and aural and equally that between sounds, also encapsulates the revolutionary reaction of an entire colonized people and begins to rearrange a space that should have never been shuffled in the first place. That is to say, colonialism constructs a space that alienates the colonized, because it does not belong to them anymore. It is mapped and shaped in the image of the colonizers. The postcolonial director faces a herculean task in remapping or reclaiming this space visually. No matter how much is shown, and in however many distinct ways, the visual space comes across as if it had been established by the colonizer; it is still there thanks to the shadow of the panopticons and, really, also thanks to the very medium of cinema, which originates from the West. But Mambety finds less resistance in the attempt to build an aural space that is uniquely African, or in this case Senegalese. It is the construction of this space that may allow the true independence of the postcolonial subject.

How do these maps get mentally drawn? It is the figure of the flaneur that makes it all possible. Baudelaire's flaneur is not necessarily an easy one to transpose into the postcolonial context, given that he defines a time (the advent of modernity) and a place (the City of Lights) that are to be seen in stark contrast with the postcolonial space. Indeed it is the well-lit and efficiently organized Paris that Fanon opposes to the colonized space. Nonetheless, both the flaneur and

Mambety's *caméra-flâneur* have a right to the city, in the way meant originally by Henri Lefebvre (as a right to the urban space, to urban life that meant being part of a society), and later by David Harvey, who declares:

> What kind of city we want cannot be divorced from the question of what kind of people we want to be, what kinds of social relations we seek, what relations to nature we cherish, what style of life we desire, what aesthetic values we hold. The right to the city is, therefore, far more than a right of individual or group access to the resources that the city embodies: it is a right to change and reinvent the city more after our hearts' desire. It is, moreover, a collective rather than an individual right, since reinventing the city inevitably depends upon the exercise of a collective power over the process of urbanization. The freedom to make and remake ourselves and our cities is, I want to argue, one of the most precious yet most neglected of our human rights. (2012, 4)

The separation between the individual and the collective is in fact a reference to class segregation, which means that everyone has a right to the city, not just the privileged. If the process of the Haussmannization of Paris may serve as an example, the poor and the workers were dispossessed and could not enjoy the result of their labors as the bourgeoisie did: "This nearly always has a class dimension, since it is usually the poor, the underprivileged, and those marginalized from political power that suffer first and foremost from [urban transformation]" (Harvey 2012, 16). The end result was that the city of Paris effectively went through a process of quasi colonization, which resulted in a class power struggle between the bourgeoisie (colonizer) and the poor (colonized). Even in terms of time, this was a lengthy process much like colonization.[9] In this problematic urban context, the flaneur did exercise his right to the city, to the new Parisian setting that followed Haussmann's drastic reconfiguration of the capital in the nineteenth century; through his meandering, the flaneur made that new city his own and gave it life. One can extrapolate that relationship to the postcolonial context. Analogous to the urban space of Haussmann's Paris that elided the poor, the postcolonial space of Dakar does not belong to the Senegalese; it belongs to the memory of the colonial. Mambety's *caméra-flâneur* reorganizes the relationship between the locals and *their* city. And whatever revolutionary instinct the director nurtured when making his films, it was adequately placed in the urban context because as Harvey asserted, paraphrasing Lefebvre, "revolution in our times has to be urban—or nothing" (Harvey 2012, 25).

Caméra-Flâneur

The flaneur plays the capital role in unearthing the modern city. Walter Benjamin's discussion of the Baudelairian flaneur in the *Arcades Project* transforms the wanderer into a full-fledged character, whom the author considers to be a byproduct of the city of Paris: "Paris created the type of the flâneur" (2002, 417). Since the city is already an emblem of modernity, the flaneur becomes the epitome of modernity. However, the flaneur plays as important a role in creating the city himself as the city does in giving him birth. It is a symbiotic relationship. The wide boulevards of Haussmann's Paris come to life not simply because they are built, but because the flaneur walks on them, because he is, as Lynch implies, in touch with them (1960, 1). A symbiotic relationship, yes, but also visceral.

The flaneur is a stroller, traditionally someone educated, perhaps even wealthy. He mixes in with the crowd and uses anonymity so that he can freely observe the surroundings: "The observer is a prince who takes pleasure in his general anonymity" (Baudelaire 1976, 692).[10] The wanderer finds pleasure in walking aimlessly and leisurely through the city, but can never associate with or be assimilated to the crowd, and thus he stands alone and remains unique. Elizabeth Wilson declares that the flaneur's foremost trait is his detachment: "detached observer, skimming across the surface of the city" (2001, 78). Yet, he still does all this without being aware of any it: "The city is the realization of that dream of humanity, the labyrinth. It is this reality to which the flâneur, without knowing it, devotes himself" (Benjamin 2002, 429–430). Thus, the flaneur is in fact trapped in the city—a labyrinth that one cannot escape, and in which one dwells in solitude.[11]

Aloofness is definitely a common trait in French New Wave characters—which occasionally extends to the filmmaker, the auteur—as they move through the city and through life propelled by unclear motives. Unawareness is unquestionably a common feature of Mambety's characters too, as they move through the city driven by obvious and not-so-obvious reasons, especially in *Badou Boy*. The lack of awareness is a key element that allows us to align the flaneur's point of view with that of an inanimate object like the film camera. Furthermore, the fact that the flaneur prefers anonymity, to remain hidden, is also a cinematic trait, as the camera is to remain obscured from the view of the audience under classical rules of continuity. Here is Baudelaire again describing the pleasures of the flaneur: "seeing the world, being at the center of the world, and remaining hidden from the world" (1976, 692).[12] Therefore, in a world of commodities, and as a creation of luxury, consumption, and marginality, the flaneur becomes the archetypal expression of alienation and modernity.

The Benjaminian flaneur prefers the arcades of nineteenth-century Paris and treats the exterior like an interior. He has the power to transform the boulevard, the outside, into an interior because of his affinity for the arcades. He looks on the city in a panoramic way, and from his detached point of view it becomes a phantasm, almost a fabrication. He has a close relationship with the objects he gazes on in shop windows because he himself is a commodity: the flaneur inserts himself into the geography of the city and becomes a moving part of it that can catch other people's attention. He is a subject and an object at the same time. He walks in a city that he creates, and Paris takes shape according to his observations. The city of Paris exposes its duality by having an interior and an exterior, but both are in some sense on the *outside*. It is the arcades that allow for this duality to take shape. The arcades were passageways in nineteenth-century Paris covered with glass roofs, so that visitors were neither outside nor inside. The passages were full of shops, a sort of city within the larger city, much like the little vignettes attached to several different shops in the Colobane market in Mambety's Dakar. The reason the flaneur feels so at home in this setting is the overlapping of interior-exterior boundaries; his personality is also at a crossroads between interior and exterior worlds, because he is marginal and can be both active and intellectual (or reflexive) at the same time. He dwells in contemporary urban space but can look back to the past. The city is constantly shifting shape because of the development and modernization process, and along with it so is the flaneur, in their symbiotic relationship. It is interesting to note that ceaseless transformation also marked Benjamin's writing of the *Arcades Project*, which was never fully finished and remains fragmented.

Even as recently as 2013 authors were still enamored of this figure: Tomasz Swoboda reconstructs the modern city through the eye of the flaneur and declares that "the flâneur is an urban animal born out of social, economical, technical, political and psychological transmutations that have transformed the homo sapiens into a being simultaneously anonymous and public, more intimate and present than ever before in history" (2013, 223–224).[13] Moreover, Swoboda argues that the act of *flânerie* is not necessarily a physical activity (i.e., reliant on movement) but can be a mental one: "The one who is the subject [of mental *flânerie*], in order not to become anachronistic, can and should traverse the map of the world at a faster speed that his Baudelairian ancestor" (2013, 231).[14] The mental speed to which Swoboda refers could be equated to another attribute of montage: the ability to move easily through and between spaces (shots).

Anke Gleber's book *The Art of Taking a Walk: Flanerie, Literature, and Film in Weimar Culture* (1999) associates the camera with the activities of the flaneur. This is a study of the rebirth of *flânerie* in West German literature since the 1970s, but the author's findings are applicable to other contexts. She defines *flânerie* as "a metaphorical extension of both photography and film" (1999, 137). According to her, the flaneur is "a camera, a kino-eye, an author as director, the flaneur shapes reality into an ongoing film; he acts as a spectator-turned-reader-turned-writer" (x); he moves "in the streets as an active, observing camera" (16) and becomes "a kind of camera" (156). She continues, "The aesthetic dimension of the flaneur's approach can be read in the quasi-photographic and filmic footage that the camera of his eyes retrieves from the world" (138). It would appear to be the subject who transforms himself into an observation tool. This chapter suggests the opposite in the case of Mambety's *caméra-flâneur* (a unique type of camera movement by which the camera takes on most of the traits of the Baudelarian/Benjaminian concept): the subject disappears and it is the camera itself that garners agency. That agency comes in particular from a lack of point-of-view shots, which means that the camera "floats" around the city and the characters without getting attached to a point of reference—a visual *acousmêtre* as it were. Gleber does link *flânerie* with filmmaking more precisely in the following observation: "His art of taking a walk introduces an aesthetics of movement that, more than any other artistic form, reveals an affinity with the long, extended tracking shots of a camera whose movement approaches and embraces the visual emanations of the exterior world" (1999, 156). Furthermore, she points out that Dziga Vertov's *The Man with a Movie Camera* (1929) and its kino-eye represent another approximation of the relationship between flânerie and filmmaking (1999, 157). All in all, however, the relationship described here is hinted at rather than fully delineated.

For a clearer point of reference, I turn once more to Godard. The tracking shots of Michel and Patricia on the Champs-Élysées are very good examples of the *caméra-flâneur*. Some of the passersby look into the camera (this is not done on purpose; because the film is shot on location, these are actual people who exhibit some curiosity). The fact that they look into the point of view of the *caméra-flâneur* validates the status of the camera as a quasi-person. However, the point of view of the reverse shot (to the pedestrians) fluctuates between Michel's and neutrality, which makes it harder to pinpoint as a *caméra-flâneur* instance. By contrast, in Mambety's postcolonial city there is more of an insistence on neutral point-of-view shots.

Contras' City, for example, follows several vendors and purchasers in the market. This is a place in which Mambety will shoot a longer sequence in *Touki Bouki*, as already discussed. People constantly look into the camera as they buy fruits and vegetables. Some of these "intruders" even emerge from the background, popping their heads just into view of the camera. The camera seems to enjoy simply observing people; young girls, but also mature women, wait their turn to get water. Large containers of water are hoisted up on women's heads, and then they walk away, tracked in several shots. The many occasions on which people return the gaze and look straight at the camera cannot be ignored. Given the exotic nature of the camera in 1968 Dakar, this is easily understandable from the locals' perspective. But Mambety definitely lingers on these returned gazes. The eye of the camera is met by several characters. Since no point of view is assigned to the camera itself, the glances of the walking public assign a point of reference; they are looking at someone then, and someone *is* behind the camera. It hardly matters who it is. The *caméra-flâneur* is born, not necessarily out of what it observes, but through the reversed gaze of several impromptu observers.

The beginning of *Contras' City* is also a great example of a *caméra-flâneur*, in spite of the lack of traveling shots. Instead, the movement of the camera is up-and-down. The movement, coupled with the lack of an actual point of view, suggests a different kind of *flânerie*—one that has to do more with witnessing than with observing. The up-and-down movement of the camera dominates the beginning of the film, and it is also worth noting the increased use of the handheld camera. The vertical movement downward is repeated, once with the baobab tree under which people get their hair cut, then during the episode in front of the church as the camera tracks down one of its columns. In its motion the camera comes off as stuck, as opposed to moving left or right, which would imply narrative progression. Patrick Chamoiseau's concept of "*trace-mémoires*" sheds more light on the vertical movement of the camera. Briefly summarized, the concept refers to the historical transmission of memory in a predominantly oral tradition; in contrast with that, "the monument always bears witness to a rooted, vertical dominant force" (1994, 16).[15] The verticality of the camera movement along the column of a building or monument reinforces the legitimacy and power of the colonial. Another possible explanation is that traditionally the orientation of maps is read on the north-south vertical axis (not to mention the global North and South division),[16] which would suggest that just as the postcolonial space of Dakar is subjected to the rigidity of maps, the movement of the camera suffers, too.

City of Contrasts

Contras' City is startling from its very title because the English word "city" stands out. While it could represent a simple refusal to use the French language (*ville, cité*), it is nonetheless significant that the director should use another Western language. The first word of the title is also problematic, inasmuch as it could be coming from either English or French (contrasts or "*contrastes*"). But more crucially, the word sounds Latin: "*contra*"—against the city, or more precisely, against the colonial ownership of the city. In the case of "contra" as "contrasts," the word would constitute an abbreviation, which in itself represents a literal breaking of the word that in turn may be interpreted as an attack on the very form of language. The apostrophe is—literally again—what provides the link between the two words. Simultaneously, it is ambivalent: it either marks the ellipsis or suggests the possessive (the City of Contrasts—the usual English translation of the title). The possessive option makes for an awkward expression, though, because the apostrophe would have to indicate both ellipsis and possession (contrasts' city), so we are left with "city of contras." By taking the Latin angle, the title begins to make more sense in the oppositional postcolonial and historical context. Months before this film went into production, several demonstrations and riots against President Léopold Sédar Senghor took place in Dakar. The events spanned May to June 1968, which correlates with the uproar happening in France.

Andy Stafford strengthens this transnational connection: "Despite the internal causes of Senegal's revolt, we can now see that the links with France and its own uprising were undeniable. One example is the continuously popular figure of Senegalese legend Omar Diop (aka Diop Blondin). Diop Blondin started his militant career as a key Paris activist, having also had a major part in Jean-Luc Godard's radical 1967 film *La Chinoise*" (2009, 132–133). The connection to Godard perseveres. The street demonstrations in Dakar verged on revolution, as some fifty thousand people took to the streets to oppose Senghor's administration. The movement, started by students (Niang 2002, 51–52), quickly turned confrontational, and according to Stafford, "one student was killed and over 900 were arrested" (2009, 129). However, the events did not get much media coverage in France; Stafford, in an analysis of both May events, theorizes that the reason was that France had difficulties with its own "maelstrom" (2009, 129). In the same essay, Stafford also analyzes Senghor's deft use of rhetoric. In a shrewd political move, the president denounced neocolonialism and blamed the disturbing events in Senegal on France. Behind the scenes, though, Senghor continued to rely on foreign powers for support (Stafford 2009, 134). In the end, taken as a commentary *against* the city, the entire film can be interpreted as political propaganda against the power establishment.

The power establishment is noticeable from the beginning sequence. The first shot of the film reveals a white clock tower through tree branches. The shot through the branches suggests distance, if not a certain voyeurism. On the soundtrack, classical music is being played. The immediate impression is that the building must be somewhere in western Europe. What the audience hears and what it sees are in perfect union at this point. The second shot moves in closer; we can see the spikes of a metal fence in the foreground, and in the background the same white building but from a different angle. The third shot moves even closer, into a close-up of the fence, whose metal work is reminiscent of a fleur-de-lis—a symbol of French heraldry, and consequently of the military and colonial force of the empire. This last visual detail reinforces the feeling that we are presently in France. The act of moving in closer underlines the symbolism of the fence in case it was missed the first time around: entry is not permitted. Of course, in the case of Sembène's *Camp de Thiaroye* (1988), the director's blunt critique of the treatment of the Second World War Senegalese Tirailleurs, a wire fence encloses the soldiers and prevents escape: exit is not permitted. The beginning sequence of *Contras' City* evokes Orson Welles's brilliant opening scenes in *Citizen Kane* (1941).

In both cases, trespassing is forbidden. In fact, Welles's film opens on a sign that literally warns "No Trespassing"; penetration of the private space is not allowed, but unsurprisingly, Welles's camera ignores these rules. Slavoj Žižek calls this break-in a poisonous gift, the secret treasure we gain access to that immediately turns horrific because we get more than we had asked for (2008a, 86–87). Significantly, Mambety's film is different. In the fourth shot, the camera moves back and basically copies the second shot, albeit at an angle. The next shot returns to the fleur-de-lis but then immediately begins to zoom out. Instead of penetrating beyond the fence, Mambety's camera encounters an obstacle it cannot overcome. It is not privileged, as is Welles's or another Western camera, so it must maintain distance and "know its place." This, of course, is an approximation of the colonial relationship.

The next shot may be the most characteristic of the film; it marries the visual with the aural and is the first instance of the aural kind of counterpoint that will be established as part of Mambety's authorial (sonic) style. At first the camera looks up at the sky and then it proceeds to descend slowly. The same white clock tower is revealed to be a part of the facade of the building. As the music continues, two voices, one female and one male, are heard on the soundtrack. The two talk about France, which again raises the probability of being in western Europe. Moreover, the building also bears the French words for city hall ("*hôtel de ville*"). Nevertheless, the male voice, which actually changes pitch as it declares the following, quite sarcastically elucidates the mystery: "Dear, this is Dakar" ("Mon petit, ça c'est Dakar"). The familiar "mon petit" must refer to the spectator, who has just been fooled. The sarcasm in the voice-over suggests that this is an unfortunate turn of events and implies forcefully that it is not desirable to be in Dakar. The change in pitch points to the director's playfulness when it comes to sound and voice. If the first two voices speak "proper" French, the third (responsible for "Mon petit, ça c'est Dakar") pronounces the name of the city more loosely, with a heavier African accent and a roll of the letter *r*. The aural counterpoint occurs immediately following the discovery that we are indeed in Dakar, when the camera reveals the Senegalese flag on the building. At this juncture, the music sputters as if it were played on a defective record. This playful artifice creates a sense of disruption and a conflict is born between the steady flow of the image and the broken soundtrack. The fading of the music, even if it is distorted, supports the downward movement of the camera. We are returning to ground level visually and aurally. The music continues to spiral out of control as the defective record comes to a stop. When the visual returns to eye level, the soundtrack falls silent.

The sound is clearly added postsynchronously, which facilitates the director's manipulation of aural space. According to Niang, the director lends his own voice to the soundtrack (2002, 54), which further connects him to Godard (and also Welles, who uses his own voice throughout *The Magnificent Ambersons* [1942]). In *Two or Three Things I Know about Her*, there is a particularly illuminating moment when the narrative voice-over wonders aloud about how to express something. Juliette goes to the garage to meet her husband. As they talk, Godard covers up the soundtrack with his own voice (Sterritt 1999, 190; MacCabe 1980, 175–176). He wonders about the narrative in front of our eyes, "But are these the words and images to use? Are there no others?" He calls himself "writer and painter" (as Alexandre Astruc imagined), and then wonders if he should show Juliette, the character, driving away from meeting with her husband. Instead, the camera zooms in on a tree and we continue to listen to his whispering voice. As if to prove his point about the futility of representation, the director shows us Juliette's car twice entering the garage—the exact same shot is shown twice—in each instance accompanied by loud honks. Several voices overlap in Godard's film, but the voice of the director reigns supreme, as does Mambety's over the aural space of his film.

As soon as the camera in *Contras' City* moves slightly away from the Beaux-Arts City Hall, the soundtrack changes to Senegalese folk music accentuated by string instruments (the score features original music by Djimbo Kouyaté). In the frame, coming from the left, a cart makes an appearance. This intrusion has to be a direct reference to Ousmane Sembène's first film, *Borom Sarret* (1963), which likely influenced Mambety as much as *La noire de . . .* did. *Borom Sarret* tells the story of a cart driver who has to go from the outskirts of Dakar to the center, or the plateau, which is the predominantly rich neighborhood downtown. Interestingly, Sembène too uses his own voice for the cart driver, thus involving himself in the process of searching for common ground but also setting himself up as being on the margins of society. This twenty-minute film becomes an odyssey because it is impossible to reconcile the two classes, the rich and the poor—there is no peaceful coexistence. When the main character finally passes the borderline, the distinction between the two worlds is emphasized by a radical change in the soundtrack; we move from the simple, quiet Wolof stringed instrument, the xalam,[17] to Mozart. Thus music marks the social discrepancy between the rich and the poor. The power of sound and music underlines the separation between the social classes through an opposition between a traditional instrument and Mozart, who embodies Western high culture. In addition to the social commentary, both Sembène's and Mambety's directorial choices also take on a political aspect, since the music indicates the historical transition from the precolonial to the colonial (or the dubious transition in power from colonizers to neocolonizers). Sound—as music—tells multiple stories.

The cart in *Contras' City* is a clear improvement over Sembène's, and is used not only as homage to the latter but also as an opportunity to propose another game of doubling: there is a camera on the cart. The metafilm game played by Mambety is not original,[18] but there is something to be said about revealing the apparatus of cinema; this is a film about the bare bones of the city of Dakar, but also about the bare bones of filmmaking. The film returns to the motif of the cart in the last two shots, and also in *Badou Boy*. Badou helps an older man harness and hitch a horse to the cart. They are on either side of the horse, and the man addresses Badou several times using the French "ça va," which can be taken to mean both a question, "How's it going?" and an answer, "All right." The obnoxious repetition of the question/answer, to which Badou does not reply, may be addressed to the audience rhetorically. The voice of the old cart driver is but one of the several narrative voices in the film that contribute to the overall atmosphere of cinéma vérité, a genre that relies on plain street interviews to advance its "story."

Similarly, in *Contras' City* the voices on the soundtrack overlap and compete for aural space. There is also a mixture of French and English comments, an amalgam of voices and sounds that echo Godard's quasi-nonsensical meanderings. In effect, the film employs a sort of stream of consciousness, again à la Godard, that is sometimes difficult to follow. The choice to use English again (as in the title), is still startling because English, like French, is the language of a vast colonial power. Underlining that authority is the intertextual reference to Shakespeare. The first time English is heard, the narrative voice quotes selectively from Shakespeare's *Macbeth* (the italics mark what makes it onto the soundtrack):

> O worthiest cousin,
> *The sin of my ingratitude even now*
> *Was heavy on me. Thou art so far before*
> *That swiftest wing of recompense is slow*
> *To overtake thee.* Would thou hadst less deserved,
> That the proportion both of thanks and payment
> Might have been mine! *Only I have left to say,*
> *More is thy due than more than all can pay.*

Beyond the abrupt use of English, the episode comes off as simply an odd inclusion in spite of Mambety's penchant for theater, which is confirmed years later when he adapts a play by Friedrich Dürrenmatt into *Hyènes*. There is no obvious way to justify the inclusion of Shakespeare other than perhaps suggesting a double mimetic process, since both theater and film mimic reality. There also may be some value in a discussion that sets up the Scottish as (historically) subaltern to the English, and the tragic ending that befalls the oppressed who overcame their condition through violence.

If one continues with this metaphor, the fragmentation of the chosen citation elicits a new reading, particularly of the last two lines, which state that Duncan is so indebted to Macbeth that he could never repay him properly. What then is the debt that Mambety transposes to the colonized-colonizer situation in his own country? Is it an ironic debt, and therefore a subtle call to revolution (i.e. one must pay back the colonizers "in kind")? In fact, the voices that follow attempt to eliminate any connection to theater—"No it's not a theater. What do you think this is?"—even though a few shots later the camera again reveals posters at the Sorano Theater (the first one even gives us a date, May 13–14, 1969) that advertise *Macbeth*, to be played in April 1969. This is the site of the National Theater, inaugurated by Senghor in 1965.[19] A few frames later, the camera returns to a close-up of a poster for *Macbeth* to solidify the connection between film (or rather its message) and the play. The voice-over that asks, "What do you think?" implicates the viewer, and fuses him or her into the loud and complicated fabric of the film. To pick another appropriate quote from *Macbeth*, the film is "a tale . . . full of sound and fury." The rhetorical question addressed to the audience (and presumably about the film) seems taken straight out of Godard again. Visually, the panning shots of grey apartment complexes also underline the connection with the French auteur; the apartment complex circular shot is used heavily by Godard in *Two or Three Things I Know about Her* in an attempt to suggest the spatial oppressiveness of the Parisian *banlieue*. Correspondingly, Mambety shrinks space by limiting the cinematic movement and by having the camera focus and move between these rigid frames. In short, the camera is encumbered. The film seems to stop, as it records fixed images, posters, and photographs—single frames.

Another important soundtrack voice belongs to the (fake) president of the republic, who declares that the Senegalese woman should be given full access to culture. His enunciation is mocked as he lengthens certain words in a sort of melodic effect (as in the word "indeependeence"). The voice of the president replaces the map of the country and Conley's national anthem; in this case, the aural map of the country is discernably erroneous. Immediately following the president's declaration, in what may be the most interesting scene of this film, two women peruse several magazines in front of a newspaper kiosk. They begin to make sexual noises, moaning as they flip through magazines; this is the "culture" to which women have access in Dakar. The episode points to the intrusion of Western culture, which is not seen as positive; anything related to Western culture can be perceived as promiscuous, and reading French magazines does not constitute culture.[20]

Amid all the voices and noises on the soundtrack, the visual mapping of the city creeps in slowly; there is a shot of the highway, then several other shots focus on the bridge from *Touki Bouki* and on the neighborhood seen from the bridge. The eye of the *caméra-flâneur* is finally set free and it travels to multiple destinations around Dakar.[21] Coincidentally, this is where Sembène shot the last few frames of *La noire de . . .* If in that film the little boy reveals himself from behind the mask in the concluding shot, in Mambety's film the camera proceeds to show a smiling boy first picking up a mango, and then, in a close-up, happily eating it. Sembène's serious tone is undercut by Mambety's playfulness.

The camera begins to move without restriction about the neighborhood and its market: a man carrying fruit, a display of sunglasses, a cloth salesman, women shopping, fabrics blowing in the wind, belts for sale, trees—these are but a few of the fast-moving images that construct the market. The Colobane market is famous for its wealth of products: "You can find anything in the world at Colobane Market,"[22] say the residents of Dakar. The market is the heart and soul of the neighborhood, and the fast-changing shots of various vendors recreate the "visual chaos of the modern city" (Lynch 1960, 5). At the same time, the market also occupies "an important place in the collective consciousness of West Africans. Every market is surrounded by legends and ghost stories. West African folklore abounds with market stories in which human beings conduct transactions during the daytime and the spirits take over at night" (Diawara 1998, 143). Within the space of the market, the modern city collides and meshes with the oral tradition, which yields a sense of freedom highlighted by the free-flowing movement of the camera.

From the market, the camera moves to an outdoor barbershop at the base of a large baobab tree. This episode may have an anthropological purpose, but the act of cutting is quite often referenced by Godard. *Pierrot le fou* (1965), for example, has a tremendous shot of Anna Karina moving scissors across the frame from right to left; the scissors open and close, and as they reach the far left of the frame, they cut the frame itself and the film proceeds to the next shot. The metaphor of the scissors continues in Mambety's film when the camera moves on to shots of tailors; first a very visible sewing machine appears, and second, a seamstress with a pair of open scissors in her hand is seen in two different shots, making it hard to ignore the symbolism behind the scissors. The camera cuts through the neighborhood and the editing stiches it back up together; just as film is actually born in postproduction, the city and the neighborhood are being reconstructed and therefore reappropriated.

The next sequence of the film follows several people at prayer time. These shots culminate in the source of sound for the scene—the loudspeaker attached to the minaret that blasts the voice of the imam into the city (see figure 5). This is what controls the city and its space; the loudspeaker is visible (an image that will come back repeatedly in this and other films), but in spite of its vantage point it does not observe the city like the typical panopticon. Instead, it is heard and obeyed; it is an acousmatic panopticon. The unconvincing voice of the fake president from above is in stark contrast with the aural power and singing enunciation of the imam. However, even the powerful acousmatic voice of the imam is suddenly challenged by ringing bells, as the film begins to evoke Christian-related images as well.[23] The voice of the imam disappears, but for a few seconds the two sounds coexist on the soundtrack. One of the most obvious contrasts of the city, then, is that of religious separation between Christianity and Islam.

Several shots of various architectural designs follow (the beautiful architecture of the market of Kermel particularly stands out; see figure 6), and on the soundtrack multiple voices sing and repeat the word "rococo." This could either be a reference to the actual architectural style, or more likely to the word "fancy"; in either case, it is used sarcastically. The architectural contradictions (emphasized by the unusual treatment of sound that contradicts the visual) point again to the social and cultural divisions in the city. In an online essay, Steve Nelson (2008) elucidates the importance of architectural design in Dakar, and I will quote him at length here because he reinforces the earlier comments on the urban colonial presence:

> From the appearance of the first French buildings in 1857 in the nascent city of Dakar, the metropole had created an architectural language to suit its imperial mission. When the colonial capital was formally established in 1902, new governmental structures, such as the 1907 Presidential Palace and the 1929 Chamber of Commerce, were modeled on their Parisian counterparts and heralded the ascendance of French power in the region. Other buildings, such as the 1908 Kermel Market and the 1932 Institute of Social Hygiene, were designed to incorporate what the French understood to be the architectural idioms of the region. This stylistic merger articulated both the French policy of assimilation, in vogue before World War I, and association, which became the guiding colonial paradigm thereafter. A polyglot architecture was meant to assert French power by physically inserting an imperial presence in Dakar, while simultaneously claiming to respond and adapt to local customs and taste. Architecture became a means for psychologically controlling and assuaging the colonized.

In *Guyane: Traces-Mémoires du bagne*, Patrick Chamoiseau argues that through their mere existence monuments idealize and glorify the legitimacy of the colonial, and thus they preserve pain (1994, 14). By contrast, the traces of memory he refers to in the title of the book are often effaced because they were transmitted orally, and "the word does not make history, the word does not make memory" (1994, 14).[24] The memory of the colonized is passed from generation to generation through song, words, and an entirely different spatial referent—not architecture, but nature. In other words, Chamoiseau opposes architecture (or the monument) to the word. By the same token, the architecture of Dakar, like the map, is criticized by the director's aural choices using an advanced medium of modernity to pass down memory and knowledge. The shrieking rococo noise is meant to undermine the inherent power of the colonial buildings, which function as reminders (remainders) of the previous domination. In short, the buildings function as large fetish objects. These objects are fine examples of indirect colonialism, or what Said terms a "general cultural sphere [and] specific political, ideological, economic, and social practices" (1993, 9), in which imperialism still loiters. As a compelling alternative, it is the images from the market, from the heart of the city, that are to represent the *actual* Dakar.

At the very end of *Contras' City*, the male and female voices return in dialogue, and now they sound positively French. The male accuses the woman, who likes the city, of being "sentimental," which could mean that she is nostalgic, that she (the colonizer) regrets having lost this beautiful city. The final sequence of the film shows a billboard that advertises going to Saint-Louis;[25] then the camera departs, moving right to left in a long tracking shot of a building, while the sound of a train emerges in the background. Suddenly the camera stops moving from right to left and begins a descending movement yet again. As the camera moves more slowly and the noise diminishes, just as in the first scene of the film, the camera reveals a poster of a Senegalese woman and a train behind her. Only the word "*moi*" ("I") is decipherable, although the subtitles offer the translation, "Me . . . is so much us." The next frame shows the word "*Arrivée*" ("arrival"), and the film, not coincidentally, is also pulling into its last stop. The end of the train route corresponds with the end of the movie, but we get two more shots that come across as add-ons. First the cart driver returns, and while he stands next to his horse and turns his head toward the camera, another voice-over utters the word "dialogues." The final shot begins on the word "*fin*" ("end") scribbled in chalk on a clapperboard; the board is attached to the cart that moves away, taking the word "end" along with it. The pertinent observation is that the ending of the film blurs the line between the diegetic and the extradiegetic, a technique that prefigures Mambety's overall aesthetic choices for the rest of his career.

Authorship and Sonic Style

Mambety stands out cinematically thanks to his expertise at both the level of the visual and the aural. To reiterate, Sembène is not as subversive as Mambety and Godard in the way he uses sound. He advocates natural sound and rejects heavy doses of music on the soundtrack. On the other hand, Sembène does sometimes go against the norm and chooses to subvert conventional filming techniques in terms of images and shots; this is less often the case with sound, such as the distorted or amplified noises in *Emitai* (1971). Similar amplification or reduction of sound is used in *Xala*. Other sound-related choices of Sembène's are revealed in his interviews with Françoise Pfaff. He first tackles the topic of sound by saying he is interested in silences, giving an example from *Emitai* of two children walking in a forest. The natural sounds of the leaves and the trees bring about the "cinema of silence" (Pfaff 1984, 63). Thus silence can be understood as a complete lack of any sound on the track, but also as natural sounds occurring without dialogue. In *Xala*, there are no such silences; even the trip that El Hadji takes to a village is accompanied by music on the soundtrack. To Sembène, then, "music is made to stress, to accentuate, or to intensify the action of the film. . . . music works like a signal" (Pfaff 1984, 65).

Considering Sembène's classical aural tendencies, Mambety's true affinity, as has probably become obvious by now, is not with his Senegalese contemporary,[26] but with Godard and the aesthetic of European auteur cinema. If Mambety was influenced visually by atemporal editing, intellectual montage, jump cuts and other cinematic techniques preferred by Godard, when it comes to sound he adds a significant layer that distinguishes him. A recent volume edited by James Wierzbicki, *Music, Sound, and Filmmakers: Sonic Style in Cinema* (2012), aims to frame the concept of an acoustic auteurism. For example, Elizabeth Fairweather coins the term "sonic fingerprint" in her essay on sound in Andrei Tarkovsky: "Meaning is generated from these sonic fingerprints. . . . The recurring use of a certain sound in a variety of different situations causes that sound to act as a refrain" (2012, 34–35). Fairweather explores the general idea that a unique use of sound and music can be the element that defines a particular director's cinematic style. Similarly, Lisa Coulthard discusses Tarantino's particular sonic style, drawing on research by Tony Grajeda, Jay Beck, and Claudia Gorbman to conclude that the role sound and music play leads to "a new kind of auteurism that considers a director's concentration on sound and music as proof of his or her authorial signature" (2012, 165). Mambety's aural style came into being well before Tarantino's, and, as elaborated in the first two chapters, his use of sound certainly elicits a claim to auteurism. For now, the focus is just on sound, but the role that music plays in Mambety's auteurism will be discussed in the chapter dedicated to *La petite vendeuse de soleil*.

Cow Boy

The connections between Mambety's first two short films begin with the titles, which contain one English word each: "city" and "boy." This is another peculiar choice reminiscent of the inclusion of spoken English and the reference to Shakespeare in *Contras' City*. As one navigates through Mambety's films, certain visual and aural repetitions in the director's work will develop more and more clearly. In the case of sound, what may initially be perceived as monotonous movement becomes a kind of incantation. Thus, repetition allows for access to the essence of things, to things unseen. Since repetition is a characteristic feature of African art according to Senghor, its use would place Mambety in harmonious dialogue with Negritude aesthetics. There is, however, a more mundane way to comprehend the director's penchant for repetitions; they could be used to improve his craft. In other words, he revisits certain approaches so that he can create a better final product.[27] The six fictional films he made are connected thematically and aesthetically, and this study intends to demonstrate the vast improvement between his first, *Contras' City*, and his last, *La petite vendeuse de soleil*. The point is that having running themes throughout his oeuvre inextricably links all his films. To that extent, these first two are also connected. In fact, *Badou Boy* smoothly emerges from *Contras' City*. If taken together—the latter as a longwinded, meandering preamble, and the former as a narrative incarnation of the latter—the two films make more sense. The titles, then, too, complete each other: Badou boy of the city of contrasts.

One last important remark on the two titles: if they are combined, we get either "boy/city" or "city/boy." The first thought is that "boy" must refer to Badou's youth, but a more likely explanation is that Mambety sees his character as a cowboy. The motif of the cowboy is sufficiently widespread throughout Mambety's films to warrant this explanation. In *Hyènes*, Draman herds cows. In *Touki Bouki*, the student companions catch Mory with a lasso, which Mory later uses himself to "tame" his motorcycle. In the last part of the same film, Mory wears a cowboy hat that he hangs on to even when running desperately. His decision not to leave with Anta has already been explained, but there is yet another layer to be peeled off here. His running away primarily means a refusal to emigrate. But Mory also rejects settling down with Anta, presumably for a better life. That is one of the defining characteristics of the cowboy, the man who must push the limits of the wild frontier, and who cannot settle (because classical cinema does not permit the cowboy to complete the oedipal cycle and marry) or cannot remain still. The last attribute of the cowboy—his compulsion to be constantly on the move—closely resembles that of the flaneur's smaller-scale stroll through the city, which would also properly explain the connection between (cow)boy and city in the two titles.

Badou boy, as a predecessor to Mory (both have a penchant for small-time crimes and constant movement) nurtures similar western genre fantasies. At one point in the film, Badou is actually on a horse, as opposed to Mory, a more modern cowboy who owns a motorbike. When Badou and his horse go left, a motorcycle goes in the opposite direction, but its sound is heard on the soundtrack well before the actual visual confirmation. This disorienting aural technique is of course later refined in *Touki Bouki*. Badou then helps a man attach the horse to a cart, and they both drive away. The camera follows them and a very excited Badou mimics the movements of a cowboy, as if he had a lasso in his hand, which represents another double play on fantasy and on mimesis: an actor pretending to be Badou, who pretends to master an invisible lasso. On the soundtrack the music changes from traditional Senegalese sounds to music typical of a western. Tom Conley identifies the western as one of those that "have exceptional affinity for cartography" (2007, 209), because within the genre "space is the object and modus vivendi of narratives that tell of the founding of new political orders or claims staked to new lands" (2007, 209). Badou, alongside the *caméra-flâneur*, does not explore new territories per se, but he might as well be doing so. Both he and the camera stake a claim over a land that was stolen from them and that they are now in the process of reappropriating. Finally, added war cries and whoops of Native Americans indicate beyond the shadow of a doubt that this is indeed a reference to the western genre.[28]

These last sounds are added to the soundtrack, and they exemplify one of the many interesting aural techniques displayed in this film. The whoops of the Native Americans are clearly added postsynchronously, so their source could be considered either non- or extradiegetic.[29] But these sounds perfectly match the desires of Badou, or how he sees himself in that moment. The added sound does not generate dissonance in this case; instead, it underlines a character's fantasy, and it allows the audience to partake in the same fantasy. *Badou Boy* presents itself as a film about music and sound more than anything else; it is a quasi-exercise in sound editing that attempts to reinstate the primacy of oral storytelling over image. The treatment of sound, noise, and music is so careful that the story takes a secondary role. As a matter of fact, there is not much of a story: a police officer chases Badou boy through the city.

In contrast with the previous film, Mambety's second cinematic effort begins with loud, 1970s-themed music bolstered by African percussion in the background. We witness the return of the actual apparatus of filmmaking, the camera, in the first few shots as the credits roll. It is a much more pronounced insistence on filming the camera, along with a few shots of people taking photos; one of these shots is a direct return, a quasi–reverse shot toward the actual camera currently filming. The music is once again an original effort, this time by Lalo Dramé. As the credits continue (including several actors already used by Mambety for his first film), the main character walks away with a kora on his back. Mambety again steps outside of the diegesis to reveal the bare bones of the apparatus. The boy with the kora on his back moves away from two different cameras: the "real" one and the diegetic one (see figures 7–9). The presence of a double camera blurs the lines between the diegetic and the extradiegetic again and suggests the layering of stories in various narrative planes. There is a lot of circularity in this film; this is obvious at the level of sound, because most sounds or pieces of music are repeated or demarcate radically different passages: for example, moments of silence are placed between identical synthesizer pieces. The beginning is illustrative of that process, as the crew prepares to shoot the film—this shot is flanked by background music, while the shot itself is covered by African rhythms, mostly percussion. There is also a tune that sounds like an organ mixed with drums that keeps replaying from a synthesizer and eventually leads to a sharp noise outburst, a sort of climax. This tune is repeated, sometimes more softly than at other times; it remains the theme song. There are five instances when this tune is used; often the officer comes into the shot, as if that were his cue.

The actual film begins with the stumbling, rotund officer, who reminds us of the equally corpulent postal worker from *Touki Bouki*; government employees have difficulties moving around the city, which belongs to the people. The officer catches up with Badou and presses him against a wire fence with the camera placed directly behind them. Badou has his arms spread out horizontally in a typical martyrlike pose. The reference to Jesus cannot be gratuitous. It is quite the reverse of Said's orientalism, which establishes how Jesus's foil, Muhammad, is turned into an impostor (Said 1979, 72). Badou carries a Muslim name, so his Jesus-like sacrifice challenges Said's dramatic boundaries of imaginative geography. In other words, it offers the Muslim perspective and understanding of sacrifice. The officer is awkward and as he attempts to spread the boy's legs, presumably for a pat-down, the gesture certainly looks sexual. The music is ominous, fast-paced, and in unison with the visual—this is a terrible situation for Badou—but then we quickly realize the scene is a flash-forward.

Two close-ups of the officer's face interrupt the long shot of the struggle between the two characters. Framed from a slightly low angle emphasizing his position of superiority, the cop represents the neocolonial power, as Fanon explained. His voice is audible on the soundtrack, but he stumbles in his speech, as he does when walking. He has difficulty speaking French during a conversation with his superior, a commissary, whose French is considerably more polished. The film finally shifts to the storyline involving the boy, who is being admonished by an elder woman. It is unclear who she is, because her voice is never actually heard in spite of her yells. She is filmed twice in close-ups yelling determinedly at the boy. However, on the soundtrack we only hear a song whose rhythm mimics the movement of her lips closely. The nondiegetic music takes away the voice and replaces it with another aural signifier. Suddenly the woman begins to cough, but oddly, the noise on the soundtrack belongs to a man. The coughing continues, exaggerated greatly on the soundtrack, and the boy finally decides to help her out, only to get chased out of the house compound. The aural effect suggests counterpoint and disunion yet again, as the sounds of the film mix to unveil another sonic rack focus effect. In spite of a few examples that come close, the sonic rack focus effect is not yet well defined by the director who masters the technique in *Touki Bouki*. In *Badou Boy*, Mambety relies more on a chaotic mixture of sounds:

loud coughing, women's voices, the noise of children playing soccer in the street, dogs barking, and the officer's voice-over.

The commissary ridicules the officer's spoken French ("Your French is not improving at all"). The audience never sees the commissary, yet his presence is felt significantly because his voice reigns over the film in an acousmatic manner. He spectrally signifies the law that one cannot escape. Concurrently his voice, which pours forth a more traditional ("pure") French accent, represents the long, unyielding arm of colonization. It is another sound cue, like Conley's "Marseillaise" or the fake president's voice, that replaces the map of France and the organization of space according to the French rules. As the commissary still talks about making a decision regarding the boy soon, the film transitions into another shot of megaphones atop a minaret, and a siren is heard simultaneously with the voice of the commissary.

If within the diegetic space of the film there is no visual alternative to the map of the metro—a counterproposal from the Senegalese that shows they can map their own land—that possibility exists aurally. The "Marseillaise" is countered with music, voices, and noises that are quintessentially Senegalese and that belong to Dakar. The minaret also counterpoints the voice of the commissary. This constitutes the second occasion, following *Contras' City*, on which Mambety spotlights the minaret megaphones whose sound is interrupted (by church bells in the first film). But that only means that the acousmatic panopticon can be reduced to other sounds, not just the call to prayer. In the cinematic context, all the sounds we hear as an audience are perceived as coming from the same source, so if the megaphone can play the part of an acousmatic panopticon, then so can another sound that accompanies it. As the dialogue ceases, the volume allocated to the siren begins to diminish. A foot strikes a makeshift ball, and the sound this action makes interrupts the fading sound of the siren visually and aurally. While the siren sound-bridges over to the next shot, it actually dies out completely at the exact moment when the foot makes contact with the ball. It then immediately returns to the soundtrack in a still descending, dying tone. As the film transitions to the next shot,[30] the siren is barely perceptible. By the time it dies out completely, the music on the soundtrack returns to pick up the aural slack. Mambety interrupts the flow of the sound, which makes us aware of its dominating presence.

The narrative importance of sound in this film is also comprehensively underlined by the constant diegetic reappearance of the kora. Badou goes by a blind man playing another kora, the same instrument the former carries on his shoulder in the beginning of the film. Years later, the blind-musician motif will play an important part in *La petite vendeuse*, in which the main character's grandmother is also blind and sings in the street. The camera persists on the blind kora player and emphasizes the value of the instrument. The film goes back to the image of this instrument many times as the old man plays it, his eyes blinking rapidly, almost as if in a trance, half praying, half playing music. He is in the middle of the city, and he is always surrounded by chaotic movement and accompanied by other sounds, like the ones noted in *Touki Bouki*: there are kids playing, dogs barking, and of course, the inevitable street noises, including traffic and cars honking, which accompany the blind man's song most pervasively. The audience never sees the highway in this film, unlike the one shot in *Contras' City* that changes the tonality of the entire story. Instead, the noises heard around the blind man, noises that really envelop the singer, create aural narrative planes that are pursued mentally by the spectators. A transference, like an aural point of view, occurs: the audience hears the city through the blind man. In short, the noises create a mental map on the city.

It must be a loud map. Since the audience hears the noises through an intermediary—the blind man, who is likely to have heightened hearing—the power of the sound is once again emphasized. Beside the exaggerated aural map of the old man, even though the road and the cars are not seen, the images from the previous film (and from those of Sembène) last in the consciousness of the audience that has experienced both films. They remain in a corner of the mind and reemerge in *Badou Boy*. While the blind man sings, Badou is seen urinating against a wall on which is written "défense d'uriner; sous peine de poursuite" (no urinating, legal penalty). Another shift occurs: the law of the colonizer, the voice of the commissary that one cannot escape may be in danger. Perhaps the law does not have a strong enough arm, because Badou blatantly ignores it. Not only that, but it is soon revealed that Badou was urinating on the officer's bicycle, when the latter picks it up from the same corner. When Badou finishes urinating and walks away, the sound of a toilet being flushed accompanies him. This is an extradiegetic sound that clearly does not respect the laws of classical cinema—both the character and the soundtrack elude the law. The sound of the toilet overcomes the voice of the blind singer, who is relegated to the aural background in yet another sonic rack focus effect.

Among his many recurring activities, the officer looks at a photo of Badou as he attempts to identify him. This gesture seems taken directly out of the plot of *Breathless*, in which pictures of Michel constantly appear in the newspapers. Badou, Michel, and the future Mory, would-be gangsters, are built from the same cloth. From the officer looking at the photo, we move to Badou looking at the city. As a flaneur, Badou takes his time to observe the city.[31] While he is looking for clients for a florist, Badou moves his head left and right in a very long medium shot (it lasts for twelve seconds), and then in a much shorter close-up he is still looking away, observing. He walks through the slums, he passes by the musician, he interacts with friends, and so he appears to be constantly on the move. In the one moment of the film when he tries to rest, he fails. Hidden between two little buses, he puts his head down. Two people walk by him and bother him, to which he reacts with disdain. When the camera returns to his observations, he is coupled with a shot of the blind man singing; the montage here suggests that Badou is looking directly at the singer, but that is not the case. This is another faux shot / reverse shot formation; the alternation of shots between the waiting boy and the singing blind man makes it seem that the two are connected in spite of the spatial distance. The singer is not only connected to Badou, he represents a musical linchpin that keeps the entire film together narratively—he is the musical flaneur corresponding to Badou's actual walking. His singing voice may get lost in a soundtrack inundated by several other voices, and yet it always maintains a level of presence. Furthermore, in the many scenes that highlight his voice without showing the audience his body, the singer incarnates one very important visual and aural marker: the radio.

As a paradigmatic acousmatic voice, the radio in *Badou Boy* functions as a space unifier, another acousmatic panopticon. After Badou rides the cart to the tune of the western genre music, the vehicle comes to a screeching halt at a stoplight. The noise it makes is an obvious extradiegetic add-on: the sound of an actual car is matched to the rudimentary cart. Immediately afterward, a voice takes over the soundtrack, and we soon realize it is the voice of a radio DJ who announces the music he will play. The aural montage is such that the western-themed music we just heard may have come from this invisible radio station. As Badou meets and eats with some friends, the next few scenes are completely taken over by this acousmatic voice and music. No radio is in sight, so the voice is still likely to come from a nondiegetic source. The station goes from soft music back to the voice that announces the political news, to more dramatic drum-based music, back to the voice that announces the diffusion of more soft music, to the voice again, followed by organ music, and back to the voice that finally ends the radio show. The aural lines between the diegetic, the nondiegetic and the extradiegetic are completely eradicated in this aural sequence.

A few scenes later, completely unrelated to the radio show, a man in a red hat comes into view. He listens to the radio, but the music he hears (as we do) is initially drowned out by dialogue coming from a completely different diegetic area. When the man raises the volume on his little boom box radio, cheerful radio music takes over the soundtrack. When he changes the station, the music on the soundtrack changes promptly, too. The physical presence of the radio does not de-acousmatize the earlier voice, because that voice does not return to the soundtrack. In addition, the music is different. However, the sight of the radio further blurs the aural lines by adding the diegetic level to the previous non- and extradiegetic levels. They all combine to build one unified, though not perfectly harmonious, aural space: is it even really important any more if the sound is nondiegetic, extradiegetic or diegetic? The soundscape controls the visual space of the film, unifies the city, and offers access to the city to everyone.

In its conclusion, the film circles back to the fence from the beginning, with Badou facing the camera while the policeman is to the side of the frame. The whole movie is about this chase, but it singles out these two scenes, from beginning and end, which anchor the entire narration of the film. The music is subdued, but at the moment when the officer puts his hands on Badou's neck, the soundtrack goes completely quiet. The silence is followed by a loud noise, resembling an explosion, as the officer moves away from, presumably, Badou's dead body: this is an effect I call a sonic jump cut. My concept of the sonic jump cut is based on the already existing visual counterpart that Jean-Luc Godard made famous.[32] The jump cut is the abrupt cut, and consequently rough transition, between two shots. It is the opposite of a match cut, in that it actually seeks to create discontinuity by attempting to connect two moments that are not a match in terms of space or time. The transition in time and space disorients the spectator, who has to struggle to suture back the momentarily lost narrative. Godard popularized the use of this alienating technique, and to this day, his name is heavily associated with the jump cut. Producing the same disorienting effect as the visual, the sonic jump cuts help unearth a space of fantasy, a space in which the audience can no longer trust that what they are seeing is true. As the officer walks away and off screen, Badou staggers a little, and suddenly more loud noises, this time resembling loud gunshots, overwhelm the soundtrack. It is as if Badou were being executed against the wall. Then he falls down. Visually, the shot loses focus and becomes blurry. The next shot begins in soft focus and transitions back to the officer. Was it all a dream? Was it all in Badou's head? These are rhetorical questions posed at the conclusion of *Touki Bouki*, too.

The veracity of the narrative is in doubt, especially when it comes to the blind singer. In the denouement, the soundtrack contains a mixture of children laughing, voices from a random crowd, and a more pronounced voice-over giving a speech; in all, an amalgam of voices. The blind singer joins the choir of voices, and now it is a revolutionary call, led by Badou's friend. When the latter sees the officer, he takes off running scared and is soon caught. The music intensifies with a stronger drumming rhythm and the parallel editing cuts between the officer and the singer, singing furiously as if in a trance with his eyes aimed toward the sky. At the very end, he plays the kora on the bridge that connects Colobane with the rest of the city. This is a high-traffic area because the bridge goes over the major highway of Dakar, the N1, so space is generally congested. Badou, suddenly alive again, gives the old singer a purse with coins, and his reaction is quite strange. He appears to gain vision, abandons the instrument, and runs off into the neighborhood. The scene is edited in an accelerated mode typical of early slapstick comedies, which contradicts the overall tone of the film. Badou picks up the instrument, and with it over his shoulder, walks away—this closes the narrative cycle because it is the shot that originates from the diegetic camera in the opening credits, the one placed directly behind the actor.

This game of doubling, of blending the diegetic with the nondiegetic, of fantasy, will develop into a well-defined aesthetic in Mambety's next films. One minor character from *Badou Boy* presages the significant role that fantasy will play in those films. In the visual and aural chaos of the denouement it is easy to lose track of marginal characters, such as the little boy who carries colorful balloons. Every time the boy appears, he is on the verge of losing the balloons. One must wonder if they are a reference to the colorful balloons from Albert Lamorisse's popular *The Red Balloon* (France, 1956). Perhaps Mambety creates a transnational connection via fantasy. In the French film, the main character, Pascal, a very young flaneur, escapes the labyrinth of the city when he is pulled up and toward the sky by the balloons. It is a wondrous symbolic escape from the past and from constrictions. The *caméra-flâneur* effectuates a similar type of escape. Unfortunately, in contrast, the little Senegalese boy does not control the tools of his impending flight. Not yet. It is a failed fantasy. In fact, his balloons often explode, and when that happens the sound heard on the soundtrack resembles that of a gun going off. Again, attaching these shots to the respective choice of noise or sound disorients the audience; we do not know which story to follow anymore, the one on screen or the one on the soundtrack. It is not imperative to decide, though. What is essential is that sound is almost an entity of its own, almost independent of the image, and in its flight away from the image, it helps remap the postcolonial city.

3 Trauma and Zombie Narratives in *Hyènes*

As an adaptation, *Hyènes* (*Hyenas*) is a narrative and aesthetic departure for Mambety. The director offers two reasons for his choice of adapting Friedrich Dürrenmatt's play *The Visit* (1956). First, other than age the cineaste does not perceive any distance (by which he likely means, creative distance) between Dürrenmatt and himself (Niang 2002, 9). Second, as already mentioned, Mambety tells Ukadike that during the previous twenty years he had been (metaphorically) searching for Anta from *Touki Bouki* and that he had finally found her in this play (Ukadike 2002, 124). As a sign of gratitude, Mambety dedicates the film to the Swiss playwright in the end credits. Moreover, he opts for an encompassing "we" in the dedication ("Nous d'Afrique"—"we Africans," or "we of Africa"), painting with a wide brush over the cultural differences between specific countries.

While it is not a unique gesture, as African directors often refer to their own work as African rather than Senegalese, Malian, and so on, the collective approach in this particular case is indicative of the Marxist direction on which Mambety embarks in the making of this adaptation. The people as a group (whether as humans or animals such as hyenas, peasants, choirs, or as an innovative and subtle incarnation of the zombie) overtakes the diegetic importance of individual characters. The film also offers several points worthy of exploration, beginning with the simple fact that it is an adaptation from the theater. A text that is typically Western finds an appropriate form in the postcolonial cultural context. Transposing the play to film poses issues that can be explained by eliminating the misperceived opposition between Antonin Artaud and Bertolt Brecht, and suggesting a dialogue between the two theatrical and aesthetic forms. As stated by the director himself (Ukadike 2002, 124–126), in some ways the film represents a continuation of his previous exploration of relationships of power and their connection to the postcolonial world. These relationships extend to the narrative as it struggles with the restrictive theatrical space of the original text.

Niang remarks that this is the first African film that broke continental, racial, cultural, and linguistic barriers (2002, 146). Whatever iconoclastic status this film may have, it is effectuated through a return to the written text.

An adaptation is actually a reenactment of something previously existing, previously "alive," so the narrative itself denotes a sort of walking dead, a narrative coming back to life. The overarching argument of this chapter will be substantiated by a discussion of three interconnected elements: individual trauma; Gorée Island as a postcolonial acousmatic panopticon and as the physical place that gave birth to an original, collective trauma (slavery); and finally the representation of the collective sufferers as zombies. Given that the intersecting point of these elements is fantasy, this chapter is framed as an extended reflection on the *imaginaire*; although most of this particular reading is not directly about sound, it will substantiate the previous conversation on imagined space and sound and will also help delineate the concept of spectral sound—sound that cannot die or that "returns."

Deeply connected to fantasy and trauma—individual and collective—this film features several fragmentations. For example, the postcolonial space finds an adequate embodiment in the rift between the diegetic limits of theater and those of cinema. That fragmentation is also evident at a micro-level in the bodies of Mambety's characters, who are either broken, suffering, or artificially repaired. Chronologically, Mambety's work puts forward cinematic characters who are increasingly damaged, artificial (literally having artificial limbs in the case of Ramatou from *Hyènes*), or dismembered. This progression culminates with Sili, the main character of *La petite vendeuse de soleil*, who is paraplegic, and a marginal character from the same film, Moussa, the wheelchair flaneur with no legs. In summary, it is necessary to explore several types of fragmentations and fissures concomitantly —theater/film, city/body, oral/written/visual, sound/image—that will help demarcate the unique cinematic postcolonial space of *Hyènes*. This postcolonial space, as depicted by Mambety, elongates in order to encompass Western forms of culture and discipline: theater and Michel Foucault's panopticon, respectively. Moreover, as observed before, the panopticon finds another instance in the particular use and manipulation of diegetic and nondiegetic music—it becomes an acousmatic panopticon that combines visual and aural to rearrange and further the control of space. Finally, although *Hyènes* represents an aesthetic departure from the preceding films in terms of its sustained treatment of aural narrative planes (i.e., it relies more assiduously on the narrative powers of the visual), it still is acoustically rich and exposes an interesting link between music and the collective.

The plot of the film follows Ramatou, an elderly, rich woman who returns to her birthplace, Colobane, with vengeance on her mind. Her main target is Draman

Drameh, a shopkeeper who had abandoned her in their youth while she was pregnant. Ramatou offers a fortune to anyone who will kill him. As the most powerful character of the film—paradoxically also the most traumatized—Ramatou is generally at an advantage when she addresses the townspeople or even when she is alone. This advantage gives her a certain panoptic power, which is underlined by a very personal relationship with the island. The island, as a space, is a contradictory place where solitude and isolation collide with escape and idyllic fantasy. In the colonial world, the island may well also echo the French nineteenth-century penal colony system, a place of punishment, order, and great isolation. Gorée represents the postcolonial version of the panopticon—it is an obtrusive presence that looms over the city of Dakar as a constant reminder of colonialism. As a kernel of the Real, unlike the vestiges of the colonial in the streets of *Contras' City*, the island cannot be removed; it is always there. Even when it is not directly in sight, the inhabitants of Dakar are aware of it—the island defines the city from afar. Ramatou's power, like the island's, transcends time and space, as even her name suggests: Ramatou means "a bird incarnating the souls of the dead" (Thackway 2003, 71).[1]

This manifestation of power and the invocation of the dead announce Haile Gerima's transcendent *Sankofa* (1993) whose main character, Mona/Shola, travels in time from the Cape Coast slave fort (an island like Gorée) of modern Ghana to a nineteenth-century New World plantation. In the beginning sequence, Gerima's film succeeds in cinematically and aurally representing access to the past and to the souls of the dead; three intertwined aural levels (drums, intermittent whooping, and an ominous voice-over calling on the spirits of the dead) accompany an unusually long visual superimposition of a spirit drummer and sugarcane fields.[2] The narrative complexity of *Sankofa* offers access to different layers of time, and perhaps takes inspiration from the complexity of Ramatou, a character who controls past, present and future, in spite of (or because of) her being a manifestation of the walking dead.

Collective Trauma and Zombies

The link to the walking dead may seem ludicrous at first glance. Senegal does not have an explicit cultural tradition that involves zombies. However, the word "zombie" comes from West Africa, and the Kongo heritage is particularly implicated: "nzambi" in Kongo can be translated as "spirit of a dead person" (Davis 1988, 57).[3] The francophone area that holds the cultural monopoly over the zombie is the Caribbean, Haiti in particular. The cultures of West Africa and Haiti sometimes overlap, and at the very least one cannot deny the historical connection through slavery between the two geographical areas and the role played by Gorée. Gorée Island, off the coast of Dakar, shown and alluded to not only in this film but in many others, was the first official French settlement (along with Saint-Louis). Even though ownership of the island changed hands several times during the colonial period (it was initially settled by the Portuguese), for about two hundred years it remained one of the hubs of the slave trade with the Caribbean. Currently, the island hosts a colonial-themed museum—a highly public way to keep the memory of the colonial trauma alive. But it is the more insidious ways that need to be brought to light.

In a groundbreaking study of the zombie traditions of Haiti, *Passage of Darkness*, Wade Davis runs down the careful selection process of slaves to be sent to the New World: "As the planters found it cheaper to bring in adult Africans than to raise slaves from birth, they had to import prodigious numbers.... Although these unfortunate individuals came from virtually every corner of the continent, the plantation owners clearly had certain preferences. The Senegalese were valued for their superior morality and taciturn character" (1988, 103). Davis also investigates the roots of zombies and zombification in Haitian culture and in the peasant population, the split between physical and spiritual zombies, and the creation of zombies through spells and special powders. While zombies have been associated metaphorically with slavery (thanks in part to various interpretations of Patrick Chamoiseau's 1986 novel *Chronicle of the Seven Sorrows*), Davis asserts that

> the peasant knows that the fate of the zombie is enslavement. Yet given the availability of cheap labor and the debilitated physical condition of the zombies, there is obviously no incentive to create a workforce of indentured labor. Instead, the concept of slavery implies that the victim of zombification suffers a fate worse than death—the loss of individual freedom implied by enslavement, and the sacrifice of individual identity and autonomy implied by the loss of the *ti bon ange*.[4] It must be emphasized that the fear in Haiti is not *of* zombies, but rather *of becoming* a zombie. (1988, 9)

That fear would shape the construction of the Haitian sociocultural space, which ultimately may come, and still does according to Davis, by way of West Africa. Davis claims that the Bizango societies—the secret societies that dictated the social structure of rural West Africa—played a capital role in shaping that space, and

> may have a direct role in the creation of spirit and/or physical zombies. The creation of the zombie, or indeed the threat of zombification, is not imposed in either a random or a critical way. On the contrary, there appears to be a logical purpose to zombification, consistent with the heritage of the people and their need to protect that heritage. A zombie is not an innocent victim, but an individual who has transgressed the established and acknowledged codes of his or her society. The act of zombification represents the ultimate social sanction. (1988, 284)

The concluding scenes from *Hyènes* are a very close approximation of this exact process: a jury of men judges, condemns, and executes Draman. Davis, in his account of one of the most fascinating cases of zombification, Clairvius Narcisse, discovers that before Narcisse became a zombie, he was in fact "taken before a tribunal, judged, and condemned. The possible link to the tribunals of West Africa was obvious" (1988, 239). But what is the semiotic value of the zombie, if it is not to be understood as an incarnation of and a protest against slavery? The zombie and zombification that we witness in *Hyènes* carry a similar metaphorical value to the "regular" walking dead that have invaded our contemporary times, with a few crucial distinctions like the lack of visual gore. In spite of the differences, the one concept that unifies all zombies is their connection to trauma of many kinds, whether collective or individual, whether issuing from physical or emotional wounds.

Ruth Leys links trauma and the wound in the following way: "Trauma was originally the term for a surgical wound, conceived on the model of rupture of the skin or protective envelope of the body resulting in a catastrophic reaction in the entire organism" (2000, 19). It is worth noting that a parallel process takes place in montage: the visual is first cut (wound/rupture), then spliced back together; when sound is added according to countercinema aesthetics (i.e. in a manner that does not harmonize with the image), it triggers more "trauma" in the visual, and the overall narrative needs readjustment (what Leys calls a "catastrophic reaction"). In citing Leys, I move past psychoanalytical connections and focus on trauma's physical, temporal, and cultural embodiments.[5] In other words, I am more interested in how one's wound (or trauma) leads to the catastrophic reaction at a national level, and even at a larger, international scale, because trauma has the ability to provide us with "the very link between cultures" (Caruth 1995, 11). According to Fanon, the national wounds are the gateway to a new subjectivity and the black intellectual man has to maintain awareness of all historical wounds: "I need to . . . see the ashes, the segregation, the repression, the rapes, the discrimination, and the boycotts. We need to touch with our finger all the wounds that score our black livery" (2008, 163–164). There is an important physical component to Fanon's approach that connects all emotional traumas; the black postcolonial subjects need to maintain direct contact with their wounds.

The always-fresh memory of the wound can bring on a collective awareness of trauma. Cathy Caruth further defines trauma: "To be traumatized is precisely to be possessed by an image or event" (1995, 3–4). That image or event remains imprinted in one's memory, but in the case of a nation, of a collective memory, it is only the event that defines the evolution of trauma. The event that cannot be forgotten, slavery and colonization taken as a whole, still generates a reaction, it still hurts because it is a traumatic experience that has not been dealt with appropriately: "If something is to stay in the memory it must be burned in: only that which never ceases to *hurt* stays in the memory" (Nietzsche 1969, 61). But it is acceptable that it has not been dealt with appropriately. In fact, consistent with Fanon's observation above, this is the preferred alternative. There should not be any healing; the wound should continue to hurt. This choice reflects a refusal to move past the atrocity of slavery; oddly, the message is that the pain should continue to play a part in everyday life. If this is the case, it ensures the continuation of a combative spirit, of a revolutionary desire—the fight against colonialism is not over yet.

Like Draman, Ramatou has endured deep personal trauma. She declares, "I've forgotten nothing. The pain is etched on my heart." She could be referring here to different types of pain, most of them undoubtedly from the past: the pain of having been betrayed by her lover, the shame she suffered as a young woman in the eyes of the community, the pain of losing her child, the pain of having to prostitute herself, or the physical pain that comes with surviving a plane crash and losing two limbs. Ramatou is in possession of every type of pain possible, which almost makes her seem an unlikely, "unreal" character. Or rather, she is an unlikely human, one who cannot die physically. Undoubtedly, the events she experiences exacerbate the pain. In contrast with her pain and the acknowledgement that she has not forgotten anything, Draman says, "You never forget pleasure like that." However, his response is to Ramatou's question about missing her and is driven by remembering pleasure and not pain. The two characters are at opposite ends of the pain and trauma spectrum, and only Ramatou's are exaggerated. One reason for this hyperbole is that it accentuates the transference from the individual to the collective—no one soul could suffer that amount of pain, so Ramatou, through tremendous loss, ascends to the status of a symbol, a stand-in for an entire people.

Dominick LaCapra uses the term "wound culture" (2001, 28) to ground his argument about differentiating loss and absence in historical writing.[6] In LaCapra's opinion, ignoring or not recognizing this difference can exacerbate historical traumas needlessly by creating unnecessary tension. LaCapra uses the examples of apartheid and concentration camps to illustrate what he means by historical traumas, traumas that the national consciousness has yet to deal with appropriately—unmastered trauma. There are other examples in our human history, though, both in the Western world and elsewhere. For example, Adam Lowenstein argues in a book about the place of the horror genre in cinema that "To speak of history's horrors, or historical trauma, is to recognize events as wounds" (2005, 1). Auschwitz, Hiroshima, and Vietnam are such events, and Lowenstein aptly links them to the horror genre because "the modern horror film may well be the genre of our time that registers most brutally the legacies of historical trauma" (Lowenstein 2005, 10). *Hyènes* is not a typical horror film, not by a long shot, and the presence of historical trauma is much more subtle, but it is present nonetheless.

Another theorist who refers to the concentration camps as the perfect example of historical trauma is Slavoj Žižek. He asks rhetorically, "All the different attempts to attach this phenomenon to a concrete image ('Holocaust,' 'Gulag'...), to reduce it to a product of a concrete social order (Fascism, Stalinism...)—what are they if not so many attempts to elude the fact that we are dealing here with the 'real' of our civilization which returns as the same traumatic kernel in all social systems?" (2008b, 51). We can grasp at the meaning of this quotation without a lengthy discussion of the value of Lacanian theory; the current pervasiveness of the subgenres of horror (mainly zombie and body horror) in popular culture finds a suitable explanation in the unconscious decision to make ourselves face the most gruesome and malign events of our entire historical existence over and over again. We return repeatedly to the original site of the trauma of humanity, because the memory of the Holocaust (or whichever unmastered trauma haunts us) still chases our collective subjectivity. In the case of Mambety's film, it is the unmastered trauma of slavery and colonization that still hangs over the postcolonial subject. The Holocaust probably plays a lesser role in the common consciousness of Africans; instead it is slavery that haunts their present and future. Thus Ramatou's return home is also a return to the site of the original trauma. At an individual level, that trauma is caused by Draman, who had refused to acknowledge their child and thus chased her away from the community in shame. But at a higher level, her reappearance marks the return to the origins of slavery, to the island from which thousands of slaves were sent to the Caribbean.

Ramatou's return to a home she had thought was gone forever fits in well with the topos of the return of the dead.[7] In both cases the return also implies death, which for Ramatou is not so much a physical death as a symbolic one. One can identify the expulsion from the town when she was a young woman as the key moment in her life; the person she had been up to that point basically ceased to exist. Žižek once again retraces Lacan's conversation on multiple deaths, the real ones and the symbolic ones, in order to give us a remarkable insight: "This place 'between two deaths,' a place of sublime beauty as well as terrifying monsters, is the site of *das Ding*, of the real-traumatic kernel in the middle of the symbolic order" (2008b, 150). Both main characters from *Hyènes* find themselves between deaths in the middle of the symbolic order. Ramatou's return is a variation on the return of the ghost of Hamlet's father.[8] In other words, she comes back to settle an unpaid debt, as Žižek explains: "The return of the dead is a sign of a disturbance in the symbolic rite, in the process of symbolization; the dead return as collectors of some unpaid symbolic debts... persisting beyond physical expiration" (1992, 23). Moreover,

> "the return of the dead is" . . . the reverse of the proper funeral rite. While the latter implies a certain reconciliation, an acceptance of loss, the return of the dead signifies that they cannot find their proper place in the text of tradition. The two great traumatic events of the holocaust and the gulag are, of course, exemplary cases of the return of the dead in the twentieth century. The shadows of their victims will continue to chase us as "living dead" until we give them a decent burial, until we integrate the trauma of their death into our historical memory. (1992, 23)

Ramatou is also well on her way toward an actual death as her body declines and is gradually replaced by artificial limbs. The last scene reinforces her symbolic death; she goes down the staircase of a bunker and disappears into the shadows after Draman's death—she may endure multiple symbolic deaths. Mambety's soundtracks use a spectral kind of sound in the same way; he returns often to the same sound or tune, which disappears only to reemerge at a later moment. Sound also transcends the "death" of the visual, as it often continues beyond the end of the film; sound may "die" diegetically, but it is revived nondiegetically through music. Ramatou's disappearance inside the bunker is not yet her physical death. Draman actually points to Ramatou's departure as the moment he was no longer himself, so he appears to invoke the same moment as his symbolic death. However, that is simply a specious transference on his part. His symbolic death takes place when Ramatou asks the town for his physical death, and from that moment it is only a matter of time until the townspeople turn against him.

Unlike Ramatou, though, Draman does go through physical death, and a violent one at that, as a horde of zombies swallows him. Nar Sene notes, albeit in a different context, that Draman suffers two deaths: "Draman Drameh, with his heavy D's that sound like the last two signs of life of an elephant; here, the sound 'D' means death. Draman Drameh dies twice: a first time in his consciousness, Draman. A second time in his 'disappearance,' Drameh" (2001, 30).[9] It is also thanks to the two characters' multiple deaths that we can discuss the return of the dead, which is "possible only within the space of the death drive, which according to Lacan, is the space between the two deaths, symbolic and real" (Žižek 2008a, 112). And as already hinted at above, Žižek's points about the Holocaust can be generalized to include slavery and the colonial experience: "The impossibility of representing the Holocaust is not simply that it is 'too traumatic,' but, rather, that we, observing subjects, are still involved in it, are still a part of the process which generated it" (2008a, 276). The postcolonial subject oscillates between a state of presence and nonpresence.

Ramatou's intentions concerning the land and the people of Colobane could be construed as an engagement in reverse colonialism—she represents her people, she is her people who have come back to life, who are acutely aware of the wrong that was done to them. Now she seeks vengeance, which includes reclaiming the land that was rightfully hers, and since Ramatou is metaphorized and used as a symbol, that repossession can be extrapolated to the larger community. Thus by association, her involvement in reclaiming the land means that everyone is still dealing with the effects of the original colonial period. When Ramatou claims ownership of the city, of the land, and even of Gorée Island, she returns to the original site of trauma. And returning to the original site of trauma is clearly linked to the return of the dead. In the citations above, the Holocaust presents itself as the traumatic source for the fundamental fantasy of our current mass culture. The same can be said about the horrors of Gorée Island: there is no decent burial on the trail to the Caribbean. In a discussion of Joseph Gai Ramaka's film *Karmen Geï* (Senegal, 2001), Kenneth Harrow mentions "the spirits of the dead slaves on Gorée" (2013, 121). The shadows of the individual slaves and the bigger shadow of slavery as an event both haunt the contemporary human consciousness.

What about actual zombies? The blundering, awkward and yet driven movement of zombies can first be read metaphorically as pure trauma, or a repetition-compulsion of one traumatic, ultimately grotesque, event—death. Žižek's distinction between drive and desire is explained through one radical difference. Desire implies an ulterior motive—I want this, but to what end, what do I really want? "Drive, on the contrary, persists in a certain demand, it is a 'mechanical' insistence that cannot be caught up in dialectical trickery: I demand something and I persist in it to the end" (Žižek 1992, 21). For the zombies, the Lacanian/Žižekian desire is impossible, but drive remains. Zombies are pure Freudian id reduced to one component: hunger. In the space created in between the two or three deaths mentioned above, there is no desire, and that space is structured only by drive. The zombies cannot remember anything from the previous life, because they would gradually shift into beings of desire. This brings us back to the order of discourse in some way, to the degree that in the Lacanian account, the Real is the "primordial gash" from which the Subjects are torn loose from nature. From this gash (as Leys notes, the word "trauma" comes from Greek and means "wound"), a Subject oozes out of the primal, fusional paradise of the Real and descends into the decentering yet identity-conferring order of the symbolic. In the case of the zombies, in spite of their numerous gory wounds, cuts, scratches, gashes, and other splits, they cannot move through the symbolic; they are stuck. Following this account, does Ramatou's drive equate her to the walking dead? Likely so. But there are other references in the film that justify this uncanny presence.

Several returns and actions validate the topos of the walking dead: as stated already, Mambety returns to a form that precedes cinema (theater); Ramatou returns home when she is believed gone; there are constant references to hyenas, animals that prey on dead carcasses; and most importantly, a horde of men "eats" Draman at the denouement of the film. Given that the film leans toward Marxist theories overall, the theoretical hook for this chapter has already leaned heavily on thinker Slavoj Žižek,[10] who also places the subject between the Lacanian Symbolic and Real, but outside of himself or herself (in direct opposition to German idealist thought). In other words, the subject cannot look inward in order to define his or her subjectivity; instead subjects define themselves in tandem with, or through, Others, through what we think they may want of us or from us, which is in essence Žižek's rhetorical *che vuoi?* It is through this question, posed to the colonizer, that the postcolonial subject has been defining himself or herself. This definition of the Lacanian Subject $ applied to Dakar circa 1992 explains the two main characters of *Hyènes* and their relationship very well, as both define themselves through the other with mixed results. They are also the only two real voices that dominate the film and challenge the overall emphasis on community and the collective.

That collective (the walking dead) is evident from the first few scenes. The film starts in slow motion, as the camera tracks a herd of elephants moving right. Only their legs are framed. In the second shot, the same herd of elephants goes left, accompanied by soft, instrumental music, composed by Mambety's brother, Wasis Diop. It is the second herd motif that the director employs, following the cows of *Touki Bouki*. The aesthetic choice of slow motion is fascinating; it is as if the film were waking up from lethargy—it is coming to life. The subject of the shot is not haphazardly chosen either. The elephant has long been an endangered species, a dead man walking as it were. More importantly, the elephant is a power symbol, known for its grandeur and effective communication within the herd. There is also the popular belief that an elephant remembers everything, which suggests two questions: What is there to remember? What cannot be forgotten? As the film unfolds, these questions find several answers, and it has already been proposed that the collective trauma of slavery is one such answer. The camera jumpcuts to an extreme long shot of a group of people walking in yet another herd while the title of the film flashes on the screen. The intellectual montage unifies the two herds, and suddenly it is the people who cannot forget something of great importance. Second, the title, *Hyènes*, refers to another animal, not the elephants from the beginning, adding another intellectual montage layer from the extradiegetic level; the expectation is to see hyenas, but instead initially there are only elephants and people. The intellectual montage works at three levels, then: two separate shots plus the title elicit yet another understanding of what a group is.

The effect of intellectual montage is fully accomplished in the next shot, as the camera tracks the moving legs and feet of the human herd. They are elephants (they cannot forget) and hyenas simultaneously. The hyena symbolism is probably linked to the idea that they will feast on Draman's misery throughout the film, and eventually on his body. As the group heads into Draman's bar, the camera moves to the side and tracks the dragging of feet on the dusty roads. The group is lifeless, they walk like zombies—the herd becomes a horde—and this motif will continue to gain steam until the violent ending.

One particular episode foreshadows the violent denouement. When Ramatou demands Draman's death, the townspeople initially express shock. And yet, they soon realize that they can take advantage of the situation; for example, they can buy lots of products on credit. In Draman's grocery store, the crowd grows increasingly louder and more demanding, unlike in the first scene of the film when everyone is lifeless. The opportunity to rob Draman brings everyone to life. As Draman realizes that he is about to be ruined, that he has no leverage and must obey the crowd's wishes, he goes mad. He bellows, "credit, credit, credit, nothing but credit!" and proceeds to destroy his own shop amid the others' yells and screams. His destructive mood does not last long, and as he walks away the crowd grows even larger. Behind the counter, his wife is overwhelmed, which is surprising because in the beginning of the film she seems in full control of the grocery store (when people want to buy too much on credit, she immediately dismisses them, unlike the powerless Draman). This oncoming herd is too powerful even for her. The crowd consumes the space of the grocery store and its contents, just as zombies would, which confirms Ramatou's menacing warning: "the reign of the hyenas has come." The character of the teacher—an authority figure of sorts—will later repeat this exact line in order to emphasize the sociopolitical power shift of the town. The hyenas, or the zombies, are now in charge.

It may make sense now to jump forward to the final scene before looking at the rest of the film. There are several departures from the play, none more important than the death of the main male character. If in the play the main character, Alfred III, succumbs under suspicious circumstances (or is likely to have taken his own life), in the film it is the collective, the horde, that kills Draman. The townspeople of Colobane do suggest that he commit suicide, but he does not listen. The film portrays him as a wanted man, one who is likely headed to his death, with no escape from the situation. One physical element that underscores the impossibility of escape is the barrier that prevents him from leaving when he borrows a car to go see Ramatou. This barrier is in the middle of an unfinished road, the only construction in sight, something Draman could easily circumvent if he chose to do so. The irrationality of the barrier is highlighted by long shots that reveal the nothingness surrounding it. As he waits for the barrier to be lifted, a poster is visible behind him that is reminiscent of the western genre and the wanted man, the outlaw. It is Draman who is the wanted man, and as he drives away into nothingness, we know beyond the shadow of a doubt that his fate is set.

The town's collective makes the decision to kill Draman following long debates and ethical conundrums. In a last attempt to convince Ramatou to spare his life, Draman goes off to see her. They meet by the sea on a high platform. Her first question, "What are you doing by *my* sea?" reinforces Ramatou's power and ownership. She claims the land and she claims the ocean. As a subject who effectuates a return, Ramatou can only be the incarnation of the "wandering" postcolonial subject. The sad beginnings of her life story (ostracized by the father/male figure—the Law—and forced into prostitution) are mere images of the colonial relationship between Senegal and France, the former having been forced into (colonial) prostitution. But years later, Ramatou/Senegal can claim ownership of herself and the land and sea. Ramatou is the new Law, a purely Cartesian subject that echoes Descartes's view of man as master and possessor of nature. The two characters talk about the past, their lost child, and how they were as youngsters. This scene positions itself as a temporal mirror image of Anta and Mory atop the rock with their musings on the future and emigration. In *Touki Bouki*, the young couple dreams of a better life in France; years later, in *Hyènes*, the older couple revisits that conversation, but Draman and Ramatou's nostalgic remembrance of their youth still carries undertones of naïveté.

The focus of the fantasy has changed, though, between 1974 and 1992. If the fantasy was originally to leave Senegal, now it is to claim ownership of the country. Draman laments that he has come to the end of his life, and without a doubt his death is a necessary one. He is a version of the postcolonial subject of which one is to rid oneself. Ramatou's merciless response is "I'll have you carried to my island" and she points to Gorée, which is barely visible on the horizon (see figure 10). Her use of "my" bolsters her claim to ownership of the land, but it also poses a problem. Owning the island means rearranging the colonial past, and by suggesting that she will have Draman carried there she implies that she will turn him into a slave, which is also congruent with the Haitian version of the zombie. (Unless she means she will have his dead body carried to the island, which would make it a literal rather than a metaphorical burial ground; in that case she would partake in creating an appropriate death rite.) She adds an invitation to her threat: "Die in peace, then come join me." This is extremely interesting, because Ramatou is not yet dead and gives the impression of being invincible and immortal. Draman can join her in real death or in symbolic death, but importantly, it appears that they will both transcend physical death.

When Draman fails to demonstrate his innocence and right to live, he drives off toward the place of his sentence in the borrowed car (he is on borrowed time). Before he gets to the meeting point, he encounters a lone character, a walker in the middle of the open road. The car goes in circles around him several times, as if to forestall the inevitable. Empathetic instrumental music matches the somber mood of the episode. In fact, when Draman drives in circles, the music, too, hovers around the same note, as if its flow were momentarily suspended. Eventually, he arrives at his trial and heads toward the group. The film crosscuts between Draman driving to meet his fate and the group of men getting ready to carry out the execution. They wear garments that look like rice bags as they slowly proceed toward their target. They are unnamed, thus impersonal, further stressing the idea of the collective. As Harrow comments, they march in "single file, in silhouette, hands behind their backs—evoking nothing as much as a line of slaves, a cordelle, bound and marching to their fate" (2007, 181). However, I perceive the collective as being in a power position rather than reminiscent of slaves; they are judges, not detainees. Spatially, too, they are on the highest tip of a sand dune, which is a vantage point. The evocation of the collective also comes from the immediately preceding scenes, in which we see hawk-eagles, a choir of children singing, then the same hawk-eagles gathering, and finally the men who come together to discuss how they can save Colobane. The shots of the hawk-eagles combined with the shots of the human herd create another intellectual montage effect indicative of the power of the committee: it dominates earth and air.

Numerous shots further support the idea of the group: first, the extreme long shot that tracks the men while they walk atop a sand dune. Then the camera is placed behind the group, as their numbers multiply. All the men wear their hair in dreads, which form bull-like horns around the ears. This is truly a herd. In one telling close-up, it can be observed that most of their faces are covered in white powder. The makeup warrants three possible explanations. First and most important, the white powder is often applied in Caribbean voodoo practices to suggest a trance; here, it takes away the life from the faces, rendering the men more ghastly. Second, in the tradition of commedia dell'arte the clown, Pierrot, did not wear a mask, but did use white powder to flatten his face; to similar effect, the silent slapstick comedies (like those of Laurel and Hardy) of the early twentieth century featured actors with heavily powdered faces. If *Hyènes* is classified as a comedy (a view I reject), the powder indicates that the people making life and death decisions are buffoons. Third, the white face is reverse racism or Fanon's famous white masks: the new leaders of the country act in very similar ways to the colonizers, uninterested in the well-being of the larger community and country and immersed in a search for personal well-being.

This group of leading males of the town closely resembles Wade Davis's idea of a secret society: it is exclusive (no women are allowed), they have a sort of a uniform (the rice bag and the hairdo), and they act in the perceived interest of the larger community—they are trying to prevent their town from destitution and poverty. The herd of men proceeds to the trial. The teacher takes up the floor and people respond as one to his questions. Then the mayor speaks and everyone repeats after him while he gives reasons for Draman's killing ("not for money, not for money," repeats the crowd). During the makeshift trial, cinematically, the director shifts from long shots of Draman's car and of the herd of men to close-ups of the judges and persistent close-ups of Draman. The cinematic space literally shrinks around the condemned.

The film crosscuts again, now back to Ramatou who is still up on the high platform where Draman had visited with her. It is unclear how far this place actually is from the scene of the trial, but the editing suggests that she observes the entire process. For his last request, Draman smokes a cigarette. His executioners advance closer and closer to him while chanting, until they completely surround him, and suddenly he is no longer visible. Simultaneously, Ramatou starts walking slowly while the voices of the crowd sound bridge into her scene, and that transition eliminates the distance between the two places. Ramatou goes step by step down into the shadow of the concrete staircase, and at the last moment she looks up and away. The reverse shot of the island of Gorée that follows is presumably her point of view. It is a beautiful point-of-view shot at twilight; the ocean scintillates and it is completely quiet (see figure 11). This shot raises the question whether the island is actually the Isles des Madeleines, an uninhabited set of smaller, rocky islands to the west of the city (the geographic orientation, to the west, would support this view). Kenneth Harrow places Ramatou at Cap Vert (2013, 116), which is the southern tip of the city that faces Gorée.[11] So perhaps the shot is taken during the morning twilight. The quick shot of the island comes at the moment referred to by photographers as the "magic hour,"[12] and it is a clear temporal jump for the film. In other words, the shot is inserted into the narrative at an earlier moment during daylight. Through the magic of montage Mambety links two temporally separated moments. On the one hand, this makes the spectators doubt the accuracy of the events. On the other hand, the visual infusion of magic reinforces the connection to Haitian magic that defines the zombie. The debate over the point of view is an important one; if the shot of the island is an insert, then it has no point of view attached to a character in the film (and it is not a God's-eye view, because the camera is placed at eye level), which would mean that it "belongs" to no one, or more accurately, it belongs to everyone. So the island seen from the coast is in everyone's consciousness, not just Ramatou's. It is, essentially, a national, collective point of view.

The film silently transitions back to the location of the ersatz trial and the crowd begins to disperse. There is no sound bridge, unlike the earlier movement toward Ramatou that carried voices along; what comes back to the scene of the trial is silence, nothingness. All that is left behind is a cloth in the middle of the frame and of the sand dunes (see figure 12).[13] The shot soon becomes a long take, as people very slowly move farther and farther from the scene of the crime. Ramatou appears one more time, continuing to disorient us. It is still "dead" quiet. She disappears down the dark staircase—her descent into hell or to another symbolic death. The next shot goes back to the scene of the crime to reveal the same cloth in the sand and a man with a chicken who passes it. Niang suggests that the ending of the film is ambiguous, that perhaps the crowd takes Draman with them (2002, 151–152). It seems likelier that his disappearance is absolute—he is completely eradicated, eaten alive. The only remaining element is a piece of inanimate clothing—an "island" in the middle of the sand, a remnant of the Real. What remains of his death, the fetish object, also represents a kind of mise en abyme of the historical relationship between island, slavery, and the Senegalese: when the subject is eradicated, a kernel remains behind (the cloth); when an entire people is eradicated, a larger kernel remains behind (the island). It should be added that the first shot—the long shot that focuses on the crowd dispersing—is not necessarily indicative of Draman's disappearance, even though his shirt is clearly in the middle of it all. It is the second shot of the "empty" shirt that establishes the character's eradication; the camera moves in closer as if to verify that indeed, he is no longer in his clothes. He has vanished.

Individual Pain and Trauma

The two main characters of *Hyènes* experience pain and trauma in radically different ways. In her fundamental work, *The Body in Pain*, Elaine Scarry explores the relationship between physical pain and reality, and the impossibility of knowing the other's pain since language does not suffice to articulate pain properly: "Physical pain does not simply resist language but actively destroys it, bringing about an immediate reversion to a state anterior to language, to the sounds and cries a human being makes before language is learned" (1985, 4). In other words, physical pain negotiates its status in the imaginary and the subject is denied access to the symbolic. Scarry differentiates between the pain felt by a subject (the subject's own pain), which gives him or her "certainty," and that subject's pain imagined by a second subject who cannot possibly fully grasp its presence, its very existence (1985, 4–5). Physical pain, unlike the emotional type, is essentially impossible to express outside of the person who experiences it. The dialogues between Ramatou and Draman speak to this point, inasmuch as he certainly does not seem to understand what she has gone through. While her pain is physical, she is clearly more hurt emotionally. Seeing Draman after all these years renews her emotional wounds, and Draman acts as a probing weapon. According to Scarry again, "The point here is not just that pain can be apprehended in the image of the weapon (or wound) but that it almost cannot be apprehended without it" (1985, 16). Substituting a person for a traditional weapon is unorthodox. Yet Draman is nothing more than an instrument, and as he loses more and more power in the town his relegation to a mere object is slowly completed.

Scarry's overall argument is built around the issue of torture and the uneven relationship between prisoner and torturer:

> What assists the conversion of absolute pain into the fiction of absolute power is an obsessive, self-conscious display of agency. On the simplest level, the agent displayed is the weapon. Testimony given by torture victims from many different countries almost inevitably includes descriptions of being made to stare at the weapon with which they were about to be hurt. . . . But whatever the regime's primary weapon, it is only one of many weapons and its display is only one of many endlessly multiplied acts of display: torture is a process which not only converts but announces the conversion of every conceivable aspect of the event and the environment into an agent of pain. (1985, 27–28)

This is what Scarry must mean by "conflation of pain with power" (1985, 18), and Ramatou turns that proposition upside down. She takes charge of the weapon, Draman, that hurt her and that continues to remind her of the pain, and she has it eliminated by the townspeople she controls. Ramatou sheds the status of a tortured subject and turns the tables on Draman. In Scarry's view, the world of the tortured person is destroyed, disarticulated, and reduced to the simple reality of pain. In contrast, the world of the torturer, who maintains an emotional distance, is still recognizable by the torturer, although it is now falsely structured through the physical pain of the tortured person, a pain that cannot be comprehended by the torturer. This inverted relationship is most obvious in the context of war, and in the case of our film, the main characters carry out psychological warfare.

The past haunts Draman, too, although not to the same extent as his female counterpart. There are internal and external traumas that follow him. Nonetheless, his trauma is inextricably linked to Ramatou's. It is the trauma of the impossible couple. And the two are ineluctably linked, as even their partly homophonic ("rama") names suggest. He can only be defined through her, which emasculates him and places him in an unlikely position for a patriarchal society—he is the inferior being, and as will be explained shortly, under no circumstances is he an incarnation of Nietzsche's overman. When the film starts, though, Draman occupies an important position in the social fabric of the town. He owns a grocery store that is also a bar, and he is the hub that connects all the townspeople. His status, like that of the colonizer must be torn down before the rebuilding of a truly independent nation can begin.

After the initial few shots that establish the herd/horde motif, we move inside Draman's bar/grocery store while he talks to a friend, and three women come in to buy rice. The camera stops moving. From a fixed stance, it records Draman talking to the friend, who is also a client, and then to the women. Given the length of this fixed long take (over a minute), there is a strong theatrical feel to the shot, as if the camera no longer has the freedom to move. Draman is initially presented in a position of power accentuated by his command of the store as well as the universally recognizable red Coca-Cola crates behind the counter. The Western symbol behind him, which later disappears from the store, enhances his political weight in the town's hierarchy. Naturally, this is an artificial enhancement like most commercial, Western intrusions in African cinema (recall that Sembène's El Hadji only drinks Evian water and Anta owns a bottle of Vittel). Draman also ascends the social ladder of the town very quickly, because the collective initially proclaims him the future mayor of the town. The townspeople do so in exchange for a promise that he would be the negotiator in dealing with Ramatou. Another mise-en-scène detail on the bar side of the grocery store is a pinball machine that no one plays. The pinball machine is a cultural French symbol, used to great effect by Godard in *Two or Three Things I Know About Her*, in which the machine aurally punctures the space of a café. In Colobane, though, the machine remains unused. The pinball machine is on the same symbolic level with the architectural buildings of Dakar from *Contras' City* that function as remainders of the colonial past, but here it is largely ignored.

The mise-en-scène of each theatrical shot is very carefully composed, in particular the one containing Draman and his friend: coffee containers, Coke crates, and a poster of a warrior vaguely resembling Samori Touré, the legendary Dyula leader (see figure 13).[14] Without getting too far into theory about photographs, one particular citation from Roland Barthes reconnects the argument to the presence of the undead. In his analysis of photography, Barthes signals that the photos that contain people no longer alive symbolically hold a terrifying truth: "the terrible thing which is there in every photograph: the return of the dead" (Barthes 2010, 9). The friend wears a soldier's helmet that slightly obscures the drawn poster of Touré. It must be a conscious decision, because no one else wears a metal hat. Later it is revealed that the helmet-wearing man is not a soldier, but operates the needless barrier in the middle of nowhere. The film contains one more drawn poster—actually a painting. One of the characters, Ibu, makes a painting of Draman, which is promptly destroyed in a fracas in the bar. The destruction of the painting prefigures Draman's eventual demise.

The Return of the Overwoman

The cinematic setup for Ramatou's homecoming is carefully directed, and the insistence on high angles makes it clear that the entire population merges toward the train station to welcome the supposed savior of their town. The fact that an entire town physically moves to the site of the arrival suggests that an element of entertainment is at play—entertainment to be consumed by the masses, like television or the movies. The arrival scene also immediately exposes the visible trauma that accompanies the main character. She takes a walk with Draman in order to reminisce about the past. They walk together in the sand as soft guitar music and harmonies are played on the soundtrack, and they revisit the place where they first made love. The melancholy quality of the music matches the content of the scene perfectly. Ramatou reminisces about being seventeen, and in another nostalgic moment, she asks him to herd the cows for her just as he did as a twenty-year-old. Draman follows every single instruction that she gives, but his herding is more or less an empty gesture because he does not even come close to the actual herd. Instead he shouts at the animals from afar. Just as amid the townspeople, his voice is wasted and lost. He is an older, less effective version of Mory, "a bankrupt grocer, in a bankrupt town," in his own words.

If this film is indeed a continuation of *Touki Bouki*, then Mory's decision to stay behind no longer seems to be the correct one. Ramatou accuses Draman of having married another for money and his only defense is that they were young. In the meantime, everyone else waits for the two to arrive at the bar, presumably with the news that Ramatou will save the town. The same tune covers both scenes aurally, as the visual narrative crosscuts between the waiting collective and the couple. Running out of things to say, Draman observes the birds flying around them, saying "It's like the past, the same birds," and then wonders rhetorically, "Who can turn back time?" Ramatou's unexpected answer, "I can," points once again to her supernatural powers. As a matter of fact, she is "super" in several different ways. After seeing her artificial leg, Draman asks if she is entirely artificial, in response to which she reveals a fake arm. His naive follow-up is to remark, "But you're all of iron." She tells him that she had gotten her injuries when she survived a plane crash. Now she has an artificial leg and arm, so the physical trauma is pushed to the foreground. But it is not a trauma that impedes her much. She is unique in that she appears indestructible; she is made of iron and seemingly cannot die. She is essentially the female version of Nietzsche's overman ("Übermensch," often translated as "superman"), the overwoman.

Referred to in *Thus Spoke Zarathustra* (Nietzsche 1937, 27–35), the Übermensch is a superior being, someone who can overcome the meaninglessness of life ("somber is human life, and as yet without meaning," 35), someone willing to risk everything, his life included, in order to enhance the quality of that life: "Man is something that is to be surpassed" (Nietzsche 1937, 27). The Übermensch is capable of imposing his own values and rules in the world, which means that he can rule over the others. He can affect history. By contrast, the woman's role is simply to give life to this history-altering creature (1937, 79–81). The roles are reversed in this film. For example, one of the first things that Ramatou does once she is off the train is to give money to the women's fund. When the mayor informs her that there is no such thing in Colobane, she decrees that it be started. Thus from the very beginning she establishes herself as a changer of rules and laws, and also as someone who will challenge the social power discrepancy between men and women. In fact, given all the cinematic links between men and animals (elephants, hawk-eagles, owls, and hyenas), Mambety's version of the man is closer to the animal, as opposed to this superior version of the overman ("Man is a rope stretched between the animal and the Superman—a rope across an abyss," Nietzsche 1937, 29).

There are indeed several shots of animals throughout the film: owls and hyenas, occasionally hawk-eagles, two references to elephants that begin and end the film, and a solitary monkey tied to a pole in the grocery store. The latter is perhaps a doubling of Draman, who finds himself a hopeless prisoner of the situation. Continuing with these animal metaphors, the sacrifice of the bull upon Ramatou's arrival also foreshadows the sacrifice that Draman will endure. The variety of the animals is confusing, though. The connections between the townspeople and the hyenas are obvious, but that is not the case with the other animals. West African cultures perceive the owl, seen in three different shots in the film, as an evil animal, a bird that carries with it a degree of magic. Its magic power perhaps contributes to Draman's downfall, and his impending transformation into a zombie. Whether it is birds or quadrupeds, the animal shots are always accompanied by shots of actual people: the men gather to discuss Ramatou's impeding arrival, crowds flock to meet Ramatou, a large group of men escorts Draman to the train station, several men dance and sing in the bar and in town, and a large herd of men judges and executes Draman.

By contrast with these herds (the collective) Ramatou emerges as the overwoman; she surpasses the meaninglessness of life, she makes her own rules that the town has to follow, she controls the past and the future, and lays claim to the island of Gorée. Quite easily, she affects history. She had given birth to a daughter who died in her first year, suggesting that she cannot or is not meant to be a mother; she creates herself, as it were—a self-made overwoman. Ramatou has control not only over Colobane and Draman, but over other races. A very intriguing character follows her: the Asian woman who appears in several scenes. Perhaps she embodies another reversed representation of what is exotic,[15] or, following Said on orientalism, perhaps this is a case of orientalism within orientalism, a mise en abyme of orientalism. The Asian woman, "acquired" ostensibly during Ramatou's international trips, sits in the back of the horse and buggy that Draman and Ramatou take on their first walk. She is a servant. Niang observes that she wears clothing à la Michael Jackson and that she reads the *Herald Tri-*

bune (2002, 138).[16] Both are references to the United States, and yet the character is Asian—West and East meet in Colobane, the new center of the world.

Amid all of this Draman is suddenly an outcast who cannot even speak properly anymore; people tell him rhetorically, "What peculiar things you say." He is lonely, and he declares, "I'll be my own judge. I'll do what's best for me." The townspeople, though, will take that power away from him. Even when he seeks refuge in the church, the priest advises him to leave Colobane. As he walks in, Draman can see that the church was making interior improvements by installing a new chandelier, which suggests that Ramatou's financial reach had extended to the clergy. In the basement of the church, Draman watches TV briefly. The program looks like a documentary about poor living conditions in Africa, in which a young boy tries to feed himself from a barren breast. It is an odd inclusion, bordering on cliché, but the young boy in the documentary symbolically solidifies Draman's new social status in the town—he is a famished subject with no positive future prospects. Draman, the under(whelming)man finally breaks down completely, and he cries.

Adaptation and Theater

Among the staunch opponents to the practice of adaptation, François Truffaut is at the top of the list. As mentioned in the introduction, Truffaut's influential article "Une certain tendence du cinéma français" touches on the role of cinematic adaptation, which the author dubs the *"cinéma de papa."* The films in this category were mostly literary adaptations, and in Truffaut's opinion their quality derived solely from the prestige of the original source. The main difference that Truffaut sees between this type of cinema and the *politique des auteurs* is at the level of the characters. In a "tradition of quality" cinema, the characters are manipulated too much, while in his type of cinema the characters are shown more respect and are allowed to flourish on their own. Mambety finds a way to walk the fine line that allows the characters to grow from the original play and take on entirely new diegetic values.

But the issues of adaptation expand far beyond the way characters are treated. One of the most common problems encountered and analyzed by adaptation theorists is that of fidelity: "For a film to be a successful adaptation, then, it must be faithful to the original" (Elliott 2003, 127). This undertaking is difficult to accomplish given the translation issue (words to images), and adaptation is likely to fail according to Kamilla Elliott (2003, 128). The solution lies in a compromise: "The task of adapting literature to film must therefore be one of deliterarizing literature in order to make it cinematic" (Elliott 2003, 129). Elliott's book *Rethinking the Novel/Film Debate* is more concerned with the nineteenth-century novel and its impact on the cinematic world (allowing two new coinages, "cinematic novel" and "literary cinema") but it also sheds light on the connections between theater and cinema. For example: "Theater was film's primary obstacle to becoming the seventh art, for it always made film look like a bad recording of itself" (Elliott 2003, 115), and "Theater . . . has been the dominant aesthetic influence on film and the art form with which film shares the most affinities" (Elliott 2003, 125). Alfred Hitchcock's not so veiled disgust with the advent of sound (the original traumatic event of cinema) found expression when he compared cinema to theater in his interviews with Truffaut:

> When we tell a story in cinema, we should resort to dialogue only when it's impossible to do otherwise. . . . It seems unfortunate that with the arrival of sound the motion picture, overnight, assumed a theatrical form. . . . One result of this is the loss of cinematic style, and another is the loss of fantasy . . . whenever possible to rely more on the visual rather than on the dialogue. Whichever way you choose to stage the action, your main concern is to hold the audience's fullest attention. Summing it up, one might say that the screen rectangle must be charged with emotion. (1983, 61)

So most of the affinities between theater and film have to do with the role that the spectators play in either form, as is also evident in the following declaration: "Practices of film consumption further undermine claims that film's closest aesthetic relative is the novel and again places its primary affinities with theater" (Elliott 2003, 121). In the case of Mambety's film, the audience is often treated to static shots, like the one in the bar, that mimic the single theatrical point of view (i.e., from audience toward the stage), rather than the omniscient, multiple points of view available to the novel.

In her seminal book, *Reading Theater* (1999), Anne Ubersfeld defines theater as a mélange of several elements: text, reader, director, actor, representation, and the audience. In brief, theater is "text + metatext" (74). Theater is only theater when all these elements are taken into consideration together or in conflict with one another. This poses an interesting problem in the context of adaptation from a play, which has to be quite different from traditional adaptions of novels or short stories. Mambety takes the text of Dürrenmatt's play and adapts it cinematically. In doing so, he brings with him only one of the elements that make up the body of the play, while everything else is either bypassed or transformed. But by extracting only the text from *The Visit*, Mambety essentially becomes a theater director. In other words, he offers an interpretation of the text, a unique representation and mise-en-scène for the text. Is this still adaptation or merely a mise-en-scène? According to Ubersfield, the text of a play is "perhaps the least important element" (1999, 7), from which (via Barthes) the definition of theatricality arises—a theater without text (ibid.).

Antonin Artaud and Bertolt Brecht

Artaud's ideas about theater hover around the central theme of the spectacle. Drawing on Eastern practices of theater, Artaud expresses his belief that occidental theater should use dance, song, and pantomime in order to "restore theater . . . to its original destiny which it presents as a combination of all these elements fused together in a perspective of hallucination and fear" (1958, 53). A theater of the senses is born: "the theater is the only place in the world, the last general means we still possess of directly affecting the organism and, in periods of neurosis and petty sensuality like the one in which we are immersed, of attacking this sensuality by physical means it cannot withstand" (1958, 81), and "a theater in which violent physical images crush and hypnotize the sensibility of the spectator seized by the theater as by a whirlwind of higher forces" (1958, 83)—in brief, a theater of cruelty. Artaud builds on this theater of the senses, a "pure" (ibid.) theater of cruelty, by calling for the creation of a "language of gesture to be developed in space, a language without meaning except in the circumstances of the stage" (1958, 61). This language is just one of the elements that places the spectator in the middle of the artistic process, in the middle of the spectacle: "In this spectacle the sonorisation is constant: sounds, noises, cries are chosen first for their vibratory quality, then for what they represent" (81). Of particular relevance to us is the observation that initially only the physical quality of sound is important and that the narrative content is of secondary importance. Here is Artaud's detailed explanation of what he means by a spectacle:

> Every spectacle will contain a physical and objective element, perceptible to all. Cries, groans, apparitions, surprises, theatricalities of all kinds, magic beauty of costumes taken from certain ritual models; resplendent lighting, incantational beauty of voices, the charms of harmony, rare notes of music, colors of objects, physical rhythm of movements whose crescendo and decrescendo will accord exactly with the pulsation of movement familiar to everyone, concrete appearances of new and surprising objects, masks, effigies yards high, sudden changes of light, the physical action of light which arouses sensations of heat and cold, etc. (1958, 93)

This definition is not dissimilar from Bertolt Brecht's theatrical practices that led to the separation between stage and audience, except, crucially, that the spectator is no longer in the middle of the spectacle, but rather removed from it. To Brecht, both theater and cinema are processes of alienation—they have to achieve and maintain a certain distance from the audience. Although the bulk of Brecht's work concentrated on theater and what he called "epic theater," which he opposed to dramatic theater, his theories definitely apply to the world of film. The goal of epic theater is to "shock the audience into an awareness that both social life and art are human creations and therefore can be changed, that the laws of a predatory society are not divinely inscribed but subject to human intervention" (Stam 1985, 211). As part of an audience, one always has to remain aware of the fact that one is in front of a fictional work. In order to make sure that no one drifted away, shocking associations of stylistic devices were employed in Brecht's theater: for example, flooding the stage with very bright light for no apparent reason except "waking" the audience back to reality. To achieve what he believed to be the goals of epic theater, Brecht suggested other specific techniques that should be used: creating a narration that is fractured, not using stars, or maintaining a double distanciation between the actor and the role he is playing and between the character portrayed and the spectator. He also advocated that every scene should be independent of the others and each track, music, lyric, or passage of dialogue has to be "in a certain tension with other tracks" (Stam 1985, 213). Sound is meant to be an independent part of the artistic process. Separating sound from image would create a certain discontinuity, which would help fuel the feeling of alienation, and should make the identification of the audience with the characters on stage or screen impossible. The separated elements should be able to exist on their own; they should have their own meaning. Given the radical fragmentation of his films, most Mambety sequences or segments could be taken as individual pieces. However, this is not really the case in *Hyènes*, which remains closer to a play and a spectacle than it does to experimental cinema.

Kaja Silverman's *The Threshold of the Visible World* challenges the schematic way of looking at distanciation. Silverman first clarifies that the German name of Brecht's aesthetic model, "Verfremdungseffekt," is mistranslated into English as "distanciation," and that it should rather be rendered as "alienation effect." She continues, "A quintessentially Brechtian theater or cinema would be one where the representational scene is in all respects more 'removed' from the spectator than is customary. In fact, Brecht's aesthetic turns upon distance in many respects. It promotes in the spectator a critical detachment from or irony toward the spectacle and its ideological values. It also isolates textual elements from one another so that each can comment on the others, rather than seeming to be part of an ostensibly harmonious whole" (1996, 86). Drawing on theory from Walter Benjamin, Silverman states that Brechtian theater (and cinema by extension) attempts to place the theatrical or cinematic event on a "continuum with the auditorium," and consequently it strives to equalize spectator and spectacle (1996, 86). Silverman advances the notion that Brecht wanted his audience to feel right at home in the auditorium, as if they were in their own living room; instead of what is generally understood as alienation, rendering the familiar strange, Brecht's theater is in fact an attempt to do quite the opposite: making the strange familiar (1996, 87). Consequently, Brechtian theater searches for closeness, instead of creating distance; in that respect it actually resembles the Artaud spectacle. If one follows Silverman's convincing argument, then the auditorium and stage are brought closer together in terms of space, and the communication window between the two is opened. Both Silverman's interpretation of Brecht, that the strange should become familiar, and the more traditional interpretation that the familiar should become strange hold true in some way. It comes down to the individual spectator and his or her own negotiation with the stage or the screen. These contrasting views on Brecht's alienation are not as easily applied to film because of Brecht's fundamental issue with the cinematic text: the spectator cannot intervene or alter the cinematic text while it is being projected on screen. While this is certainly true from a physical point of view, this study will eventually entertain the possibility of such an alteration in terms of spectatorship, agency, and perception.

The setup of *Hyènes* as theatrical performance is apparent in several scenes and episodes. Throughout the film diegetic audiences double the actual extradiegetic audience, as in the episodes when Ramatou arrives in town. During that scene, while the entire town welcomes their lost daughter, the camera cuts away to a solitary dancer. The dance of the woman in the street is framed in a long shot, away from the crowd—the diegetic crowd disappears. Suddenly it is simply us, the "real" spectators who witness a (side) show. This shot illustrates Žižek's opinion that cinema "is a subgenre of the theater—a theatrical performance in which the spectator, by means of his stand-in (camera), moves forward into the space he observes" (2008a, 111n7). During this shot, though, the camera does not move forward. Instead, it simply observes from a distance. The dance of the woman could be one of the Artaudian elements, a small part of the larger spectacle.

A moment later the narrative is back at the welcoming party and Ramatou speaks to the crowd. The townspeople sit in an outdoors auditorium, which reinforces the idea of a diegetic public.[17] The town brings in a bull to be sacrificed in honor of Ramatou. The same drum music to which the bull is brought on is the music to which the lone woman dances—two shows are unified aurally. As Ramatou stakes her claim on the town (largely based on her wealth; she is described as being richer than the World Bank), she is interrupted yet again by an insert of the dancing woman (see figure 14). The sound bridge of the drums unifies the two scenes, yet they remain spatially and perhaps even temporally separated. The drummer announces Ramatou's arrival throughout the town. His voice travels throughout the space of the town and acts as a spatial unifier, but it describes the town as an abandoned space: "Colobane where trains, planes and even cars no longer stop"—it is a non-place, a stage governed by sound.

Ramatou wants to give the townspeople lots of money, but she also wants to buy their court. She had already bought their chief justice, Gaana, whom Mambety plays himself. The involvement of the director goes beyond a simple cameo, as Mambety reaches back to his acting roots. If in *Touki Bouki* he had Charlie invoke his name during the phone conversation—which implies that the director, like Mory, is something of a prostitute—in *Hyènes* Mambety fully takes on the role of a corrupt politician, a more insidious type of prostitute. Gaana belongs to Ramatou, who is clearly on a vengeful tear: "Life made me a whore, and I will make the world a brothel." In this episode the audience also learns that Draman had refused to recognize Ramatou's child as his own. Not only that, but he claimed that two other men slept with her, an accusation that led to her fleeing and turning into a prostitute. Ramatou declares in front of everyone that she had roamed the world, which makes her into a walking prostitute—the only possible flaneuse, according to Susan Buck-Morss.[18] She offers an incredible amount of money to whoever kills Draman, possibly transforming the film into a story about money, which goes directly against one of Artaud's strictures: "Stories about money, worry over money, social careerism . . . have nothing to do with theater" (1958, 76). Even though the people initially refuse the offer so as not to become savages—"rather starvation than blood on our hands"—the balance of the town is thrown off.

In spite of that, the city prospers, but on the strength of a heavy infusion of Western items. Several objects replace the Coke crates behind Draman from the beginning of the film: everyone gets air-conditioners, refrigerators, an amusement park, and TVs. The intrusion of the West is comprehensive, and it occurs in other films, most notably in Sembène's *Xala*; El Hadji is only comfortable when indoors (or in his Mercedes) where he can enjoy the air conditioner to which he is addicted. In Sembène's view, as with Mambety, the dependence on European gadgets points to the malaise and alienation of the contemporary African man and woman: "We know all these little signs that are in the film, the air-conditioner and other things, and we observe that they alienate the individual" (Ghali 2008, 74).[19] The character of El Hadji never suffers too much because of this alienation. He is unaware of its effects on him until it is too late. His love for all things European positions him as an opposing force to tradition, which is exactly what happens to the townspeople of Colobane.

The (Acousmatic) Panoptic Island Fantasy

This section of the chapter reassesses the role played by the island in the national consciousness of Senegal, which will be explained mainly through a psychoanalytical consideration of fantasy. That in turn will allow us to revisit the previous idea of an imagined phantasmagoric space and sound. *Hyènes* is only seldom exemplary in terms of sound use, but it is quite useful when it comes to discussing fantasies, particularly the fantasy of the panoptic island. Thus, throughout the next section I will use references from *Touki Bouki* to facilitate the discussion of sound. However, given that the two films present a sense of continuity and that they both allude to and showcase islands, *Hyènes* will remain an important point of reference.

At the first level, sound has to be analyzed through the spectators' perception of it. There are several theoretical suggestions that sound produces an imaginary space. Bela Balazs proclaims, "As listeners, too, we are transferred from our seats to the space in which the events depicted on the screen are taking place" (1985, 125). His view, of course, is seen as complementary to the usual visual transference that happens to the spectators in the theater. To take another example, André Bazin claims that montage transforms "something real into something imaginary" (1967, 50). Although he refers to visual montage (i.e., what we see in and from the breaks between shots), a similar process takes place with sound. Just like visual montage, sound is also "put together," edited in such a way that it leads to something imaginary while covering the "wounds" in the text. It is not just that we can imagine sound when it is missing from a shot, as spectators did early on during the silent years of cinema. We must also imagine what sound creates within the diegesis. The dog that barks in Anta's neighborhood in *Touki Bouki* is invisible to the eye, but when we hear it the natural reaction is to revert to whatever mental image we have formed in our mind: "Any familiar noise calls forth inner images of its source as well as images of activities, modes of behavior, etc., which are either customarily connected with that noise or at least related to it in the listener's recollection" (Kracauer 1997, 124). The signified comes to life in spite of the lack of visual signifier. The aural signifier supplants the necessity of a "real" visual signifier, but the aural signifier is as real as needed. It suffices. And it leads us, the spectators, into Bazin's "something imaginary," into fantasy.

The incursion into fantasy starts by delineating the concept of the unconscious. In *The Ego and the Id*, Freud predicates the concept of the unconscious on repression: "The repressed serves us as a prototype of the unconscious. We see, however, that we have two kinds of unconscious—that which is latent but capable of becoming conscious, and that which is repressed and not capable of becoming conscious in the ordinary way" (1952, 698). These two kinds constitute the first level of the unconscious, the descriptive unconscious. One of the main ways to access this unconscious is through dreams, which according to Freud represent a fulfillment of unconscious desires. There are other ways, which Freud calls "parapraxes," most notably the slip of the tongue,[20] but also spotty memory or misreading. The condition of "neurosis" develops when certain unconscious desires try to emerge from the unconscious but fail, which leads to an internal conflict. Manifestations of neurosis include obsessions (like having to touch something repeatedly), being hysterical (developing a physical impediment without being sick) or phobic (having unreasonable fears of things, situations, or animals). Such occurrences are not common in the films of Mambety, at least not at an obvious level. It is not the characters who suffer from neurosis (one might claim, reductively, that it is an occidental ailment). However, when looking at the overall narrative of *Touki Bouki* one finds several such obsessions, both visual and aural. So, crucially, it is the text of the film that proves to be neurotic.

The parapraxes mentioned above allow access to another type or level of the unconscious, the dynamic one, which is more of a fluid negotiation between tension, displeasure, and the desired state of pleasure than is the descriptive unconscious. Finally, the third level or type of unconscious—the systematic unconscious—gives way to Freud's triumvirate of subjectivity: id (searching for immediate gratification), ego (suppressing and controlling urges according to the reality principle), and superego (enforcing rules, and providing our internal voice, a voice that can never be quieted). The superego can be further divided into conscience and ego ideal. Conscience tells us what is right and wrong, and forces the ego to inhibit the primary needs of the id so that subjects can pursue goals that are more morally acceptable than pure gratification. The ego ideal places the individual on the "correct" path of life, which is to say toward the ideal goals as established by society. In this pursuit, the mind attempts to make up for the loss of the perfect life experienced as a baby.

The Lacanian model for subject identity builds on the Freudian one and adds a few important nuances. To Lacan, the human subject comes to his or her identity through language, and the unconscious is in fact structured like a language because it consists of signifiers rather than signs.[21] The subject necessarily emerges from this progression split between the conscious and the unconscious. The child moves from the mirror stage and the imaginary order (a state in which we begin to make identifications but actually experience a misrecognition of ourselves) to the symbolic order. Access to this order is achieved through a recognition of the human subject's relations to the other subjects around him or her; identity is thus built through differences, similarities, and absences. It is this observation that leads Eagleton to claim that "language is 'empty' because it is just an endless process of difference and absence: instead of being able to possess anything in its fullness, the child will now simply move from one signifier to another, along a linguistic chain which is potentially infinite" (1985, 145). This is where Lacan's definition of desire comes from, because desire springs from a lack, an absence, which the human subject tries to fill. Once one enters the symbolic order through the act of speech, through language, one becomes separated from the mother's body and independent as subject. And that is the object that one will spend one's life trying to recapture. This is the crucial moment of sacrifice, of traumatic loss, the denial of *jouissance* (that is, castration), when the subjects are cut from the primordial object of desire, and forced into a system (the Law) in which they must pursue that special lost thing. Since that initial object cannot be recaptured, other objects are substituted for it; Lacan calls them the *"objet petit a,"* and they are inevitably insufficient.

How is this psychoanalytic detour relevant to Mambety's films and use of sound? In the postcolonial world, subjectivity must come to fruition in radically different ways from the cases exposed by Freud and Lacan, especially because the postcolonial subject has to deal with another level of reality. He or she must become a subject and access the symbolic order not just through the process of difference and absence generated by his or her countrymen, but also through a mediation with the colonized space. The ego ideal sets the subject on an incorrect path, but one that is required by the political milieu of the colonized space. There are in fact, two adjacent ego ideal paths and two symbolic orders, and the postcolonial subject must deal with both of them simultaneously. It is my belief that the use of sound in Mambety's films helps us understand and navigate this predicament and gives us the psychoanalytical solution: cinematic sound functions like a veil of fantasy meant to protect and help the postcolonial subject better negotiate his or her subjectivity.

The question of fantasy emerges from the discussion of the unconscious and is equally complicated. Slavoj Žižek's reading of Lacan helps us place fantasy at the core of the Freudian unconscious, which is "fragments of a traumatic, cruel, capricious, 'intelligible,' and 'irrational' law text, a set of prohibitions and injunctions" (1992, 152), as well as "knowledge that doesn't know itself" (2007, 52). Freud himself explains the process of fantasy through a well-known scene that progresses from a sadistic component (the child sees that the father is beating a child who represents a rival) to a masochist phase, and on to the final, impersonal form, "a child is being beaten" (1958, 186). Constance Penley observes that in the logic of this fantasy the girl "identifies, during [the] three stages with the adult doing the beating, the child being beaten, and with herself as a spectator viewing the beating. She can thus be both subject and object, or identify with the entire scene itself" (1989, 48). In contrast, boys experience a variation in terms of who is doing the beating ("I am being beaten by my father" progresses to "I am being beaten by my mother"), but in the end boys also adopt the sadistic position through an identification with the beating adult in the third stage. Freud's description of the beating fantasy and Penley's subsequent observation show that fantasy invokes multiple identifications; this is especially true in the context of the spectator-film relationship, which also implies an immediate fulfillment of those fantasies.

This is not the case for Lacan, in whose opinion the fulfillment of the fantasy has to be postponed. The postponement is very similar to what happens in the Freudian anal stage, in which the child learns to derive pleasure from the expulsion of feces but also learns to manipulate pleasure through withholding. For Lacan a fantasy is not a satisfiable need but an unsatisfiable desire. After the oedipal trauma—the separation from the body of the mother—the human subject has to constantly search for that eternally lost object. Fantasy will sustain the desire. That fantasy is never meant to come to fruition: "The fantasy is the support of desire, it is not the object that is the support of the desire" (1978, 185). In *The Plague of Fantasies*, Žižek agrees with this assessment: "A fantasy constitutes our desire, provides its coordinates; that is, it literally 'teaches us how to desire'" (2008a, 7). In *Seminar VII* Lacan's algorithm of fantasy, $\$ \diamond a$, explains the dynamic between the desire of the subject ($\$$) of and for the object ($\diamond$) that has substituted the Thing (a), or the *objet petit a* (Lacan 1992, 99). This is essentially an unobtainable object of desire. According to Kaja Silverman's reading of Lacan, the outward and inward movements designated by $\diamond$ allow the subject to achieve heterogeneity (i.e., to come fully into one's own), but the "subject returns from this journey with 'empty hands'" (Silverman 1996, 76). This tragic event takes place because the object does not really exist in the traditional, palpable sense.

As becomes apparent in the conclusion of *Touki Bouki*, this is Mory's destiny, too: to finalize his journey empty-handed. By comparison, Draman is actually the one being emptied, in an extreme manifestation of this journey. So Mory might be the better $\$$ example. At the very end of the film, he sits dejected and contemplates the broken horns from his motorbike—even the horns, the quintessential *objet petit a*, are broken. Naturally, the analysis can be pushed even further to suggest that the broken horns represent Mory's broken masculinity: not only does he come back empty-handed, he comes back less of a man than before. In his famous preface to Fanon's *Wretched of the Earth*, Jean-Paul Sartre identifies a "colonial neurosis" that affects the native and that can only be eliminated "through force of arms" (1968, 20–21). Without directly referring to neuroses, Fanon advocates freedom through violence against colonialism, which has therapeutic effects (1968, 86, 94). Even though Mory makes the "correct," idealistic decision, he seems further defeated as a neocolonial neurosis emerges. His refusal to leave is a symbolic violent act against neocolonialism, expressed materially by the break-up with Anta and supported cinematically by the chaotic visual and aural montage that follows his decision. Yet it is hardly a cathartic moment for Mory. The hybrid fetish object of the motorcycle with horns on it initially brings together two cultures, the Western world and Africa, through their respective semiotic values. The fact that at the end Mory is left with broken horns and most likely a malfunctioning bike (not unlike Draman's car that drives in circles) is a clear reminder of two realities. First, there is no "recipe," no compelling therapy for healing oneself of colonial and neocolonial neuroses. Second, in spite of the general bent toward hybridity in Mambety's work, the Western world and Africa (and perhaps the non-West in general) still have plenty of incompatibilities.

It was Mory who started the journey by suggesting to Anta that they go to France, and in the end he pays the price. His demand jump-starts the Lacanian drive, which in turn becomes desire and eventually leads to unsatisfiable fantasy: "[There is an] intimate relationship between drive and demand. A drive is precisely a demand that is not caught up in the dialectic of desire, that resists dialecticization" (Žižek 1992, 21). The subtle difference is that the demand almost always implies that one wants something else (and Mory actually does not leave, so he does want something else), while the drive cannot be shaken, which is the case with Anta, Ramatou, and the undead.

In its most radical form, the drive becomes the death drive, which does not mean that the subject yearns to die: "the death drive . . . is *the very opposite of dying*, it is a name for the 'undead' eternal life itself, for the horrible fate of being caught in the endless repetitive cycle of wandering around in guilt and pain" (Žižek, 2008c, 293). So the death drive means immortality, the impossibility of death rooted in a compulsion to repeat. The zombie is clinically dead, but the pure death drive remains so it keeps walking until it is killed again. Ramatou is also dead symbolically but her pure drive, the pursuit of vengeance, endures. Thus the difference between the zombie and the subject is that the latter hovers in the space between the symbolic and the Real, while the former is presymbolic or possibly already in the Real. It can be argued in fact that Ramatou herself dwells in a Real created by her overwoman powers. When there is nothing left but death drive the subject can no longer be disjointed, split, dislocated. It simply ceases to be. The Freudian notion of death drive is capable at any given moment of ruining the symbolic framework built in order to sustain subjectivity. The embodiment of the zombie, or of Ramatou, speaks exactly to this point, to the creation of an excess of life or a surplus enjoyment, as Žižek would phrase it. The death drive is exactly this add-on, whatever can be added to life itself that makes it more than just life. In other words, the zombie survives its own death drive en route to immortality.

Fantasy mediates the relationship between drive and desire relentlessly. In the words of Žižek yet again: "fantasy is the very screen that separates desire from drive: it tells the story which allows the subject to (mis)perceive the void around which drive circulates as the primordial loss constitutive of desire" (2008a, 43). The case of the flaneur is instructive in this context, too. He finds himself in the middle of the city, a part of it and yet removed from it. He also negotiates his fickle relationship with the Real through a fantasy—the crowd around him acts like Žižek and Lacan's screen, the protective veil. In cinema, the desire to see the source of the sounds emerges from a prohibition, from the fact that we are not allowed to see their visual markers. In classical cinema, these occurrences are rare because one strives for the impression of reality. But when countercinema practices deny the audience knowledge of the source of sound, we are basically denied *jouissance* in the Lacanian sense. As spectators, we continue to want to see those images, images that are "lost" to us. Fantasy allows us to negotiate the pain that comes from desiring what we cannot have, and thus desire and *jouissance* can never coexist in a relationship of contingency. The way to deal with this pain is, of course, also through the *objet petit a*.

Žižek offers a simple definition of the *objet petit a*: it is "not what we desire, what we are after, but, rather, that which sets our desire in motion" (2008a, 53). It is worth noting that Žižek's take on Lacan's *objet petit a* is perfectly exemplified by the objects surrounding the characters of *Touki Bouki*. The list of multiple forms the *objet petit a* takes visually includes the boats that Anta and Mory observe from atop the cliff, the treasures they are after (the trunk, clothes, cars), and of course Gorée Island, which is shared by *Hyènes*. One important detail clarifies the definition of the *objet petit a*: it only becomes apparent when looked at "from the side," with a distorted look of desire:

> This is precisely the Lacanian *objet petit a*, the object-clause of desire, an object which is, in a way, posited by the desire itself. The paradox of desire is that it posits retroactively its own cause, i.e., an object that can be perceived only by the look "distorted" by desire, an object that does not exist for an "objective" look. In other words, the *objet petit a* is always, by definition, perceived in a distorted way, because, outside this distortion, "in itself" it does not exist, i.e., because it is nothing but the embodiment, the materialization of this distortion. . . . *Objet petit a* is "objectively" nothing, it is nothing at all, nothing of the desire itself which, viewed from a certain perspective, assumes the shape of "something." (Žižek 1989, 34)

In light of this last definition, I posit that the ultimate visual *objet petit a* in Mambety's films and in West African cinema in general is Gorée Island itself. The characters of the films always look at the island from a distorted perspective and the island itself is rarely in clear focus. Moreover, there are no examples of scenes shot *on* Gorée Island in any of Mambety's films.[22] It is never explained why there are all these references to the island, and thus the reasons behind the desire that connects the characters with the island are elusive. In fact, the representation of the island is merely a presence, a contour on the horizon, and one that cannot ever be appropriated. If the director had brought the island to life cinematically instead of keeping it on the horizon, it would have lost its fantasy quality—it would have become real.[23]

In *Hyènes*, the fantasy of eating Draman conceals the horror, the Real, which is only glanced at by Ramatou and embodied by the oppressive island. Because Mambety does not physically set his films on the island, the characters avoid direct contact with the Real. Harrow's recent study on trash explores the film *Karmen Gei* (2001), whose action partially occurs on the island: "The camera taking us across to Gorée to pan the features of those mourning the dead, those of the past, yesterday's debris, the slaves gone by, the business deal and its sordid value to be remembered and then supplanted" (2013, 122).[24] Mambety's camera avoids getting caught in this horror of the past, thereby refusing to make it present directly. Inevitably, though, while the horror of the Real (that this is a place where slaves were killed or shipped off to the Caribbean) is concealed behind the fantasy of the return of the dead, the fantasy also makes that horror present. Ramatou experiences something quite similar; she goes from an unsatisfiable desire (she can no longer be with Draman, whom she still loves, because he has married another) to a satisfiable need after realizing that she can at least accomplish her vengeance. In effect she punishes Draman for the trauma she had suffered. She breaks a cardinal rule of fantasy, achieving a fleeting sense of satisfaction by traversing the fantasy when she "witnesses" Draman's execution. She can accomplish both actions, look at the island and at Draman's execution simultaneously because she controls the Real, and rules no longer apply to her. From the vantage point of the platform by the sea, Ramatou becomes the latest incarnation of the Foucauldian panopticon, but a version that is split between observing and maintaining the past alive on the Gorée side, and disciplining and punishing lowly Draman on the other side.

The subject $ must separate from the *objet petit a* in order to fully come into his or her own, but in these films the postcolonial subject seems incapable of doing so. The island is an important marker of lack and of the traumatic event at the core of the symbolic order for the postcolonial subject. Ramatou's claim in *Hyènes* that she owns the island unveils the ultimate postcolonial fantasy. It is not quite clear yet, though, what the actual fantasy entails. To be the colonizers as opposed to the colonized, to reverse the roles, to own land, to own history, to own the past? Perhaps all of these possibilities together. It does not suffice just to be the colonizing entity (France); but a reversal of fortune is needed, one that sees the postcolonial subject own its past. The problem is that in the process, the postcolonial subject would also own potential slaves to be sent to the Caribbean. Could this be the fundamental guilt from which the postcolonial subject is trying to remove himself or herself? The Lacanian Real is more terrifying than whatever version of reality is witnessed daily, which is a fantasy construct anyway. This Lacanian reading allows Žižek to build an argument for an ideological fantasy that structures reality itself (2008b, 44). Furthermore, Žižek's powerful reading of the 9/11 events in *Welcome to the Desert of the Real* proves to be a vital counterpoint to this postcolonial fantasy. According to him, America saw its worst nightmare (that is, fantasy) come to life following years of blockbuster movies that proposed similar scenarios (2002, 15–17). By contrast, the cinematic subject in the postcolonial context is still safe from any such horror. This happens mainly because there is a set of fantasies that is not quite so obvious—not visual—that occurs only at an aural level. As spectators, we are thus doubly removed from a potential fall into the Real, protected first by the visual fantasy and then by an aural one because the aural frequently follows a different narrative path from the visual.

Thus resisting the drive and not fulfilling one's fantasies are exactly the appropriate ways to deal with the postcolonial situation. The ultimate postcolonial fantasy can never come to fruition, because it would mean entering the realm of the Real—Lacan's third and final stage of subjectivity. The Real is an impossibility. It can also be described as the symbolic order that carries something traumatic at its core—Lacan called this entity, via Freud, *das Ding* (the Thing). It is the element that does not allow the symbolic order to attain perfect balance, since it cannot appropriate this core. The Thing is that which could swallow the subject, and the *objet petit a* is a fragment of the Thing after it has gone through the process of symbolization. So seeing the Real would annihilate the subject. In our context, the Thing is colonization itself, while Gorée Island plays the part of a fragment of that absolute void. Once again, the island, as the *objet petit a*, is nothing at all. Gilles Deleuze's study of islands in one of his early essays, "Desert Islands" (1953), claims that islands are in fact always deserted because of the inherently problematic spatial relationship between the island and the sea. According to Deleuze, the sea can cover up the island and swallow it at any given moment, which means that even if inhabited the "island doesn't stop being deserted" (2004, 10). It remains empty, nothing at all, a remnant of the Real that cannot be accessed.

Turning back now to a very familiar example from *Touki Bouki*, a few more wrinkles can be added. In the case of the sounds that surround Anta while she writes at the table, the accompanying images are never visible. Is the baby crying simply because he is hungry or hurt? Perhaps the unseen dog is a stray animal, which is not unlikely for Dakar. Perhaps the dog then projects the real image of a shantytown as opposed to an expansive metropolis. Perhaps the siren belongs to an ambulance that carries the mortally wounded. There are multiple possibilities, but it is quite likely that the phantasmagoric space constructed by this scene is actually another fantasy meant to protect the viewers from the Real. In this context, the Real is that the country of Senegal has yet to adjust to its postcolonial existence, and presents itself as a fragmented space in which retaining or even attaining one's identity is impossible. The images are taken away from us, and in their place sounds give us an attenuated version of the truth and a sense of protection; it is, yet again, the acousmatic panopticon that effectuates a role radically different from the initial intention laid out by Foucault.

However, this feeling of protection may be naive. Fantasy protects us, but it can also reveal the exact object of our horror (Žižek 2008a, 6). Žižek complicates this issue even further: "If what we experience as 'reality' is structured by fantasy, and if fantasy serves as the screen that protects us from being directly overwhelmed by the raw Real, *then reality itself can function as an escape from encountering the Real*" (2007, 57, emphasis in original). The aural reality does not always match the visual reality throughout Mambety's film. The aural/visual schism prevents us from actually seeing the reality, and therefore "we never pass from the spectral Real to reality" (Žižek 2008a, 201). The spectral Real is a perfect embodiment of the sonic phantasmagoric space, since they are both figments of the imagination. As a result, it becomes imperative to consider sound a necessary ingredient in the creation of both the postcolonial fantasy and its space.

The ambiguous nature of fantasy is analogous to how spectators perceive the film's narrative with or without the contribution of sound. Žižek makes a similar point about fantasy: "Fantasy is the primordial form of *narrative*, which serves to occult some original deadlock" (2008a, 11). He refers here to the myth of primordial accumulation, but one can generalize the idea of a deadlock to the visual and sound. Classic Hollywood cinema uses sound in order to enhance the image, or to complete what the image is telling us; sound should not be "noticed." This is the original setup—the deadlock that needs to be broken—and this happens also to be the Law. The unorthodox sound in Mambety's films may be considered a transgression. The film and its sound go against an established Law and from that point of conflict, sound emerges solitary and independent. Lacan makes a similar point about conflict in *Seminar XX* (1998, 58–59) at a more personal level. This point explains how fantasy works with the following famous declaration: there is no sexual relationship. We can never have an ideal partner; instead we make our actual partners (in our heads) into one. This idea is illuminating in the context of image and sound understood as a "couple." In other words, in Mambety's films the relationship between the two is not always harmonious. His work challenges the conventional structure according to which spectators perceive and judge image and sound together, so it challenges the (Lacan and Žižek's) big Other. Therefore, it is necessary to explore further the Law of the Big Other, which in the case of Hollywood-style cinema refers to the rules according to which image and sound should coexist.

Among his many contributions, Rick Altman gives us a capital volume, *Silent Film Sound*, on the history of sound in the cinema from the very beginning.

His study is a tremendously ambitious project that marks important moments in the timeline of the relationship between sound and image. It begins with establishing sound as discontinuous at first in its relationship with the image (2004, 92–93). It then moves slowly toward the unification of the two, bypassing the "oppressive" period of vaudeville (during which film was secondary to the theatrical act, 2004, 104–115), and the early nickelodeon years to arrive at the conclusion that sound and image together could "create realistic pseudo-events" (2004, 155), a point on which Edison also insisted (2004, 175). The general direction toward marrying image and sound, or standardizing sound, slowly eliminated attempts such as placing voices behind the screen or music that might have competed with what happens on screen for the attention of the audience (2004, 318). The process ends in a simplification: "limit the soundscape to a single sound source, standardize sound practices, gentrify sound choices. In this classical approach film exhibition found its first stability, and cinema thereby its initial identity" (Altman 2004, 390).

Michel Chion, in the first part of his book *Film, a Sound Art*, follows a similar historical path (2009, 2–18), beginning with the suggestion of sound through images (2009, 4–7). Chion also originally discussed the "dream" of voices in *The Voice in Cinema*; to him, cinema was never silent, it was deaf, and every time we saw the actors' mouths move we must have dreamed (for our purposes, "imagined") what they were saying (1999, 7–9). This separation of our senses, of our understanding of what happens on screen, was what threatened the state of cinema at the time. From the last points it results that sound in general must have been imagined (e.g., if a vase drops, one must imagine the sound it makes when hitting the ground). Yet a reversal is taking place in the films of Mambety and in the examples already covered. There is direct access to the sound, but not to the image, which must be imagined, and in turn sound leads to the creation of an imagined space. Bazin explains how the film comes to "life" in the minds of the spectators: "we need to believe in the reality of what is happening while knowing it to be tricked . . . so the screen reflects the ebb and flow of our imagination which feeds on a reality for which it plans to substitute" (1967, 48).

It is no longer the case that sound is being passed over in favor of the image, as more and more studies are focused on the effects and affects of the soundtrack. Mambety's aesthetic goes distinctly against some of the early theory on sound that claims sound must match the sound of the "real" world closely. Theorists such as Christian Metz and Jean-Louis Baudry were proponents of that similarity in "Aural Objects" (1980, 29) and "Ideological Effects of the Basic Cinematographic Apparatus" (1974, 47) respectively. Hollywood's efforts to conceal the cinematic apparatus include "hiding" the sound—matching it to actual, seen sources; in a word, synchronization. Postproduction dubbing provides the auteur with an opportunity for innovation and artifice. A familiar example: in *Contras' City* male voices proceed from female bodies. This violation is comical on an unsophisticated reading, but in fact it challenges the reality of sexual difference as well as the rules of continuity. In another instance in the same film, the postsynchronous dialogue does not match the tempo of the action, which appears to be a deliberate choice. This creates an obvious discrepancy between sound and image; the image is chasing the sound, basically trying to keep up with the *real*, primary story. That story is further complicated by the inclusion of the voice and song in the films of Mambety. All these intrusions, of the voice, of noise, of music, could not they be considered incarnations of trauma in relation to the film and the visual, as already hinted at before? The sound cuts the spatial integrity of the visual, wounds it as it were. In classical cinema sound has largely remained "invisible" as to preserve rules of continuity and the impression of reality. However, when it does not, it traumatizes the film.

Panoptic Music

Besides the new scopic regime implemented by Ramatou, the panopticon can also be found at the aural level of the film in the music. To reiterate, music normally functions as a way to enhance the visual narrative—empathetic music (e.g., the music on the soundtrack matches the rhythm of the horse and buggies in *Hyènes*); if the rhythm or melody of the music goes against what happens on screen, it is anempathetic. Nar Sene writes the following about the role of music in *Hyènes*: "Here the music and the history crawl forward together, so much and so well that we don't know if it's the history that creates the music, or if the man built his film starting from the music. The latter seems to me more certain" (2001, 27).[25] An example of a scene built from and around music occurs when Draman walks into the church looking for comfort. At first the nondiegetic music comes from an organ, so the space of the church is marked not only visually but aurally, because that is the type of music one associates with Catholic churches. Yet the organ music is not purely Western, and soon after Draman's entrance drumbeats are added to the soundtrack. An aural clash ensues, as sound splits the space of the church into traditionally Western and traditionally Senegalese segments. The split extends to the outside, too. Right before Draman exits the church, dejected, very soft instrumental music plays on the soundtrack and subtle drum sounds are added.

Moreover, the soundtrack goes beyond this conflicting mélange; a faint choir comes in, followed by the notes of an electric guitar, as the shots sound bridge into the next sequence. The choir—symbolic of the African collective—is integral to the churchgoing experience in Africa. This is not the only choir in the film. In a seemingly arbitrary episode, the camera briefly follows a children's choir singing in the street, and never revisits them; there are also a few instances when women's choirs are heard, but their location is never revealed. The diegetic and the nondiegetic overlap once again. From the church, the film moves outside to the celebration of the town, and people are clapping to the tune of fireworks. The aural progression from the organ, to drums, then choir and electric guitar, literally explodes in fireworks.

Yet, the film's most important aural contribution occurs at the very end. Nondiegetic music begins shortly after Draman's death, a few moments before the end credits commence rolling. Draman's death had brought on an eerie silence, a death of sound. The song emerges from that silence and slowly takes over the soundtrack. Sound is coming back to life. In a parallel action, bulldozers come in and level the place. The town is about to begin rebuilding. But it was already in ruins because the process of disintegration had already begun when the mayor's office got rid of the furniture in Draman's desolate grocery shop. The bulldozers are mechanical equivalents of the elephants from the first shot—same body register, but from radically opposed ontologies.[26]

The camera moves into an establishing shot of Dakar from afar; the loud noise of a descending plane carries on and dies out while the visual narrative transitions into a shot of a lone baobab tree in the far background. The film steps outside of itself, outside of theatricality, and outside of any connections to the play. In fact, the end reads like an addendum. Superimposed on the shot of the baobab, the emblematic tree of Senegal, the film's dedication appears: "We Africans dedicate this ballad to the great Friedrich 1922–1990."[27] As the song starts, the visual narrative returns to the elephants and thus to the beginning, in order to close off the narrative circle. Nonetheless, the song continues to live outside the narrative, it continues to tell a story (this is a narrative effect that will come into more focus in Mambety's last two films), and it unifies diegetic and extradiegetic spaces.[28] It functions like the acousmatic panopticon that rearranges the postcolonial space (a metaphor underlined by the bulldozers that level the town). Musically, the song has a modern beat, raplike, combined with sounds of owls. The story it tells is a narrative about the ramatou bird that flew away and returned. The lyrics read, "Get up and get to work, if you don't get up in good time and start work, how will you find your freedom?" The song carries Marxist undertones because it aspires to render work meaningful by offering the most desired postcolonial condition—freedom—as reward. Through meaningful work in the material world, the postcolonial subject can become unalienated, in the Marxist sense: no more loss of control over labor, no more separation from the product of labor.[29]

Through this song, the film continues its emphasis on the collective, because suddenly multiple voices are heard singing. The chorus, which originally appeared in the church episode, effects a process of transference of our emotions according to Žižek: "Chorus in classical tragedy: we, the spectators, came to the theater worried, full of everyday problems . . . but no problem, there is the Chorus, who feels the sorrow and the compassion instead of us—or, more precisely, we feel the required emotions through the medium of the Chorus" (2008b, 32). It is, therefore, no accident that the choir makes an appearance during Draman's worst emotional moment, while he cries in church, and reappears at the end of the film following his death. Not only that, but the chorus as a part of the soundtrack lives outside the diegesis—not quite alive, not quite dead—which leads to the spectralization of sound. More specifically, it is sound as voice that textually matches the walking dead of *Hyènes*: "Voice is neither dead nor alive: its primordial phenomenological status is rather that of the living dead, of a spectral apparition that somehow survives its own death, that is, the eclipse of meaning" (Žižek 1996, 103). Spectral sound, like Ramatou and Draman, lives in between deaths.

4 Voice(s) in *Le franc* and *La petite vendeuse de soleil*

THIS LAST CHAPTER continues to explore the narrative spaces produced by sound and the visual, the acousmatic panopticon, and particular attention will be paid to the roles played by voices and music. In the midst of it all, the postcolonial body is portrayed as being metaphorically and literally maligned; the director's last film follows the odyssey of a socially misfit quadriplegic girl. A similar journey takes places in *Le franc*, a seldom-discussed film but an essential one for understanding Mambety's work. It is also the only one that relies consistently on physical comedy, in ways reminiscent of Charlie Chaplin and Laurel and Hardy, which complicates the discussion of the postcolonial body. These last two films revisit previously discussed themes—sound manipulation (alternating diegetic and nondiegetic music), sonic fantasy space, narrative connections to orality, the postcolonial social struggle, fragmentation, and the pains of the individual and his or her body—but they are all secondary to the acoustics and the acousmatic panopticon that dominate the aural spaces. It is also noteworthy that the narrative construction of these two films follows the typical structure of Western fairy tales and the actantial model, as well as several narrative elements associated with African folk stories. This mixture is particularly evident in *La petite vendeuse*, which borrows heavily from structures and formulations encountered in folk stories. Thus a new narrative model is needed in order to explain the fusion of Western and African traditions exemplified by Mambety's cinema.

Le franc was meant to be part of a trilogy about "the little people" (*les petites gens*), which Mambety did not get a chance to complete due to his untimely death. The plot concerns a poor and indebted musician, Marigo, who wins the lottery, but encounters problems when trying to cash in the winning ticket. The film traces his wanderings while presenting itself as an ode to music and musicians; in the end credits, the director even dedicates the film to all the musicians of the world. At the center of the film, besides the actual character, a musical instrument, the congoma, resides. This is an instrument used for a particular style of music, the goumbé, usually played at social events. The style hails from a neighboring country, Guinea-Bissau, which means that the director, who persistently crosses cinematic boundaries, also crosses geographic boundaries in what may be an attempt to unite Africans under one sound.

As mentioned in the previous chapter, Mambety has a rightful claim to acoustic auteurship, and several other theorists have commented on this aural phenomenon. Among them, Mervyn Cooke considers Scorsese, Tarantino, and Lynch to be modern sound auteurs because of their unique acoustic styles (2008, 483–489). Influential critic Claudia Gorbman uses the French term *"mélomane"* to describe the acoustic auteur: "More and more, music-loving directors treat music . . . as a key element and a marker of authorial style" (2007, 149). She explains the idea of the *mélomane* in the article "Auteur Music":

> A confluence of factors has led to the preeminence of auteur music. Over the last twenty years the advent of digital recording and storage of music as well as of digital video editing have made it possible for directors to exert much greater control over the selection and placement of music in their films, and has liberated the music soundtrack from the rarefied province of specialists. The strictures and underlying aesthetic of the classical rules of film music simply no longer hold. Melodies are no longer unheard, song lyrics are perceived to add rather than detract from audio-viewing and the sky's the limit with respect to the possible relations between music and image and story. (2007, 151)

Furthermore, Gorbman's discussion of Jean-Luc Godard when defining the concept of *mélomane* helps us understand Mambety's penchant for sound and music, too: "For Godard, music is a montage element, subject to radical disruption and placed in dialectical relationships with the image and other soundtrack elements. On one level, Godard's music foregrounds the arbitrariness of all film elements; it is difficult to experience it as 'invisibly' reinforcing the mood of narrative scenes. On another level, music carries cultural meaning" (2007, 158).

Gorbman's observations about the role of music expose a play of aural counterpoints between music and other acoustic elements, such as dialogue, noises, and the like. While such contrasting sounds, as well as oppositions between the visual and the aural, abound in his earlier films, Mambety's use of music has not necessarily provided the audience with comparable dialectical struggles. Instead, music attempts to unify the narrative space of the film, and in doing so to create the likeliest incarnation of the acousmatic panopticon. To reiterate the idea stated in the introduction, if the visual panopticon as described by Foucault unifies and normalizes power, the acousmatic panopticon challenges that power by seeking to unify and normalize the diegetic space of the films, at a first level, and the larger postcolonial space of an entire country at a second level. Gorbman's reference to music and cultural meaning reiterates the logical inference that cultural meaning is specific to each country, region, or director. It is that specificity that hints at the creation of a space that could be uniquely Senegalese, uniquely Dakarois, or uniquely Mambetian.

One of the main theoretical issues concerning the role of music in films comes from its contentious place within the diegesis of the film. For the most part, theorists have not considered music an integral part of the actual space, the actual diegesis of the film. It was regarded as an add-on (as sound itself was originally theorized to be) that carved its own niche in the larger production of the film on the soundtrack. Music was used to manipulate the feelings of the audience, but by and large it was perceived as an outsider, and therefore labeled nondiegetic. As Robynn J. Stilwell puts it:

> It is true that nondiegetic scores tend toward subjectivity and source music to a kind of realistic "objectivity," which would seem to make them synonymous with empathy and anempathy, but they diverge from a single point, the point-of-view/audition/feeling of a character in a diegesis. Empathy/anempathy is the relationship that the audience . . . has with the character: they recognize and identify with the feelings that the character is experiencing, and may feel them, though in an attenuated form. When we talk about subjectivity in film and film music, the connection between character and audience is more intense and more enveloping. (2007, 191)

Recall that diegetic sound (or music) occurs within the confines of what is seen on screen, and thus has a clear source; nondiegetic sound comes from offscreen and is seemingly not connected (at least directly) to the diegetic. Two other terms define the remaining possibilities: "extradiegetic sound" is sound connected to the diegetic but that has no place being heard on screen (the perfect example is a familiar one: the sound of the toilet goes off on the soundtrack, even though the character urinates in the street); and "intradiegetic sound" is sound whose source is known but that the audience cannot see at that particular moment. There is a great deal of overlap and dialogue between the four types of sound, which has led to narrative tensions, especially between the diegetic and the nondiegetic. The struggle between diegetic and nondiegetic music generates a fantastical gap,[1] to use Stilwell's term: "The trajectory of music between diegetic and nondiegetic highlights a gap in our understanding, a place of destabilization and ambiguity" (2007, 186). That gap "is a transformative space, a superimposition, a transition between stable states" (2007, 200). What better metaphor to describe the postcolonial than the fantastical gap between the colonial and a universe that has yet to take full shape?

At a smaller scale, but one equally ambiguous and transformative, the emergence of subjectivity can be closely linked to sound and music, too: "Hegel mentions an ancient Egyptian sacred statue, which, at every sunset, as if by miracle, issued a deep reverberating sound—this mysterious sound magically resonating from within an inanimate object is the best metaphor for the birth of subjectivity" (Žižek 1996, 92–93). But the true object's voice must remain mute, unarticulated, because the moment it escapes, the moment it is spoken or articulated, the object disappears in order to give way to "$, the barred subject lamenting the loss of the object" (Žižek 1996, 93). In this context, music functions in a role akin to that of the island and of the fantasy, as a protective shield against the horrors of the Real: "Music: it is a lure, a screen, the last curtain, which protects us from directly confronting the horror of the (vocal) object" (Žižek 1996, 93).

In order for the music to serve properly as the last curtain in *Le franc*, Mambety places songs and voices in various physical spots around the city—in the center of Dakar, but also at the periphery. As a result, songs and voices travel through space and rearrange it; they yield spatial powers, but also temporal ones. They return at several moments during the day, just as the loudspeaker of the mosque announces the five prayer times, or the radio brings news to the entire city. As a more detailed example, Sili of *La petite vendeuse* walks out at daybreak while a faint song plays on the soundtrack. The song becomes a real diegetic song, sung by the character's grandmother, but later in the day. The result is a spatial and temporal displacement of the song, as the aural shows off its malleability.

So why place the same song in separate physical and temporal areas? Could the faint song at the beginning of the film be in Sili's head (perhaps because her grandmother sings it often)? With a nod to structuralist Gérard Genette, Claudia Gorbman calls this type of music "metadiegetic music"—music imagined by a character in a film (1987, 22). Yet it is not certain that Sili does imagine that song, or more accurately, remembers it. In fact, at the beginning of the film the song can only be purely nondiegetic. Later information resituates the source of the sound, and the undeniable fact that the same song occurs in two separate places renders it a perfect example of what Jeff Smith calls "spatially displaced sound" (2009, 14–16). This notion plays a crucial role in the creation of a unified space; a song or sound that exists simultaneously in multiple places exposes the visual as lacking complete narrative strength once again. If the camera moves about the city, the image it shows must necessarily change, which breaks the space up into fragments. The same song being played at various locations accomplishes the opposite effect.

Jeff Smith's work on music sheds much-needed light on the differences between diegetic and nondiegetic. He dismisses the notion that the sound/music is ever nondiegetic when viewers are confused about the source of the sound. Instead, to him, it always remains diegetic. So in effect there is no transition between diegetic and nondiegetic or vice versa, because the apparent transformation is actually "produced as an effect of the film narration's communicativeness" (Smith 2009, 22). Furthermore, building on Gorbman's research, which follows the traditional definition and describes diegetic music as music that comes from a source within the narrative, Smith explores the boundary between the two types of music, challenging previous misconceptions—such as the faux dependency between "realistic" and diegetic, aural fidelity, and sound's volume—in order to posit that "the nonrealistic treatment of diegetic music is merely comparable to other kinds of expressive devices in the cinema, such as the use of slow motion in action or fight scenes" (2009, 4–6, and 14). Smith supports his findings with examples from Hollywood-style movies. As may have already become obvious, Mambety's use of sound is even more nuanced.

Franc Sounds

Le franc begins acoustically with saxophone music, which is interrupted by the loud voice of an imam calling to prayer in yet another aural counterpoint. The call to prayer, or rather the megaphone from which the voice emanates, is a perfect approximation of the acousmatic panopticon, particularly because initially the visual referent is missing. The call to prayer penetrates all the nooks and crannies of the city at a sonic level, but the audience knows that it must come logically from an actual minaret (which makes it an intradiegetic source). The minaret doubles as a panopticon that relies on the proliferation of sound rather than the visual. The tower structures the space of the city and the lives of the inhabitants through the call and the voice that control the people who inevitably respond to it. The imam himself is rarely seen, replaced by the loudspeakers that are so prevalent in Mambety's cinema. The Senegalese director is not the only one obsessed by the loudspeaker/megaphone. For example, it is also at the center of the Algerian director Merzak Allouache's film *Bab-El Oued City* (1994), in which the main character, Boualem, rips off the loudspeaker next to his bedroom so that he can get some rest. His action sets the plot of the film in motion, but what is germane here is that he attacks the acousmatic dominance of the mosque. This attack makes more sense in the context of Algerian cinema, which relies on more pronounced, potent social commentaries within the confines of a country that has stood up violently to France.

That same social commentary comes off in much more subtle ways in Senegal. It is the voice of the unseen imam that travels and calls people to the action of the prayer. The clash with the saxophone music points to the struggle between Western and local (or Other) acousmatic powers. Jazz, an American art form, fights for the aural space of the film. While the credits roll, the first shot of the film begins, a shot of the ocean waves. Water is certainly a leitmotif for the director, and in this context it works congruently with the music. However, it is the visual that changes the meaning of the aural, not the other way around; the visual again takes a temporary backseat to the aural. The saxophone and the voice do not take turns dominating the soundtrack, so this is not an example of the sonic rack focus effect. Instead they overlap one another, they clash like waves, making it hard to understand the words of the imam or to focus entirely on the music. A third noise joins them momentarily: in the neighborhood, a woman airs out grain in a makeshift bin. The sound of the grain being flung up in the air rhythmically matches the music of the saxophone, which means that a jazz improvisation element is added diegetically. This last aural element fuses the diegetic and nondiegetic aural spaces in an innovative manner, shrinking the fantastical gap and therefore limiting the destabilization effect; the aural space evens out the fragmented narrative.

The soundscape slowly switches to a choir of children's voices, which take over the soundtrack. At this point the aural map of the film includes, in order: a saxophone, a man's voice, "grain" percussion, bird chirps, and the voices of children. This amounts to a veritable symphony of noises. Through sound bridge transitions—for example, the camera moves from the neighborhood to a long shot of children sitting around their teacher in the street—the aural unifies and structures the cinematic visual space. The children are learning the Qur'an and they all read off wooden tablets; the teacher (a visible imam) sits in the middle and recites along with them. Oddly, he wears sunglasses, which obscure his eyes—he has something to hide—and Mambety's commentary against religious groups continues.

The children are loud: their voices grow a little quieter when the camera moves inside Marigo's room, but they can still be heard within the new space. The voices that control and unify the aural space of the neighborhood penetrate all the way inside people's homes. They move outside and inside, breaking down physical barriers and walls. The voices of the children are local or localized, concentrated in one spot, right next to Marigo's room. The imam's voice from the minaret has a much wider reach across the neighborhood and farther out across the entire city. Nevertheless, because they both make up the same soundtrack (i.e., they are actually in the same place), they both attain acousmatic powers.

Indoors for the first time, the shot that introduces Marigo is exquisite. It is structured diagonally without being a Dutch angle, which appears to be done on purpose: this is an elegant alternative to the film noir oblique angle that suggests conventionally that something is amiss. In this case, too, as the audience soon learns, the situation is tragic. A few scenes later, Marigo and his friend Lobster walk in a market and they are framed in an actual Dutch angle, which confirms the predicament of the main character. Back in Marigo's room, the diagonal is pulled off through the mise-en-scène. In the foreground and to the bottom far right of the frame there is a lit lamp; in the center of the shot Marigo lies down, his head toward the lamp and his legs up the wall (see figure 15). In the background and upper left corner of the frame a poster adorns the otherwise empty wall. The three elements—lamp, actor, poster—are further connected through physical overlapping: the lamp covers up part of Marigo's head (which creates an amusing effect—it is as if his head is lit because he is having an idea), and Marigo's left foot covers up part of the poster. The mise-en-scène diagonal movement from the lamp to the poster inscribes the main character in a semiotic prison of sorts. When the camera tracks back and changes angle, the same formation reappears, but now in a horizontal progression from left to right and the entire poster to the left of the frame can be seen.

The two-dimensional quality of the poster, or of any poster that is part of the diegesis, speaks volumes to the lack of plasticity of the visual. Basically, the poster is one frame, one of the twenty-four frames that when rolling give the impression of movement. The insistence of Mambety on these mise-en-scène props stresses, through opposition, how much more flexible sound is. This particular poster, unlike the posters mentioned in discussions of other films, is very important to the main character. Upon waking up, Marigo immediately turns to it, touches his face as if praying and then touches the poster in adoration. In all the other examples, the posters and the maps remain at a distance from the characters and are not acknowledged. They are there simply for us, the audience. But Marigo physically touches this poster and almost climbs onto the wall. Since the feeble separation between diegetic and nondiegetic sound and music has been a recurrent point of discussion, it is worth remarking that a similar "confusion" occurs with this particular poster. The posters that no character refers to within the diegesis are still part of the mise-en-scène, so they are diegetic. However, at another interpretive level they are extradiegetic—they can be analyzed separately and they produce meaning from their quasi-paratextual presence. On the contrary, Marigo's poster is even *more* diegetic, if diegesis allowed degrees. It is not just a prop in the traditional sense. Instead, it grows into a character.

Back in Marigo's room, the landlady brutally expedites his awakening by pacing the yard in front of the room and yelling for the rent money at the top of her voice. She threatens to hang on to Marigo's congoma, a percussion box that he carries around his neck and plays in several places throughout the city. The children's rhythmic recitations are still overheard on the soundtrack, but now it is her voice that dominates the local aural space of the neighborhood and by extension, the soundtrack of the film. To emphasize her control, the landlady (played by renowned Senegalese singer and actor Aminata Fall) uses a whistle, which she blows several times, thus piercing the aural space. She represents the law visually (made obvious by the close-ups of her face, grotesquely contorted by the yelling) and aurally (thanks to the power of her voice and the added acoustic potency of the whistle). Tangentially, the whistle plays a key role in the psychoanalytical world of Žižek. In *How to Read Lacan* (2007) the theorist reminds us of a sequence from Chaplin's *City Lights*, in which the Tramp swallows a whistle and with every ensuing hiccup the whistle makes a sound from inside his body. Chaplin has already been visible literally in the poster in Rama's room in *Xala* and spectrally in the physical slapstick behavior of our current main character, Marigo.[2] Žižek looks at the *City Lights* episode as the perfect example of shame at its purest: the Tramp/Subject faces the excess of his body that he cannot control, and importantly, that excess is a sound, a spectral sound that does not belong to him although it comes from within him.[3] Sound is an autonomous entity, without a body of its own, inhabiting the body of the Subject momentarily. In short, it colonizes the body. As a carrier of powerful sound, the whistle is used in many contexts as an enforcer of the law, whether in sports or actual law enforcement. The sound of the whistle comes from an object, but it is through the voice of the character, through her blowing, that the sound achieves a body of its own. The placement of the whistle *within* the body certainly makes for a much more convincing argument, but is the whistle on the landlady's lips all that different? In my opinion, the sound of the whistle, regardless of where it comes from, is always Žižek's spectral sound, sound that escapes us. It is still sound that is not fully controlled, because once it leaves the body and goes through the whistle it turns into something else. That something else retains the quality of having been within, but it also becomes completely unrecognizable once expelled through the whistle—it is not a natural body sound. And is this not that exactly what happens to the voice of the unseen imam that metamorphoses when passing through the loudspeaker on its way to establishing a unified acoustic field over the entire city?

The choice of actor for the landlady role is interesting because Fall is a well-known artist whose music even features on the soundtrack, but she torments Marigo, a fellow musician. Marigo is fictional, which allows an innovative blurring of the lines between diegetic and extradiegetic: the actual musician pretends to be a landlady, while the actual actor pretends to be a musician. When the landlady briefly lets Marigo be and decides to go for a walk by the sea, she relies on a walking stick to move around, extending Mambety's cinematic trend of choosing characters that are physically limited. The landlady cannot move easily about the neighborhood, but she still towers over this particular space through her voice and through the most potent acoustic object at anyone's disposal (other than the mosque's loudspeaker)—the whistle.[4]

When Marigo finally escapes the soundscape of the landlady and leaves the neighborhood, a group of children (possibly the same children who were reciting the Qur'an) accompany him clapping along to his song. It is a bizarre sequence because there are actually two Marigos, one with the instrument and one without; the former walks left, while the latter walks right. Even during the scene with the group of children, the editing crosscuts between the Marigo surrounded by the children and the Marigo who walks all alone. Mambety experiments with temporality one more time, as two temporally separated Marigos are force-edited together and placed in a kind of existential dialogue—who is Marigo without the instrument? As the camera frames the two versions mainly in long shots, which emphasize the distance between the real and the fantasy, the Marigo without the instrument looks back longingly toward Marigo with the instrument.

From this scene the action moves to the train station, where we first meet the boy in the wheelchair who carries a boom box and who will play a much more prominent part in the next film. For now he is nameless, but he plays an integral part because he literally carries sound around the city. He is a flaneur on wheels and he too contributes to the unification of space through the acousmatic panopticon of the radio. At the train station, Mambety introduces, in voice-over, a dialogue between a caller and the Ngor Island radio station DJ; it comes from the boy's boom box, but covers up the entire soundscape as if nondiegetic. That is to say that it "sounds" as if the voice-over is limited to the nondiegetic, but because there is an actual diegetic boom box the source ultimately remains unclear. The island of Ngor is a resort with plenty of beach space next to Dakar, but to the north. It is intrinsically and geographically the opposite of Gorée Island and its colonial memories. Following the brief dialogue, the radio voice announces the devaluation of the African franc and discusses the National Lottery results. The voice represents another incarnation of the *acousmêtre* because even though one can point to the boom box as the location of the voice, we still do not know the actual location of the DJ.[5]

Mambety makes use of the radio and the voice in ways quite different from the French auteurs. The radio does feature prominently in the French New Wave, and three relevant examples come to mind from Agnès Varda's *Cléo from 5 to 7* (1962) and Godard's *Pierrot le fou* (1965) and *Two or Three Things I Know About Her* (1967). In *Cléo* the main character, a singer, talks with her housekeeper in the back of a taxi. On the radio, the audience hears news about Algeria, but the characters remain unmoved by what is being said. Yet when her own song comes on, Cléo becomes animatedly aware of the sound coming from the radio. She declares herself annoyed with her own voice, by contrast with her apathy (shown by her lack of annoyance) toward something that really matters, like the war. It must be noted, though, that her voice is trapped inside the little radio box and then, at a secondary level, inside the car.[6] In *Pierrot le fou*, when the main characters take a long car ride, the radio announces deaths in Vietnam, but they do not seem to notice it and they do not discuss it. In *Two or Three Things*, Juliette's husband constantly works on a transistor in an attempt to communicate news from Vietnam via this homemade radio.

Critically, all these examples place the radio in a limited space, so the expansive quality of the acousmatic voice is eradicated. Even though it travels inside the car (or the room), it does not reach beyond its confines. The opposite is true for the boy in the wheelchair, whose radio travels like that of a car but releases sound freely into the aural space of the city. More importantly, in the French films the characters are not always aware of the acousmatic presence; that they can ignore it takes away the omnipotent power of the aural. In summary, in the French context, the acousmatic voice is reduced, minimized, and used to expose gaps, as opposed to generating a sense of unity. Of course, the main purpose of these scenes is to point to the alienation of the subject and to criticize the French subjects' ignorance of the awful political reality that surrounds them. Varda and Godard portray the individual, the modern Western subject, as cut off from the national consciousness. By contrast, in Mambety's films the individual is woven into the social fabric through aural suture. Not only does the acousmatic voice of the radio retain its qualities, but it also augments its power. And the Senegalese, the postcolonial subjects, listen and pay attention to the radio; in *La petite vendeuse*, a man actually pays the boy in the wheelchair to play a news radio channel. In *Le franc*, as the camera treks about the station, a train arrives and several different people go about their daily activities. However, the soundtrack remains focused on the acousmatic voice of the DJ, which continues uninterrupted even though the visual changes perspective. The visual cannot escape the sound that accompanies every cut in the film; it is as if the camera attempts to flee but is pulled back by the coherence of the aural, which once again unifies space.

When Marigo meets Lobster, a little person who wears vivid colors and a backward baseball cap (this clothing item will reappear in *La petite vendeuse*) and who sells lottery tickets, the film turns comedic. They strike up a friendship, walk away together, and become an odd couple reminiscent of Laurel and Hardy. Indeed, as in *Badou Boy*, a subtle element of physical comedy emerges. A few scenes later Marigo carries the door to his room on his back. His movement is awkward, he falls down, and even hits one of the *car rapides* with the door when he tries to climb aboard. Then he falls on top of the car, on which he has a hard time maintaining balance. The physical comedy adds a dose of sympathy for the main character, who now negotiates his in-limbo status as an object (of humor) and a subject-creator (of humor). In a 2009 online essay, Anny Wynchank remarks that "the character of Marigo is burlesque, with his stiff movement, excessive gesturing, his funny faces and facial expressions."[7]

From the outside scenes by the train station, we move inside a *car rapide* where a man plays the guitar and the boy in the wheelchair reappears, which explains how he moves so fast around the city and why he is seen at several locations. The *car rapide* has no windows or back door, so the music played in the van travels freely throughout the city. The vehicle goes by the president's palace—a regular destination in Mambety's cinema—and maps the city. This trip marks a return to the visual odyssey of *Contras' City*, although there seems to be more of a concrete point of view attached to the characters in this instance. The *caméra-flâneur* and the traveling sound unite to update the map of the city; the market of Kermel, such a beautiful presence in 1968, is now shown in two separate shots, only the impressive gate still identifiable (see figure 16). The trip extends and the scene becomes a long sequence. Marigo "doubles" again, playing the congoma in the street although in actuality he is on top of the *car rapide*. The point of the scene is finally made clear as the van pulls back into the train station. There is no other destination, so the car drives in a loop that brings everyone back to the original spot. As the day progresses, the train station achieves the status of a visual leitmotif. It represents the possibility of escape that never comes to fruition because none of the main characters leave. Like the Parisian flaneur, the characters and the *caméra-flâneur* of *Le franc* are trapped in a labyrinth from which they cannot escape, stuck at the original point of departure.

When Marigo and Lobster walk away from the train station for a moment, the DJ voice regains control of the aural space of the film. The voice has now expanded its range. While the visual cue of the boom box justifies our belief that we are hearing the radio show, the voice carries much further than the range of the machine. It hovers over the neighborhood and all the characters, reminding everyone of the economic shortcomings of the country. Congruent with the announcement on economic austerity, Lobster suggests to his new friend that he buy a lottery ticket, so he can be "like James Brown." Music reaches across the ocean to offer a fleeting vision of a unified space of international music. Lobster, the quasi prophet, points to a man carrying a door on his back who had gone mad after buying a ticket from him, but in fact that man is future Marigo, in yet another temporal jump and doubling. Present Marigo follows the advice and buys a ticket bearing the number 555. When he arrives at home, he glues it to the door and then covers it up with his beloved poster, giving the latter yet another meaning—protector of riches and the future. Finally shown in a close-up, the words on the poster are legible: it reads "Yaadikoone Ndiaye"—a Senegalese folk hero, a regional Robin Hood figure (Barlet 1996, 139).

Yaadikoone was indeed a "protector of the children and the weak," as Marigo explains to the local government officer when he attempts to redeem the winning ticket. Below the image of Yaadikoone, a citation without source is legible, possibly originating with the director himself: "He dreamt of a free and grand Africa where the one who is hungry would not be trampled."[8] In the special features of the DVD for the *Médiathèque des Trois Mondes* edition, Mambety talks about what cinema and filmmaking mean and acknowledges the role that Yaadikoone played in his life; he credits the hero as the reason why he started making films.[9] When Marigo places the poster over the ticket, the imam's voice appears on the soundtrack and Marigo touches his face in an ambivalent gesture—is he praying to the poster or answering the call to prayer? Given the director's connection to Yaadikoone, a transference occurs here through which Marigo and Mambety coincide. Nar Sene spends considerable time unearthing the reasons why "Yadi," as he calls him, was such an influence in Mambety's life (2001, 15–18). Sene also notes that Yadi was made prisoner several times and sent to the island of Gorée (16), which may further explain the director's fascination with the insular spaces.

When Marigo walks out of the room, religious beads in hand, he bows to the poster again and kisses it. He walks into the city and suddenly the two primary sounds from the beginning of the film—the call to prayer and the saxophone—reemerge. However, in this instance they are accompanied by two quick shots that de-acousmatize the sounds; there is an actual saxophonist playing in the street, and immediately following that surprising shot it is shown that the call to prayer originates, as suspected, from a loudspeaker. Visually, the film returns several times to the musician as people prepare to pray. Revealing the source of the sound does not change its acousmatic powers, because it still dominates the soundtrack. In spite of the de-acousmatization that occurs (according to Chion, de-acousmatization leads to a taming of the voice and a loss of power), the sound in this particular instance still creates some impression of omnipresence, because the voice behind the loudspeaker remains attached to an unseen body. Mladen Dolar makes the following claim concerning the process of de-acousmatization in the course of an argument to establish voice as an object fetish: "The acousmatic voice is simply a voice whose source one cannot see . . . but even when it finds its body, it turns out that this doesn't quite work, the voice doesn't stick to the body, it is an excrescence which doesn't match the body" (2006, 60–61). As an example, Dolar cites Norman Bates's mother (whose voice is really Norman's); eventually he reaches the conclusion that *"there is no such thing as disacousmatization"* (2006, 70, emphasis in original). In our example, the sound coming out of the loudspeakers does not lead us back to the body from which it comes, so it is a partial, ineffective de-acousmatization. Furthermore, to add to Dolar's intriguing point, even when the sound does return to or is matched to a source, that original source does not magically become full-bodied. As suggested in an earlier note about aural dismemberment, once the voice or sound travels away as an acousmatic voice or sound, the original source remains hollowed, empty to a degree. Deleuze's idea of always-deserted islands is similar; even if people temporarily inhabit the island, it remains deserted. The aural dismemberment makes complete sense given Mambety's tendency to focus on characters who are physically limited and challenged and whose bodies are in some cases dismembered: the blind kora player; Ramatou and her artificial limbs; the landlady with her cane; the paraplegic Sili; the immobile, blind grandmother; and the boombox boy in the wheelchair.

The hollowed (as a source of sound), dismembered body also functions as the source that returns the gaze aurally. In his article "*I Hear You With My Ears*: Or, The Invisible Master," Žižek discusses the role played by the mysterious house in Hitchcock's films—a place believed to be empty, but which generates such terror in the spectators (through the diegetic character "interacting" with the house) that it appears likely that the house returns the gaze. He explains it as follows:

> The crucial point, of course, is that this gaze should not be subjectivized; it's not simply that "there is somebody in the house," we are, rather, dealing with a kind of empty, a priori gaze that cannot be pinpointed as a determinate reality—she "cannot see it all," she is looking at a blind spot, and the object returns the gaze from this blind spot. The situation is homologous at the level of voice: it is as if, when we're talking, whatever we say is an answer to a primordial address by the Other—we're always already addressed, but this address is blank, it cannot be pinpointed to a specific agent, but is a kind of empty a priori, the formal "condition of possibility" of our speaking. (1996, 90)

The undamaged structure of what one perceives as reality depends on repression and exclusion, according to Lacan and Žižek. Something must always be excluded, the *objet petit a*, in order to lead a normal life, to be in touch with the reality around us. But in psychosis "this exclusion is undone: the object (in this case, the gaze or voice) is *included* in reality, the outcome of which, of course, is the disintegration of our 'sense of reality,' the loss of reality" (Žižek 1996, 90). From a discussion of spectral sound (which in this version closely resembles Chion's *acousmêtre*), Žižek arrives at the conclusion that the body is indeed hollowed out by its own voice:

> What we have to renounce is thus the commonsense notion of a primordial, fully constituted reality in which sight and sound harmoniously complement each other: the moment we enter the symbolic order, an unbridgeable gap separates forever a human body from "its" voice. The voice acquires a spectral autonomy, it never quite belongs to the body we see, so that even when we see a living person talking, there is always some degree of ventriloquism at work: it is as if the speaker's own voice hollows him out and in a sense speaks "by itself," through him. (1996, 92)

Once again, voice separates itself from its presumed source, and yet it survives.

The film circles back to the train station and the soundtrack begins to overflow with noises, but it is dominated by the voice of the DJ, which is accompanied visually by a quick shot of the boy with the boom box. The DJ announces the winner of the lottery drawing. It is Marigo's number, 555.[10] The voice of the DJ and the saxophone continue to share the soundscape and to dominate aurally. The visual gradually disappears because it is getting darker out, and soon nothing can be seen anymore. It is pitch black but the sounds remain. Since this scene takes place by the sea, one of the two shots in the dark faces the ocean and the boats that move about slowly. In the far background, out of mist and obscurity the island of Gorée makes another spectral apparition; it returns a hazy gaze, as it were. Even though within the narrative space of this film, it makes more sense for the island of Ngor to make an appearance, given its size this island has to be Gorée and not Ngor (north) or Isles des Madeleines (west). Another clue is the geographical proximity of the main train station (Gare Ferroviaire de Dakar), from which the ferries go to and from Gorée. At the end of the film, though, the island behind Maribo is in fact Ngor (Mambety even goes so far as to thank the green boats of Ngor in the credits). Nevertheless, the island presence perseveres and frames the space of the city: Ngor to the north and Gorée to the southeast of the city. Geographically, then, the two islands and the city constitute yet another diagonal, carefully matched cinematically by Mambety's mise-en-scène inside Marigo's room.

From the open space of the ocean shore, which is drastically reduced by darkness, the film effectuates another return by revisiting the landlady's neighborhood. She plays Marigo's congoma in the backyard and sings in broken English. Aminata Fall is credited in the opening with a song titled "In the Morning"; this appears initially to be it, but the delivery presents another crossing between the diegetic and the nondiegetic. When she sees Marigo leave with the door,[11] she offers to give back the instrument, pitying the man for having gone insane in her opinion. But he does not stop, and as the landlady repeatedly calls out his name—including a last effort that turns melodic—it is now the name of the main character that moves about the neighborhood and not the whistle. Fall's voice moves to the soundtrack where the listeners hear the "real" song, also sung mainly in English. The song is vaguely reminiscent of a blues lament about a "baby" in the romantic sense of the word. In essence, the actress Fall previews the song of the singer Fall at the beginning of the sequence, then the real singer takes over the soundtrack, generating another fantastical gap of sound as music is displaced spatially and temporally.

However, the relevance of Fall transcends the use of her voice. By participating in the creation of this film both visually and aurally, diegetically and nondiegetically, Fall emerges as a larger-than-life figure who matches the reality of her cultural impact in Senegal. The singer first met Mambety while they were both upstarts at the Sorano Theater in the mid-1960s. In a brief interview with Sada

Niang, Fall describes Mambety as a close friend and repeatedly as someone with a golden heart who took care of her and was extremely generous with other artists (2002, 208–211). So Mambety may have chosen Fall for a brief appearance in *Contras' City* and the extended part in *Le franc* simply because of their close relationship, not for the singer's iconic singing. Nonetheless, the symbolic power of Fall's voice cannot be ignored. For example, in a recent article, Senegalese-born academic Babacar M'Baye analyzes a blues song by Fall, "*Yayeboye*" ("Dear Mother"), in which she sings to and about mothers. The song expresses the agony of separation between mother and child, and thus "reflects a Senegalese cosmology in which children view their mothers as sacred beings" (2013b, 111). While similar views of mothers can be found elsewhere in the world, M'Baye's essay does develop a distinctive view about the transatlantic dialogue between Fall and American blues singer Mahalia Jackson. M'Baye proposes that singing the blues represents, first, a resistance to slavery and colonialism, and second, a coping mechanism used by black mothers to help their children deal with issues such as violence, separation, or alienation. The key finding of the essay, though, is the creation of a "circumatlantic space": "These songs reveal the complex trajectories of a blues tradition that originated from Africa and travelled to the Americas, before returning back to the continent where it was first conceived" (M'Baye 2013b, 106). Not only does Fall control the cinematic space of *Le franc*, but she reaches well outside the diegesis to affect entire local and international cultures.

After leaving the neighborhood, Marigo enters the lottery office and places the door and poster in front of a female officer who sits behind a counter and a glass wall. The shot is again framed diagonally, with Ndiaye's image between the two actors (see figure 17). Yadi's face is twice framed, once by the limits of the shot and again by the small window of the counter. The poster, no longer a mere prop, is an actor in its own right, entrenched in the middle of the action. When Marigo removes the poster, the ticket, still glued to the door, is seen through the same small window, and that shows its own narrative importance. It is after all the one object that drives the plot of the film forward.[12] Just before Marigo leaves the office, the director reverses the shot and focuses on the female worker through the other side of the open window, her face also perfectly framed in the glassless semicircle. Marigo soon finds out he should not have glued the ticket to the door, and on the soundtrack mocking laughter is heard. The film cuts to a shot of the landlady throwing water at the camera, which supplants the missing Marigo; it is his point of view that gets splashed. We remember that when he first left the neighborhood in the morning, the landlady threw water in his face.

The laughter covers shots of the landlady and the lottery office, and it carries an echoic quality like Michel's gun in *Breathless*. It is also reminiscent of the witch's laughter in *Touki Bouki*, especially because the same actress plays Aunt Oumy. Not only does sound carry over between shots in the same film, unifying diegetic space, but one gets the feeling that it also moves between entirely different films, tying up Mambety's cinema and the extradiegetic space in one cohesive, aural narrative. In his close reading of Roberto Rossellini, Conley mentions a map that speaks (2007, 70), but what is even more intriguing is the note that accompanies it, in which he arrives at the conclusion that Rossellini's films "(especially when they are superimposed on one another) deal with national unification" (2007, 225). Mambety's films overlap narratively, too, to the point that one might be able to puzzle back together a large coherent story. Parallel to Rossellini's treatment of Italian national space, Mambety's films speak about and for national and African unification. They "speak" because they actually use sound and voice to clamor for that unity. They also transcend space and time thanks to an ability noted by Chion: "On-the-air sounds, usually situated in the scene's real time, enjoy the freedom of crossing boundaries of cinematic space" (1999, 76), and "music enjoys the status of being a little freer of barriers of time and space than the other sound and visual elements . . . cinema's *passe-muraille*. . . . Out of time and out of space, music communicates with all times and all spaces of a film, even as it leaves them to their separate and distinct existences" (1999, 81).

Marigo leaves the lottery office to try to remove the ticket. He still has difficulties carrying the door, which is suddenly symbolic of the weight of the past and the impossible future: the poster of Yadi epitomizes the past, and the riches promised by the ticket—which he cannot access—the future. The present is wobbly and uncertain. A future of riches remains just out of the postcolonial subject's reach. It is a perturbing thought, that salvation in whatever sense is within reach and yet cannot possibly be grasped. It is the unattainable fantasy and the ticket is the *objet petit a* that mediates the relationship between subject (Marigo) and desire (for money). Marigo finds himself stuck once again, this time temporally. The *objet petit a* has been discussed at length in the previous chapter, but it is worth mentioning that the voice is a type of *objet petit a* according to Lacan, alongside the breasts, the feces, the phallus, and the gaze. Moreover, the *objet petit a* has already been defined as something perceived when looking awry. Marigo's placement between past and future constitutes yet another diagonal movement, an awry angle that defines the world of *Le Franc* in a microcosm. It would follow logically that there must be an equivalent of looking awry in the aural domain, a hearing awry. And hearing "from aside" as a diegetic character is exactly what happens with the various aural narrative planes through which Marigo negotiates subjectivity.

Outside the lottery office, Marigo sits down and looks at Yadi, who looks back at him mutely. The shot / reverse shot formation sutures the spectator between the two, which brings to mind the famous shot / reverse shot in *Breathless* between Michel and Humphrey Bogart's photo: diegetic, fictional character meets diegetic photo of a real, nonfictional and extradiegetic actor. Michel touches his mouth, a highly problematic gesture, and it appears he wants to touch Bogart; at the very least he reinforces the fact that he is the "real" one, the flesh-and-blood man. However, they are both unreal, both two-dimensional; like their impossible relationship, Marigo and Yadi also coalesce. This process flattens the former—he is but an image—and reasserts the latter's role as a character and not a prop.

Alas, Marigo finally has a bright idea, which belatedly fulfills the symbolism of the lamp from the room. His eyes widen and the camera temporally jumps to the door being washed ashore by waves—he will attempt to remove the ticket with salt water. Visually, the camera tracks back and up to reveal that he finds himself in the middle of the rumble at the abandoned market of Kermel. It is a sad development, but one that has positive implications for the postcolonial space. If in *Contras' City* the market and its art deco walls represented a visual reminder of the colonial,[13] the director now gets the chance to rearrange the space of the city. The rumble remains, but aurally, there are crashing waves and wind. It is just nature, howling. And that emptiness clearly opposes the opulence of French art deco.

Marigo finally finds his way to the beach where he hopes to detach the winning ticket from the door. He begins to sing as he submerges the door in the ocean water. Shots of boats are interjected and then another temporal projection finds him atop one of those boats. The editing cuts again in parallel between two versions of the same character: one struggling amid the waves to retain possession of the priceless door and the other one on a boat, playing the congoma. Fragments of the island appear behind the boat opposite the sandy beaches on the Dakar side. Back on the beach, the ticket comes loose and sticks to Marigo's forehead without him realizing. He thinks he has lost it. As he covers his head in despair, he finds it and erupts in hysterical laughter. His beloved poster washes away without him noticing or caring. He lets go of the past. He plays like a child in the water and sings, but the voice clearly comes from a nondiegetic source, and instruments accompany it. Marigo is dubbed, his voice doubled by a classic *acousmêtre*, so one last time sounds mix to create a fantastical gap in which sound resides as an *objet petit a*. In that gap his laughter carries over to the black screen and the credits start rolling. The end credits reveal that Madieye Massamba Dieye is the musician who plays the congoma and the harmonica, and that he provides voice, too—it is his voice that sings Marigo's last song. Real and imagined musicians merge yet again just as they did with Marigo and Fall. The soundscape is uniform and unified.

Voice in Cinema

According to Michel Chion, sound in film is "vococentric," meaning that voice is the primary sound we hear as an audience, the sound we focus on before anything else on the soundtrack (1994, 6; 2009, 73–75). Furthermore, Kaja Silverman's seminal book, *The Acoustic Mirror: The Female Voice in Psychoanalysis and Cinema* (1988), proves that Hollywood is not only vococentric, but that the voice belongs to the male subject. Moreover, Hollywood imposes the same kind of restrictions on the female voice as on the female body: "The former, like the latter, functions as a fetish within dominant cinema, filling in for and covering over what is unspeakable within male subjectivity" (Silverman 1988, 38). According to Silverman, classic cinema employs three recurring methods that control and manipulate the female voice. First, this voice is confined to an inner textual space, perhaps a painting or a film-within-a-film, which takes away any real contribution to the actual diegetical space. Second, a woman is forced to speak and the emitted sound is the result of someone else's—typically a male's—actions. Third, the female voice is given an impediment, such as an accent or a timbre that suggests an incapacity or inability to speak (1988, 56–61). Silverman writes, "By confining the female voice to a recessed area of the diegesis, obliging it to speak a particular psychic 'reality' on command, and imparting to it the texture of the female body, Hollywood places woman definitely 'on stage,' at a dramatic remove from the cinematic apparatus" (1988, 63). These methods have been widened in the context of postcolonial cinema to include both men and women. It is the voice of the postcolonial subject, male or female, that is confined and ridiculed.

The accent plays a considerable role in the films of Mambety, from mocking the president's voice (a sonic marker, like Conley's reference to the national anthem) to the insistence on speaking regional, authentic languages and not the colonially imposed French. This strategy avoids running afoul of Fanon's warning, "There is nothing more sensational than a black man speaking correctly, because he is appropriating the white world" (2008, 19). Fanon's discussion of languages is centered on the Antillean man who returns home from France to speak only in French as a way to "underscore the rift that has occurred . . . embellished with the appropriate accent" (2008, 19), but it can be extrapolated to the cinematic context of Senegal. Mambety avoids the appropriation of the white world altogether. That is not what is at stake here. Instead, it is about appropriating the space that rightfully belongs to the Senegalese. The president is mocked because of his accent and intonation when he speaks French and because Senghor supported the use of the colonizers' language, French. The officer in pursuit of Badou is mocked because of his poor French. These are government people—like Fanon's soldier/cop who delineates the colonizer's space—who fail in the attempt to appropriate a space that does not belong to them through a language they cannot master completely. Dolar also looks at accent as one of the three dimensions of voice (along with intonation and timbre) that help us become aware of the voice as an independent entity from the body (2006, 73): "Accent... is something which brings the voice into the vicinity of singing, and a heavy accent suddenly makes us aware of the material support of the voice which we tend immediately to discard. It appears as a distraction, or even an obstacle, to the smooth flow of signifiers and the hermeneutics of understanding" (2006, 20). But in Mambety's films, space is aurally appropriated through the basic local language, which lacks an accent. Ramatou's return, for example, is not marked by a drastic change in her speech. Even though she spends considerable time away from the town of Colobane, upon her return she does not speak like Fanon's cosmopolitan Antillean. She fits right back in and there is no cultural rift.

In the films of Mambety, Ousmane Sembène, and particularly those of Safi Faye, several strong female voices dominate both within the diegesis (i.e., characters speak up) and on the nondiegetic soundtrack through music. As M'Baye pointed out, Senegalese culture emphasizes the role of the mother and the grandmother, who are often charged with decision making. They are active elements as opposed to the males, who are constantly shown in these films as passive and lazy. The quintessential illustration comes from Abderrahmane Sissako's *La vie sur terre* (1998), in which the camera follows a group of men sitting in chairs who only move around the walls of a house in order to follow the direction of the shade. The Freudian sexual dynamic—man active, woman passive—is reversed in the context of African film, which often favors the voice of women and of mothers in particular.[14]

Studies of the voice of the mother made by Guy Rosolato, Chion, and most recently Silverman have led to the concept of an "acoustic mirror." The voice of the mother and that of the child, the subject, help differentiate the limitations of the two bodies, mother and child, and lead to the formation of the subject who separates himself or herself from the body of the mother. This happens both visually, as Lacan has pointed out, and aurally. As Silverman notes, the mother, because of her primordial role of a storyteller to the child, is the first language teacher. She defines and interprets the reflected sound image of mother and child in the acoustical "mirror stage" (1988, 100). The formation of the child subject comes into full focus by subtracting—from the body of the mother in the Lacanian mirror stage, and also from the echoes of her voice, in which the "child discovers its identity and voice" (1988, 81). Dolar echoes Silverman's research, and insists on removing the gaze from its paramount importance in the subjectivity process: "Yet the voice can be seen as in some sense even more striking and more elementary: if the voice is the first manifestation of life, is not hearing oneself, and recognizing one's own voice, thus an experience that precedes self-recognition in a mirror? And is not the mother's voice the first problematic connection to the other, the immaterial tie that comes to replace the umbilical cord, and shapes much of the fate of the earliest stages of life?" (2006, 39). Indeed, the "image" of a child enveloped by his or her mother's voice "is a fantasy of origins—a fantasy about precultural sexuality, about the entry into language, and about the inauguration of subjectivity" (Silverman 1988, 74). This fantasy takes on an unpredictable form in the context of Senegal.

While the maternal voice represents a prototype in the West for the disembodied voice-over in cinema according to Chion and Silverman, that same voice is likely to be understood differently elsewhere. There are no mothers central to the films of Mambety, although there are marginal characters who do play that part. In *Touki Bouki* Anta's mother shows up in exactly one scene, during which she sells vegetables at the market and carries on a conversation with a neighbor. Befitting the brevity of the scene and the apparent lack of interest that Mambety shows in the character of the mother, in his films mothers are barely sketched and become quasi caricatures. There is no obvious, immediate explanation for this choice except to point to a cultural shift toward the importance of youth. Anta shows up during the conversation and bullies the friend of the mother who had gotten food on credit. There is nothing soft about this new version of the woman. Anta not only separates herself from the mother, but she imposes her will. She effaces the presence of the mother, which is almost a reversal of the process of subjectivity; in this case the subjectivity of the mother is perceived through the vocal lens of the daughter.

In the acoustic mirror, in terms of sound, the echoes of the voice of the mother initially function like a blanket of sound. For Rosolato it carries a positive connotation, a "pleasurable milieu," in which the voice is both emitted and heard by the child—unlike the dynamic of sight, which entails only the misrecognition. In fact, it was Rosolato who first used the term "acoustic mirror" in order to contextualize the relationship between emitted sounds and heard sounds (1969, 79). For Chion the voice not only envelops but also entraps the child: "In the beginning, in the uterine night, was the voice, that of the Mother. . . . One can imagine the voice of the Mother, which is woven around the child, and which originates from all the points in space . . . as a matrix of places to which we are tempted to give the name 'umbilical net.' A horrifying expression, since it evokes a cobweb" (1999, 57).

The beginning of *La petite vendeuse*, whether Sili hears or imagines the song, epitomizes the uterine night because the character begins walking at daybreak. The discussion of the mother's voice is completed by Julia Kristeva's concept of the "chora" (1984, 25–28).[15] The chora describes the maternal space, a sense of unity between mother and child that provides us with a more flexible subjectivity space. In other words, the chora can swallow up the infant, but it can also open up for him or her. Chion's interpretation, which suggests the emerging subjects appear trapped, is of most value in the postcolonial context and that of the labyrinth of the city, in which the cinematic subjects seem equally stuck.

Chion does attach some positive qualities to the powerful voice of the mother: "One could argue that it is the first model of auditory pleasure and that music finds its roots and its nostalgia in this original atmosphere, which might be called a sonorous womb, a murmuring house—or music of the spheres" (1999, 81). Music is the medium that allows the infant to be "in tune" with his or her mother, as the child harmonizes its sounds to those produced by the mother. In *Touki Bouki*, Aunt Oumi sings to both Mory and Anta. But she is not a mother, which points again to Mambety's insistence on pushing the character of the mother to the fringes. Aunt Oumi is not even a mother figure, because she is a rather frightening presence. However, her laughter controls the aural space and her constant movement controls the cinematic space of the film, rendering her nearly omnipresent. Chion's *acousmêtre* speaks exactly to this type of overwhelming presence; besides God, one of the original forms of the *acousmêtre* is the mother. Along with the landlady/Fall, Aunt Oumi controls the extradiegetic space between and across films. She acquires omnipotence through a nonmaternal singing voice.

Singing Voice

La petite vendeuse de soleil (The Little Girl Who Sold the Sun) (1998) follows a quadriplegic girl, Sili, in her attempt to make a living and help her family by selling newspapers in Dakar. Although Mambety's film career was cut short, this forty-five-minute film does provide the world with an encompassing and comprehensive view of all his work. It is, in some ways, the ideal film on which to conclude his directorial career and this book—a modern fairy tale that inspires dreaming and a positive outlook for Senegal. In *La petite vendeuse* the director's vision of an improved national identity is built through a type of ideology that begins at the bottom of the social strata and that proliferates through the Senegalese oral tradition. The film also openly articulates the desire of the Senegalese people to break free from Western (that is, French) social, political, and financial influences.

The resemblance between Sili and the situation of the African continent, and particularly that of Senegal, is overtly obvious from the start. Like Sili, many countries are limited by their own (socioeconomic) handicaps but still need to fight to alleviate the effects of globalization and acquire complete financial independence. In order to achieve these objectives, the film suggests, a reconciliation between tradition and modernity is needed. The director's vision of a new

Senegal is built from meshing old and new values; oral stories and songs have to coexist with the advent of technology in the current world market. Aside from the political tone, the analysis of the film will continue to establish sound and music as genuine challengers to the primacy of the visual.

There are a few important connections between the film and oral tradition. If one takes the traditional *schéma actantiel* for fairy tales (Greimas 1986, 180), the story of the film matches it remarkably well. There is a subject (Sili) who is on a quest with a clear objective (to have a job/sell newspapers) that she achieves in spite of the *opposants*, the opposing forces (mainly the band of unruly boys, but also her physical handicap and her gender). She succeeds because she has *adjuvants*, helpers (Babou, but also the businessman, the commissary, and the boy in the wheelchair). The *destinateur*, the person who initiates the quest, is the grandmother, although she does so indirectly; Sili wants a job in order to support her family, grandmother included. The last category is the *destinataires*, those who benefit from the quest. In this film, Sili and her grandmother obviously benefit from the former's job, but because Sili is a metaphor for the country, those benefits extend (sadly, just metaphorically) to the rest of the country.

What needs to be stressed here is that the schema is typical for Western fairy tales and yet it works perfectly in an African context. The film marries these traditions by filling out the *schéma* with plenty of references to African folk stories—references to the hare, to the animal kingdom in general—and by using a few other classic folk conventions. Moreover, Mambety's visual storytelling, combined with his inventive use of sound, redefines the idea of beauty. Western fairy tales such as those of Charles Perrault often focus on exterior beauty, or rather effectuate a movement from external to internal beauty. In African stories such as those of Birago Diop, and in Mambety's films, the reverse is true; Sili's beautiful soul and desire to help everyone, to share the sun, make her more attractive on the exterior. These fairy-tale connections appear most clearly in this last film, but there are traces of that orality elsewhere in Mambety's cinema. *Le franc* sets up the (oral) transition to *La petite vendeuse* very well:

> *Le Franc*, like the other Mambety films, is marked by the aesthetic of the oral tradition . . . the fantastic and the irrational that we find in traditional stories occupy an important position in Mambety's film. . . . In fact, we can consider Marigo akin to the Deceiver or the Trickster of oral stories. He manages for a long time to deceive the landlady who tracks him to claim six months worth of rent. Furthermore, Mambety introduces in his film a character of the oral stories, Kuus, who, as in the story transcribed by Birago Diop, *The Gourds of Kouss*, brings riches to the hero. (Wynchank 2009)[16]

The hero in *La petite vendeuse* is atypical. Sili begins her idealized quest for national identity in Colobane, the director's old neighborhood in Dakar—an epicenter of marginality, as Nar Sene aptly describes it (2001, 11). This community, depicted through the lens of the less fortunate, acts as the catalyst meant to ignite the desire for an ideological shift for the better. In fact, in *Hyènes* the name Colobane is used for a fictional town on the outskirts of Dakar, so it is itself situated at the periphery, on the margins. The fact that Colobane is an actual neighborhood in the city could also point to an "extraction": the neighborhood is the epicenter of marginality, but removing it entirely from the city and transplanting it to the outer layers further highlights that marginality; it is a reterritorialization of marginality. Like Conley's map that speciously tells us where we are, Colobane raises questions of space and location. In Sili's version of Colobane, space may shrink visually, but it expands aurally.

The beginning of the film reaffirms the common aesthetic choices of the director, who, as he does in *Hyènes*, constructs the visual space of the diegesis through theatrical rules while opposing the diegetic to the extradiegetic. The filmmaker restricts the space that the camera is allowed to cover and focuses on mise-en-scène details. The first shot reveals women waiting, possibly at a bus stop; the camera is placed on the other side of the highway, which means that the cars and trucks that go by interfere visually. There is no reverse shot, so through absence another waiting crowd is implied—the extradiegetic audience, us, waiting on the other side of the road for something to happen. The second shot of the film starts a secondary plot: at the market, a woman is accused of stealing and hurled into a van by a group of policemen. At the beginning of the sequence, the woman steps in front of a crowd all by herself. Everyone behind her forms a semicircle, waiting to see what will happen—this is the diegetic audience that yet again mirrors the real audience that watches the film. No one intervenes, no one says anything, and that level of passivity further underscores the role of the diegetic crowd. That mirroring effect is reinforced by the third shot, in which three policemen stand idly by a wall, presumably looking over at the same incident. The boy in the wheelchair who appears in *Le franc*, whose name ("Moussa") we finally learn, wheels himself into the shot and rotates the chair in such a way that he positions himself between the cops and the incident in the market. He puts his chin in his hand and becomes a spectator, too. Five cops who had arrived swiftly on the scene take the accused woman into custody. The camera tracks their movement and circles back to the diegetic audience, which remains impassive. Moussa advances his chair a little bit, shrinking the distance to the camera, as if to get into a better viewing position. A group of people, framed in a long shot, watches the same scene from an adjacent building. This is followed by what seems to be a point-of-view shot from inside an apartment and out the open window that faces the scene of the incident. But again the reverse shot is missing, so we cannot be certain who exactly is watching other than us, the real audience.

The movement from outside to the intimacy of an apartment announces that space will be limited in this film, that it will be constricted to a stage; the double frame of this problematic shot (the frame of the film and the frame of the window) suggests tight enclosure. The transition to a shot of the accused woman in prison, then, is flawless. Mambety moves to yet another private space and again forces the audience to maintain distance; prison bars separate the camera and the woman. She paces like a lion and whispers in Wolof: "Everyone's gone crazy in this country." In spite of her gesticulation, she does not yell, as she did in the market. As a matter of fact, the soundtrack goes quiet following her arrest. People watch the scene quietly, as well-behaved spectators should. There is no sound inside the apartment, and the accused woman behind bars speaks very softly but audibly—it is the whispering voice that marks the transition from interior to exterior, which Dolar calls "a zone of overlapping" (2006, 81). According to Dolar, whose work is closely related to Žižek's,[17] the voice exhibits an odd topology because it is caught in the gap between the inside and the outside, another fantastical gap, which it delineates: voice is "the very principle of division into interior and exterior" (2006, 71). The voice coming from inside one's body denotes the inside, while the outside is defined by the projection of the same voice into the world, a projection that cannot be controlled because the voice is "ephemeral, transient, incorporeal, ethereal" (ibid.). The madwoman's faint voice circumscribes the dialogue between interiority and exteriority in this eventful beginning.

From the ensuing silence and following the opening credits, the film introduces the main character, Sili. It is dawn and quite dark still, so the first few shots are visually pointless. Sili's small body takes shape from the obscurity; through the sound her crutches make, the spectator can determine that there is indeed someone in this darkness. A muffled song accompanies the click-clack of the crutches. It is the song of her grandmother, a song that will become the leitmotif of the film.[18] If in *Le franc* the aural return involved the voice of the imam, in this film it is the singing voice of the grandmother. Therefore, Sili is born almost literally from darkness and song—Chion's uterine night—and from the voice of the grandmother that pushes her forward.

From Sili's slow walk the film jumps into a close-up of a pair of rugged hands making gravel. The next shot backs up into a medium frame that shows the lower body of the same man. The camera tracks further back to reveal that it is an older man and almost immediately the scale of the frame changes again, this time into a long shot that shows the man sitting on a large pile of small rocks. A plane descends behind him and its sound meshes momentarily with the rhythmic sound of the hammer hitting rock. Modernity happens around the old man still stuck in a Sisyphean job. A few scenes later, a group of athletes runs by the old man, whose pile seems to have gotten bigger. New and old generations, modernity and tradition, have very little in common. The camera opens up a little bit and two establishing shots put the plane touching down in view, then the periphery of Dakar from where Sili begins her trip into the city.

The ubiquitous conflict between tradition and modernity in the film leads to an updated perspective on Louis Althusser's definition of ideology. Althusser improves on the Marxist idea of a dominant ideology by expanding the definition to "the imaginary relation of individuals to their real conditions of existence" (1971, 153). The theory of ideology (in short, a discourse that promotes false ideas about the political regime in which the subject lives) proposed by Althusser challenged Marxism, inasmuch as ideology was no longer framed on the basis of class struggle and it did not conceal the exploitative agreements on which class societies operated. As an alternative, Althusser proposed that ideology become synonymous with lived experience, meaning that ideology is born out of each individual's relationship with the world. This fits in perfectly with Mambety's film, which is part of the unfinished trilogy titled *Tales of Little People*. Senegal's new ideology builds up from the lower rungs of society instead of focusing on the upper classes. It also concentrates on individuals, the "little people," who live at the margins of society and who have had minimal impact on the social construction of the country.

Like Mambety, these marginalized people strongly oppose the system and the public institutions, and they have no faith in the current government, which makes Marxist discourse and Žižek's ideology impossible; for false consciousness to work, the people have to believe, to buy into the political structure. Again, the result of focusing on individuals is that ideology is built from the ground up; it begins with the smallest individual, and ideally, it would spread to an entire nation and then to an entire continent. Therefore, by way of Althusserian thought, a reversal of Marx's ruling-class ideology ("the ideas of the ruling class are in every epoch the ruling ideas," [1974, 64]) dominates this film; it is the idealistic beliefs of the poor and marginalized Sili that rule. Žižek agrees with Althusser up to a point, but to him we do not yet live in a postideological world, so some updates to the Althusser model are required. For example, one must replace the interpellation model of the policeman's (which like Lacan's mirror stage poses a problem of misrecognition) "Hey you there" with a larger signifier such as the Nation (another version of what Žižek calls the Big Other). Mambety adds another nuance to this new type of ideology: he advocates a return to the oral tradition of the country, which would allow the people to share their newly found sense of national identity on a very personal level, while embracing modern change and new forms of expression like a fairy-tale film.

It is through Sili that the director unveils his ideological fantasies. When Sili asks her friend why the people prefer the newspaper *Sud* to the one she sells, he answers that it is the paper of the people and that hers, *Soleil*, belongs to the government. Sili's unexpected response is that she will "stay with *Soleil*. That way, the government will get closer to the people." She innocently suggests that an ideological change is warranted. As Lieve Spaas remarks, "The optimism conveyed by the girl's victory over natural and social adversities may be read, on an idealistic level, as Mambety's dream for his country and his continent; a program promoting social equality, economic policies and a belief in change for Africa" (2000, 29). This girl is simultaneously real, someone from the slums of Dakar, and illusive in what she represents: a symbol for Senegal. The symbolism is sustained throughout the film, from the larger picture of Sili mirroring an entire nation (young and physically challenged) to such small details as the bag she carries around, which displays a large "S" on the side: S for Senegal of course, but also S/$ for Subject.

The mirroring effect between country and Sili brings Althusser back into the discussion. One of the theorist's more radical claims is that people acquire their identities even before being born because they are mirrored in preexisting ideologies (1971, 164). Sili is thus a perfect Althusserian subject trapped in a preestablished web of ideologies. Moreover, in her idealistic declaration that she would stick with *Soleil*, Sili also reveals herself as a political subject in the manner described by Žižek, who again challenges the Althusserien model of interpellation. According to Žižek, the subject does not turn around when called on simply because of that one authoritarian voice. Instead, the subject turns around because of an unconscious belief that the Law, the Big O Other, has access to what he or she had lost, to *jouissance*. Sili hopes to recapture what she had lost though her idealistic and unrealistic political allegiance.

The Sili-Senegal metaphor culminates in a surprising denouement in which the director's most important fantasy is finally voiced and traversed: the front page of the newspaper reads, "Africa Leaves the Franc Zone."[19] This headline is an obvious commentary on Senegal's financial dependency on France. The solution that the director proposes is that African countries assist one another, which is reflected in the characters' interactions. Even though Sili is extremely tough and proves she can overcome obstacles, neither she nor Senegal can manage on their own. Sili finds her sidekick in the character of Babou, a boy who helps her throughout the film and who validates the overall metaphor of the film. He represents another African country willing to work together and share resources. For her part, Sili divides her earnings among all the beggars in the street, Babou included, which overturns the Western model of capitalist competition and individuality in favor of a socialist sense of community.

Babou's most important role is that of protector. He takes it upon himself to shield Sili from a menacing band of young boys who try to put an end to her employment. The band has an authoritative leader who fittingly wears a Michael Jordan T-shirt. As one of the most recognizable figures in the world and at the peak of his dominance when the film was made,[20] Jordan embodies the capitalist values of the West. Like Lobster from the previous film, the young leader wears a baseball cap backward, which is an object fetish of the West. Wearing the cap backward was originally a defiant gesture, a social subversion by young African Americans, but it has now permeated all social strata. It is also a symbol of and for youth (Ross 1994, 228). In this film, the backward cap comes to represent the opposite of what it meant initially. If the baseball cap stands for the American lifestyle, then worn in this context by the young boy it represents a "cheap and stylish source of fantasies of Americanicity" (Ross 1994, 288). The cap is not a haphazard prop and the director carefully manipulates its placement. In the very first shot, and thus before we know what he is really up to, the young leader wears the baseball cap with the visor in the front. As he grows more callous, the cap changes positions, too. In the end, through the mise-en-scène association with the rogue boys, the West is reaffirmed as an antagonistic force.

The prevalence of newspapers in the film also underlines the Western presence in Senegal. The writing in the newspapers follows the Western norm, reading left to right. As explained before, Mambety often shoots in the opposite direction. For example, the fixed camera records the passing of a peasant pushing a cart from the right side of the frame. Once he exits to the left of the frame, the camera lingers for a few seconds on the open, empty field. Time dilates and the film captures that slower pace. Sili is also mostly shown moving from right to left, but her relationship to the newspaper is more complicated. At one point, her face is superimposed on the running print of the newspaper. One of the quintessential symbols of knowledge in the Western world, the printing press, is adorned with the face and voice of an illiterate Senegalese girl; written word and spoken word coexist briefly in the same visual. In her influential study of orality in the works of directors Dani Kouyaté and Mambety, Ann Elizabeth Willey hypothesizes that with this shot the director "coalesces the discourses of modernity, technology, tradition, and literacy" (2003, 83). Willey's reading is pertinent, but the character of Sili also operates as a means to bring people together, which goes beyond uniting conflicting discourses. Further tangling of Western and African values occurs on the soundtrack of the film, scored again by Mambety's brother, musician Wasis Diop. The thumping sound of traditional drums, the djembes, punctuates the sound of wind instruments performing elements of free jazz. It may be appropriate, then, to claim that sound can function as an ideological tool in *La petite vendeuse de soleil*. Several elements of this film intimate that the visual should be meshed with oral storytelling. The visual storytelling inherent in cinema merges with the oral tradition of the griot and with new aural heroes like the handicapped boy with a radio. The boy reinforces the notion of an aural/oral culture that is capable of subverting the domination of the image. Therefore, as it does in *Le franc*, sound assumes a more literal traveling quality, allowing technology and tradition to blend together and rearranging the space of the postcolonial city.

Sound also revitalizes the life of Sili's neighborhood. As the camera wanders about the neighborhood, various sounds or noises materialize on the soundtrack. Following Sili's footsteps and the echo of the crutches hitting the pavement, the song of the grandmother resumes and then Mambety sound bridges into an actual shot of her (see figure 18). The blind grandmother's song accompanies the rest of the sounds throughout the entire sequence, but at fluctuating levels of volume. As is evident from figure 18 as well, the shots focusing on the grandmother reveal the last stage of de-acousmatization: seeing the mouth. To Dolar, the wide-open mouth is a "gap, the crack, the hole, the cavity, the void" on the verge of which "the voice as a fetish object consolidates" (2006, 68–69). But to reiterate, the voice never fully returns. The fluctuations of volume produce more sonic rack focus effects; at moments the grandmother sounds very loud, and at other moments she is relegated to the back of the soundtrack. As a result of this effect the audience gets the feeling of moving about the neighborhood, when in fact the camera remains on Sili.

In addition to the cyclical, spectral soundtrack music, the film frequently returns to the image of Sili's grandmother, the blind clairvoyant. Her voice echoes throughout the neighborhood, and it dominates the aural space of the film as it embodies another acousmatic panopticon. Along with the acousmatic panopticon, the *caméra-flâneur* makes an appearance in this film, too. After Sili lands the job to sell *Soleil*, the city is first mapped visually. The entire neighborhood is shown in one establishing shot, while the voices of the children selling papers fill out the aural space. The camera is on the same bridge that crosses the main highway in *Badou Boy*, and without a defined point of view it moves left to reveal more of the neighborhood. The children sell papers in the middle of the highway and cars rapidly move on either side. The camera advances into a tighter frame on Sili, who is walking the streets and smiling because she has a job. The song of the grandmother appears on the soundtrack, without her being visible this time. Sili looks to her right and says, "Grandma! I'm selling the *Soleil* now," but there is no grandmother to her right and no match cut to prove otherwise. Her diegetic voice addresses the intradiegetic singing voice of the grandmother—Sili talks to the voice on the soundtrack.

Continuing to experiment with the source of sound, the filmmaker complements the grandmother's singing voice with the radio of the disabled boy.[21] The radio fuses voice and technology and allows sound to move about the community physically. Moussa's radio, which plays a popular tune, counterpoints the beautiful voice of the grandmother. As if realizing his mistake, he promptly turns the radio off, so that the voice of the grandmother can dominate the aural space once again. Then shouts of the boys who sell newspapers flood the soundtrack. Their voices are soon swallowed by the strong emergence of bagpipe music. The insertion of bagpipe music into the soundtrack seems egregious at first (like the saxophone in *Le franc*), but this artificial contrast is a noteworthy attempt to reconcile Western wind instruments with Senegalese music, which relies primarily on percussion. The aural intellectual montage fuses the two together on the soundtrack and creates a fleeting yet effective transnational musical mindscape.[22]

The oral elements of the film more forcefully suggest the reconciliation between a traditional oral culture, whose knowledge is often encapsulated in folk tales, and imminent technological development—rather than a complete abandonment of tradition. Sili's entire story presents itself as a fairy tale because her ideas are not anchored in reality. The film ends with a formula used in traditional Wolof fairy tales: "This tale is thrown in the sea,"[23] and even Sili's relationship with Babou brings forth an element of the fairy tale, given its very subtle romantic undercurrent. The two main characters, Sili and Babou Seck, are illiterate, but share a connection to spoken stories.[24] Although Babou cannot read, he carries around a book bearing a drawing of Leuk le Lièvre, canonical hero of West African folk tales. Charles Sugnet notes that this is a book cowritten by Senghor and Abdoulaye Sadji, *La Belle Histoire de Leuk-le-Lièvre* (1953), published by Hachette in Paris, and he points out the irony that Senghor's "policies failed to create an adequate school system" (2006, 1224). So when both Babou and Sili look inside the book, it is a seemingly futile gesture. However, Babou ends up *listening* to the story Sili tells him while holding on to the book. Willey understands that Mambety "suggests that the written version of the folktales that the children narrate to each other supplements the oral ones, does not replace them" (2003, 85). Sugnet also identifies this moment as a key episode that exposes Mambety's concern with primary orality (secondary orality is mediated by cinema) because the characters are in "possession of their Senegalese cultural patrimony . . . and know how to perform them [the stories] orally" (2006, 1230).

After Babou jumps in the water to retrieve Sili's crutch, the two characters retreat to a quiet spot, and she brings him back the book he had dropped. Babou asks Sili to sing a song and tell a story. In the story, which she had heard from her grandmother, Sili tells of the hare that is granted the title of smartest animal because he proves he is the youngest. He outsmarts all the other animals by yelling, "Make room, I'm about to be born," and the hopeful cry of an entire nation surfaces in his utterance. As she tells the story, though, the camera gets distracted and moves away from the characters in order to show branches rich with green fruit moving in the wind. The wind picks up considerably in volume. This is similar to the effect in *Le franc* in which Fall's song is accompanied by the growing noise of the wind. Nature's "wind" instrument contributes to forming a new aural space. As the audience listens to the voice of Sili, now the raconteuse, the griotte, it loses itself briefly in another time—*in illo tempore* of storytelling.

The telling of stories and the grandmother's constant singing reinforce Mambety's penchant for orality. The voice and the spoken word stimulate the birth of a new sense of national identity. The national identity built through song is made possible by an unlikely quality of the singing voice: "Singing blurs the word and makes it difficult to understand" (Dolar 2006, 30). The result is the creation of an expression beyond language, or a "highly sophisticated language" (Dolar 2006, 30). By telling stories through singing in this sophisticated language, the most impoverished Senegalese people who hail from the lowest social strata begin the process of self-interpellation, in yet another Althusserian connection. Althusser's example of interpellation from above leads to a recognition on the part of the person who is being addressed. That recognition and subsequent turning of the head contribute to the person's becoming a subject (1971, 168). Interpellation takes on varied nuances in the context of the black subject, according to Fanon. He offers a fascinating example of interpellation, in which a white child in the subway yells, "Look, a Negro!" (2008, 90–94). Fanon then proceeds to index the physical effects of those words on his body: "My body was returned to me spread-eagle, disjointed, redone, draped in mourning on this white winter's day. The Negro is an animal, the Negro is bad, the Negro is wicked, the negro is ugly; look, a Negro . . . the little white boy runs to his mother's arms: 'Maman, the Negro's going to eat me'" (2008, 93).[25]

The interpellation in Sili's case comes from a police officer. He becomes suspicious of the large banknote she had received from a businessman in exchange for all of her newspapers. The businessman is quite interesting, because he embodies the new bourgeoisie—he is the only character who speaks French in the film, and he is dressed in a fancy dark-blue suit. He pays ten thousand francs for the thirteen newspapers, but it is not a purely charitable act. He mentions Sili's grandmother, whom he calls "the prophet," and encourages Sili to buy some clothes.[26] As he takes the newspapers he reads a fictitious title, "Yaadikoone's son has escaped," which signals the extradiegetic importance of this character again. Sili reluctantly takes the cash, which she wants to break into smaller bills and coins. In response to the inquiries of the police officer (the money of the new bourgeoisie gets her in trouble), Sili very courageously demands that they go to the station. She leads the way as the policeman trails, suddenly hesitant. At the station, which features the same poster of Yaadikoone from *Le franc*, she speaks to the ranking officer and proves her innocence, but the entire episode is implausible. Sili shows a receipt for the newspapers, which she had signed with a picture of the sun. Nothing she says or does is questioned, and the officer—who sits throughout the scene projecting passivity—grants all of her wishes (he is a rather unusual fairy) including the release of the imprisoned woman who was yelling that she was innocent. The officer's compliance with all of Sili's demands is a fairy tale as it were—this would never happen in reality—but in the context of this film, ideology is reversed: it is the officers who heed the interpellation, and justice is no longer the prerogative of the upper class but is yielded by the "little people."

Successful in her defense, Sili breaks the bill and buys a parasol for her grandmother. From a corner, Moussa watches over the proceedings. As a matter of fact, he shows up magically where anything relevant happens (see figure 19). Medium close-up shots of the grandmother while she sings follow, and afterward Sili shares her change with everyone in the neighborhood including Babou, her new friend. The song slowly falls quiet, allowing for the clinking of the coins in everyone's hands to be heard. When Sili and Babou exit to the right of the frame, the grandmother's song increases in volume, effectively concluding the scene aurally. In the next scene, the film jumps temporally to Sili in a new yellow (like the sun) dress, dancing and leading her friends down the street to the rhythms of a popular song, which appears to be on the soundtrack. It is not entirely clear where the song comes from until Moussa reveals himself trailing the little group, and pressing stop on the boom box when they arrive at a table. He wants more money and the children pay up because they want more music. Sili puts on a pair of sunglasses with yellow frames—more sun-related motifs—and dances to the tune. In the original title of the movie, *La petite vendeuse de soleil*, the word "sun" is not capitalized, and it uses the preposition "de" ("of"), not "du" ("of the") as it would if "soleil" referred to the newspaper. This spelling cast ambiguity over the product that Sili sells. Along with the papers, she may be selling sun and happiness.

In the last episode, after the menacing boys get away with one of the crutches, Babou carries Sili on his back. They enter a hallway; while Sili keeps the book open, they walk toward the exit, toward the light of the street. The camera remains motionless and the soundtrack grows increasingly quiet until only Babou's steps can be heard. The children of the street, lined up in this hallway, move outward as if to make more room for the two. When almost everyone else disappears from the shot, a male voice-over, likely Mambety's, announces that this tale is thrown to the sea, but he does not finish the formula. Instead, it is Sili's voice that does: "the first to breathe it will go to heaven." It is a remarkable shift from the dominance of the male narrative voice to that of the female heroine of the film. Unlike Hollywood in Silverman's study, here the female voice is placed front and center. Sili first superimposes her face on the newspaper while declaring her aptitude for doing the same type of work as the men (that is, boys). At the end of the film she also supplants the narrative voice of the griot, of the male voice-over, and of the director. Furthermore, the diegetic character switches roles to a nondiegetic part. This shift is usually effectuated in the opposite direction: a voice-over begins and eventually its diegetic source is revealed (or, as is often the case, it remains purely nondiegetic). Sili breaks the rules and leaves the diegesis to take over the acousmatic qualities of the voice-over.

Sonic Space and the Fourth Wall

It has been established that a separation of sound and image occurs quite frequently in the films of Mambety and that it often causes the audience, suddenly aware of the cinematic act, to detach itself from the action on the screen. It has also been shown that in Mambety's hands sound is not just a technique reminiscent of Godard's practices, but a storytelling tool that yields greater narrative power than the visual, recalibrating the relationship between the two. But does sound ever become entirely independent of the image? According to Deleuze's argument in *Cinema 2* (1989), sound initially emerges from the image, but then splits and becomes its own entity and thus produces the sound-image. Deleuze builds his theory on analyses of silent cinema and looks at the progression of sound in film from a historical perspective: "In contrast to the intertitle, which was an image other than the visual image, the talkie, the sound films are heard, but as *a new dimension of the visual image, a new component*" (226). The progression he analyzes has its basis in the fact that the intertitle functions as another type of image since it is seen. In silent films everything was inconspicuously in front of the audience. What talkies introduced was a modification of the visual image, or rather of our perception of the visual image; we suddenly see something that was not there before, available for us through the added act of hearing. Sound, as a component of the image, makes something else visible in that same image. In Deleuze's words, "when speech makes itself heard, it is as if it makes something new visible, and the visible image, de-naturalized, begins to become readable in turn, *as* something visible or visual" (229). And then Deleuze arrives at the following conclusion: "instead of a seen image and a read speech, the speech-act becomes visible at the same time as it makes itself heard, but also the visual image becomes legible as such, as visual image in which the speech-act is inserted as a component" (234). The two elements can be taken separately or as a whole, but can also be substituted for one another.

Deleuze's argument advances and discusses the filling of that missing dimension in cinema, the out-of-field space. To him, sound in whatever form was meant to fill the out-of-field of the image, which probably refers to whatever the image could not project onto the space between the audience and the theater. He also contends that interruptions and cuts actually contribute to the sustaining of a continuous, coherent space:

> When cinema became talkie, the out-of-field seems to have initially found a confirmation of its two aspects: first, noises and voices could have a source external to the visual image; secondly, a voice or a piece of music could show the changing whole, behind or beyond the visual image. Hence the notion of "voice-off" as sound expression of the out-of-field. But if we ask in what condition cinema draws out the consequences of the talkie, and so becomes truly talking, everything is inverted; this is when the sound itself becomes the object of a specific framing which *imposes an interstice* with the visual framing. The notion of voice-off tends to disappear in favor of a difference between what is seen and what is heard. . . . Interstices proliferate everywhere, in the visual image, in the sound image, between the sound image and the visual image. That is not to say that the discontinuous prevails over the continuous. On the contrary, the cuts or breaks in cinema have always formed the power of the continuous. (Deleuze 1989, 180–181)

Even though those breaks emphasize the existence of a continuum, they also generate the sound-image. This is the natural progression; sound eventually garners independence from the image, "the sound-image is born, in its very break, from its break with the visual image" (Deleuze 1989, 251). The result is that there is always a relationship between sound and image, but that does not mean that this association has to be smooth. As a matter of fact, Deleuze calls attention to the break between the two, suggesting that an "irrational cut" takes place. Many recent critics, including Chion, think that the "irrational cut" may create an artistic effect based on that precise opposition. This is an audiovisual counterpoint, in which a given cinematic moment allows the image and the sound it features to carry opposing ideas that lead to separate signifieds.

Deleuze's immersion in cinema sound is even clearer when he tackles sound in modern cinema: "The speech-act is no longer inserted in the linkage of actions and reactions, and does not reveal a web of interactions any more. It turns in on itself; it is no longer a dependent or something which is part of the visual image; it becomes a completely separate sound image" (1989, 243). The sound turning in on itself is analogous to the folding and unfolding of the infinite fold as characterized by Leibniz and Deleuze. Permutations of sound generate multiple sounds that, just like the fold, split and develop to infinity. Sound in this instance functions like an aural fold,[27] because it fills out the cinematic and theatrical space (i.e., the space in the actual theater) through a continuous developing motion. In doing so, it establishes the space of the fourth wall as an unending interaction between the audience and the projection on screen. Moreover, the cinematic/

diegetic sound must generate a fantasy space imagined by both audience and actors. Among the many experiments with sound, it is this interaction that most fuels Mambety's innovative, revolutionary type of cinema.

The aural fold, the sound that comes from the screen toward the audience, meshes with the sounds coming from the audience and creates a spatial continuum, like the unified space of the city produced by the acousmatic panopticon. The voice of the grandmother first unifies the diegetic space of the film, and then physically unites screen and audience. The movement of the Deleuzian folds between the Leibniz Baroque house levels closely approximates this movement of sound. On a literal level there is physical evidence of the Baroque and of its folds on the first floor, and on the second floor there is a mental landscape, an abstraction of the Baroque. The infinite fold moves continuously between the two levels, but crucially it is also divided between the two, so it also expands on each floor. The constant movement within each floor, and between the two floors, completely fills up the space of the house. There is no void in the Leibniz Baroque house, because "folds are always full" (Deleuze 1992, 36). According to this model, the audience and the screen are placed on the two separate levels. The infinite interaction between the two finds its best form in the aural, not the visual. Because sound essentially disconnects from the screen in the auditorium during a film screening, the distance between spectator and the cinematic text is considerably shrunk. Noises and silences especially create an interactive bridge between the two spaces in the same way that the Baroque house levels communicate.

The space between the audience and the screen is further complicated by advancements in technology, such as Dolby sound: "Dolby . . . creates a space with fluid borders, a sort of superscreen enveloping the screen—the superfield" (Chion 1999, 69), and to the point about sound having a physical aspect, Dolby introduces "an acute feeling of the materiality of things and beings" (Chion 1999, 155). While these technical advancements in sound delivery have not influenced or shaped cinema in Dakar, Dolby does provide us with an interesting paradox concerning silence and the audience's reactions to it: "So Dolby cinema introduced a new expressive element: the silence of the loudspeakers, as well as the audience's attentive silence, which is its consequence. Every instance of silence is disarming since it seems to expose our faculty of hearing; it's as if a giant ear were turned toward us ready to pick up the tiniest sounds we make. We are no longer just listening to the film; we are being listened by it" (Chion 2009, 148).

Silence is also an incarnation of the *objet petit a*. When a soundtrack suddenly goes quiet, the film begs for more attention from the viewers, who wonder if something is missing. As a courtesy, an audience is supposed to remain quiet during a screening; that silence can be exacerbated by the silence of the loudspeakers. Absolute silence is impossible, though, because people shift their weight in the seats, eat, cough, and so on. These natural noises are covered by the noise coming from the speakers in the auditorium. The sound and noises of the film converge with the noises of the audience. In Senegal, audiences tend to be much more raucous than their Western counterparts. Going to the movies is more of a social activity and an opportunity to express oneself and one's opinions about the film on screen. If the intertitle and the sound could each bring out something previously invisible in the image, as Deleuze claims, why could not the same phenomenon apply for a noisy audience? This detail is crucial to our understanding of the fourth-wall space in African films, as the aural space that forms around the fourth wall is a space of clashing sounds from the screen and from the audience.

In their article "The Noises of Spectators, or the Spectator as Additive to the Spectacle," Jean Châteauvert and André Gaudreault discuss what the spectators bring to the aural space of the theater. Their claim is that spectatorial noise contributes to the "structuration of the sound space" (2001, 184). Through a historical approach, the two theorists uncover the process by which spectators went from being contributors to the aural space (e.g., interacting with the lecturer by the screen, inopportune noises, applause, laughter), to being quiet.[28] The sound space went from being unstructured—anyone could do or say anything while in the audience—to structured, which more or less meant that the audience was to be silent. And thus "the regime of film consumption may have let the spectator move imperceptibly from a *solidary* to a *solitary* mode of consumption" (Châteauvert and Gaudreault 2001, 190). The problem is that no audience follows the silence rule completely. If indeed there was a time when the sound space of the theater was a solidary enterprise—containing simultaneous sounds from the screen, the microphones, the music, the lecturer, and the spectators—there must be traces of that in today's African cinema.

Paul Hegarty's book *Noise/Music: A History* (2007) explores the relationship between the sounds of the audience and the sounds coming from an orchestra, which can be extrapolated to a screen. Hegarty considers alternative pieces of music that have challenged the classical understanding of what music should be or sound like. Yves Klein's *Monotone Symphony* is a forty-minute piece that consists of a single twenty-minute sustained chord followed by a twenty-minute silence. John Cage's 4'33" requires that the performer be on stage and remain absolutely quiet for the entire duration (Hegarty 2007, 25–26). Hegarty's conclusion is that music itself can be composed by incidental sounds, the sounds heard from the audience. In the case of a film, the spatial continuum between screen and audience comes to life through a meshing of the sounds, especially the silences, coming from both sides. In the context of African film, this spatial continuum even runs the risk of being overtaken by the voices of and from the audience.

Details of what happens on screen and on the soundtrack may easily be missed by the loud, distracted audience, allowing for the possibility that the meaning of the film and of the soundtrack change.

So the distance between spectator and the cinematic text is considerably shortened, just like the fantastical gap on the soundtrack. Even if the silence is not complete, a unifying aural effect occurs. There are examples in *La petite vendeuse*: the morning when Sili leaves the village and, even more clearly, when the accused woman whispers and gesticulates her frustration behind bars. Also, if Godard can serve as an example one last time, there are several moments when the whispering voice-over of the French auteur makes it almost impossible to discern what is being said. Imagine the spectators in the audience, frustrated that they cannot understand what the characters are saying. The natural reaction would be to pay more attention, to be drawn even deeper into the diegesis. Godard does not allow the spectator to take full advantage of the aural space of the theater—the spectator must work for that privilege. This effect is completely lost to foreign audiences who watch the films in a theater or on a DVD. The reason is the subtitles (likewise, the words of the madwoman are made known through translation, even though they are whispered almost imperceptibly). It becomes less crucial to hear what the characters say when one can simply read the dialogue. But how the subtitles and titles for the hearing impaired alter the cinematic experience is a topic for another project.

Figure 1. Anta and the neighborhood soundscape.
Touki Bouki, *Trigon Film, Senegal, 1973*.

Figure 2. High-angle shot: Anta and Mory on a cliff.
Touki Bouki, *Trigon Film, Senegal, 1973*.

Figure 3. Gorée Island: spectral presence.
Touki Bouki, *Trigon Film, Senegal, 1973*.

Figure 4. Metro map.
Contras' City, *Studio Kankourama, Senegal, 1968*.

Figure 5. Acousmatic panopticon: loudspeaker.
Contras' City, *Studio Kankourama, Senegal, 1968.*

Figure 6. Kermel Market.
Contras' City, *Studio Kankourama, Senegal, 1968.*

Figure 7. Diegetic kora / extradiegetic camera.
Badou Boy, *Studio Kankourama, Senegal, 1970.*

Figure 8. Diegetic camera.
Badou Boy, *Studio Kankourama, Senegal, 1970.*

Figure 9. Diegetic kora from previously diegetic camera.
Badou Boy, *Studio Kankourama*, Senegal, 1970.

Figure 10. Pointing to the panoptic island.
Hyènes, *ADR Productions/Maag Daan, Senegal/Switzerland, 1992*.

Figure 11. Panoptic island at magic hour.
Hyènes, *ADR Productions/Maag Daan, Senegal/Switzerland, 1992.*

Figure 12. Draman's disappearance; "island" cloth.
Hyènes, *ADR Productions/Maag Daan, Senegal/Switzerland, 1992.*

Figure 13. Draman's bar; Coke crates, warrior poster.
Hyènes, *ADR Productions/Maag Daan, Senegal/Switzerland, 1992.*

Figure 14. Dancing woman.
Hyènes, *ADR Productions/Maag Daan, Senegal/Switzerland, 1992.*

Figure 15. *Le franc*; Marigo diagonal.
Le franc, *Waka Films, Senegal, 1994.*

Figure 16. Kermel Market ruins.
Le franc, *Waka Films, Senegal, 1994.*

Figure 17. *Le franc*; Yaadikoone.
Le franc, *Waka Films, Senegal, 1994.*

Figure 18. The blind grandmother sings.
La petite vendeuse de soleil, *Waka Films, Senegal, 1998.*

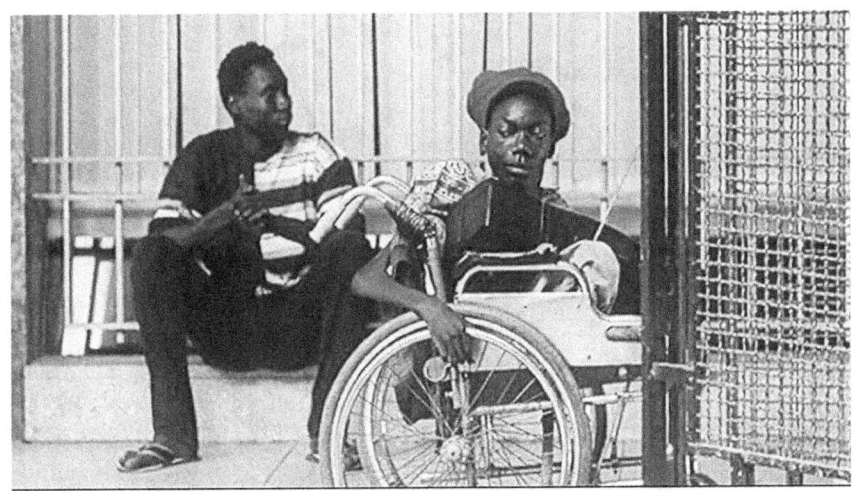

Figure 19. Moussa, the witness.
La petite vendeuse de soleil, *Waka Films, Senegal, 1998*.

Conclusion
Current Contexts and Legacies

It has been more than fifteen years since Mambety's untimely death and his last feature. Hopefully the previous pages have shown that his six fictional features are in dialogue, that they complete each other in order to create a unified narrative space, and that they answer aesthetic questions posed early on in the director's career, as well as bigger-picture questions: What is cinema? What is Senegalese cinema? What is Mambetian cinema? When one considers these films as a cohesive narrative, one may discover that the conversations between them yield a sort of social network that offers intriguing answers to the questions above. Through this network, knowingly or unknowingly, Mambety carves his niche in the history of global cinema.

Several theorists, such as Lieve Spaas, have already hailed him as "original" (2000, 172). Moreover, Spaas declares that "Mambety has found a cinematic language hitherto unknown to African cinema that is indisputably his own" (182) but does not explain unequivocally what that cinematic language is. What is without doubt, however, is that both the originality and the personal cinematic language emerge mainly through the treatment of sound. It would be too reductive to call Mambety's cinema an aural cinema. Certainly there has been a transition from the traditional oral culture to the written (in which, to reiterate, Senghor, the writer and the politician, played a large role), and then to cinema. But the origins of cinema are found on the side of the colonizer, in the West, which is why the infusion of the aural in Mambety's cinema alters how one should understand his particular brand of postcolonial cinema. It is not necessarily groundbreaking—other cinema traditions and auteurs have used sound to counter the classical rules of cinema—but it does not need to be groundbreaking. It just needs to add enough nuances so that new cinematic forms may reveal themselves. Cinema does not and did not need to be reinvented in Africa, or Senegal, or by Mambety. It just needed to adjust to the sociocultural context they share. As a result, that new form of postcolonial cinema affects the wider concept of cinema from within. And no other director in postcolonial cinema, the great Sembène included, has done so more powerfully than in these six films.

This study employs several terms to describe Mambety's assiduous ways of enhancing the presence of the aural, its narrative role, and its capacity to generate new spaces and new maps: "sonic rack focus," "sonic jump cut," "aural dismemberment," "*caméra-flâneur*," and the "acousmatic panopticon." These terms express the travels of sound in accurate cinematic language, because sound does move. And as sound moves, it displaces our perception of physical and visual spaces. Numerous displacements occur in these films, as sound bends, breaks, resurfaces, splits, and spills onto endless narrative planes. In spite of the substantial number of Western theorists who have been increasingly concerned with issues of sound during the last decades, through the continuing influence of thinkers such as Lacan and Foucault, the Occident and its thought remain strongly connected to the act of seeing, to the eye, and particularly to the eye of the camera. Though always present explicitly or implicitly, the aural has often been pushed to the background and made into a construct that could emphasize but not necessarily supplant the visual. In the Western world, the aural/oral has too often been reductively associated with African arts and storytelling. This segregation—visual/written–Occident, aural/oral–Orient—continues the orientalist traits exposed by Said, to which even I may have fallen victim. Like the characters who speak with an accent (the policeman from *Badou Boy*, for example), who cannot fully appropriate the French language, Mambety films the visual with an accent—a nod to Godard here, another to Eisenstein over there, shades of Brecht and Artaud, and so on. However, in each case the goal is misplaced; the appropriation of the French language and space should not be a goal at all. Instead it is the appropriation of one's own language and space that is important and that should not be negotiated through the colonizer's perspective. Mambety's filmic language moves well beyond these visual accents to approach and then appropriate cinema itself through his own language and space. Sound allows the virtuoso director to do exactly this, to articulate creative thought in a way that is closer to African expression and that does not completely erase the relevance of the visual. In other words, there is no segregation, just a frequent reversal in which the aural retains a primary narrative role and the visual serves as a proponent, not as an inhibitor.

Unfortunately, this particular aesthetic and Senegalese cinema as a whole have not taken off as envisioned and hoped by Mambety; but neither have they regressed. The same year as Mambety's last film, Safi Faye made her chef-d'oeuvre, *Mossane*, a film that advances Mambety's penchant for the female voice. Sembène made two more films before his death, *Faat Kiné* (2000) and *Moolaadé*

(2004), which deal mostly with social issues but also with fragmentation of space and tangentially even the aural, such as using the radio as a sonic marker. But Faye and Sembène are of Mambety's generation, the so-called pioneers of African cinema. Among the new voices of Senegalese cinema, Moussa Touré stands tall. He is particularly relevant because of two well-rounded films: *TGV* (1997) and *La pirogue* (2013). In these, Touré, currently the strongest directorial voice in Senegal, also deals with the problematic postcolonial space that continues to be a relevant sociocultural issue. So what has happened to Mambety's legacy and identity? More accurately what *is* his legacy?[1]

In 1983, Tunisian filmmaker Férid Boughedir made a landmark documentary, *Caméra d'Afrique*, which aimed to discuss the question of identity while raising awareness about several film productions of the previous twenty years.[2] The film opens with Mauritanian filmmaker Med Hondo, who offers his musings on the question of what cinema is. Hondo's question—What is cinema *to us*?—is much more honed than it was for Bazin: What is cinema to us Others, nonoccidentals? Hondo explains that because Western man invented cinema, it belongs logically to the Occidentals, the "toubabs" (white men, in Wolof). As a result, Hondo warns of a new type of colonization that comes from the monopoly of conventional Western cinema in African theaters and infiltrates the culture. The solution is that the African needs to be a producer of cinema, not just a consumer. He would revisit his ideas in an article published online by *Jump Cut*:

> Film plays a major role in building peoples' consciousness. Cinema is the mechanism *par excellence* for penetrating the minds of our peoples, influencing their everyday social behavior, directing them, and diverting them from their historic national responsibilities. It imposes alien and insidious models and references, and without apparent constraint encourages our people to adopt modes of behavior and communication based on the dominant ideologies....
>
> Dominant imperialism seeks to prevent portraying African and Arab values to other nations. Were they to appreciate our values and behavior they might respond positively to us. They believe themselves "superior" to us, to our peoples' roles in world history. We are not proposing isolation, closing our frontiers to all Western film, nor any protectionism separating us from the rest of the world. We wish to survive, develop, and participate as sovereign peoples in our own specific cultural fields and to fulfill our responsibilities in a world from which we are now excluded. (1986)

Hondo and Boughedir both speak to Africa's need for a strong cinema. Cinema is an integral part of the contemporary culture and it must develop. Making an effort to sustain this development would yield a more coherent Africa in which the filmmaker can find an identity: "Show what Africa is" (Hondo 1986). Oddly, this suggests that the identity of filmmakers be tied together by one coherent aesthetic, which may in fact be detrimental to the development of individual artistic capabilities. The challenging material dimension of cinema in Africa has long hindered these capabilities. Moreover, as James Genova points out in his careful examination of the historical conditions from which African films emerged, materialism is "a key component in the practices of early West African filmmaking. The representations of and directed at Africa/Africans during the colonial period were connected to a specific set of material relations that structured a system of Western dominance exploiting Africa (and other colonized parts of the world) for the further enrichment and development of the ruling capitalist class in Europe and North America.... Systems of representation correspond to their material conditions of production and are, as such, grounded in the historical moment of their manufacture" (2013, 15).[3] In line with the subversive vein of African cinema, African directors have made a conscientious effort—one that became a symbol of resistance—to limit the influx of production money from the West,[4] and "what they lacked in material they compensated for with vision and tenacity" (Genova 2013, 74).

Another obstacle is that the African director's identity must lie beyond the multifaceted meaning of the epithet "griot." Many directors have called themselves or have been given this appellation by theorists. Melissa Thackway remarks, "I personally see the griot as a communicator who is losing his touch. He has been left behind by modern modes of communication. There are all kinds of media that directly penetrate people's own homes and the griot can't keep up. It is therefore necessary to use these same media to be heard.... But the griot needs to be listened to. Today, griots can use film to reappropriate the word" (2003, 194). The reappropriation of the word might not be needed, but perhaps placing the word in a context—sound or soundtrack—that is more conducive to maintaining its original ontological values is. Only Mambety clearly makes a sustained effort to rely on the narrative powers of sound. The insistence on finding alternative ways to tell stories concurrently shows that Mambety was keen on using the cinema of the toubab but that he also did enough to change storytelling to make it his alone. In doing so, the director drives the postcolonial conversation forward because of the unified aural space that he seeks to construct. On the one hand, this aural space enhances the vivacity of the visual African narrative; on the other hand, it offers an alternative, an equally vibrant storytelling mechanism. In other words, Mambety employs sound to arrive at the same unified African space that his contemporaries sought and expressed in other ways (e.g., Sembène's undivided map behind Rama or Hondo's merging values and behaviors).

Moving on to the period since Mambety's death, it may be worth looking briefly at some of these more recent films. Safi Faye's last film, *Mossane*, came out about the same time as Mambety's last. Before that Faye had been mostly known for her ethnographic early films, for having worked with Jean Rouch, and for the quasi documentaries *Kaddu beykat* (*The Farmer's Voice*) (1975) and *Fad'jal* (1979). Both these films paved the way for the more polished and fictional *Mossane*. In *Kaddu beykat* and *Fad'jal*, villagers speak to the camera, as the titles imply ("voice" appears in the first and the second bears the name of Faye's native village), so for the most part Faye's cinema still was a cinema of the scopic—looking into the camera, witnessing, and revealing truths. Nevertheless, Faye also shows women singing as they work the field, and she lends her voice to the soundtrack in a Welles-like dominating and authorial gesture. In the case of *Mossane*, though, the shift to the aural is much more incisive. Narrative songs on the soundtrack accompany the ceremonies witnessed visually (sacrifices, wedding, burial), and throughout the film the choir is made up entirely of female voices. The all-female choir stresses the importance of the female voice, which normally is not given authority in classical cinema, as Silverman has instructed us. A traditional voice-over has more diegetic power, but the song is one of the oral ways in which African stories have been passed down from generation to generation. Faye subverts the domination of the male voice by constantly turning to female voices and focusing on a collective of griottes. The voice and story of the main character, Mossane, are supported and built up by the ethereal voices on the soundtrack. The result is that the voice of the young daughter is shaped by the female voices coming from an unknown, nondiegetic source beyond the screen. These acousmatic voices dominate the aural space of the film, such as the voice of Sili's grandmother, and suggest a reversal of power in the male-centric politics of gender.

The film makes use of several classical conflicts: the conflict between generations and that between tradition and the desire for emancipation and sexual freedom. The preservation of local values is important, but something has to change about the way women are treated. It is in this disparity that the work of Faye echoes that of Sembène and Mambety—they all understand the importance of tradition, of preserving one's roots, but they are also aware that many changes and adjustments are needed. However, "tradition" here is understood from the perspective of the local filmmaker, not what we Westerners deem "traditional": "The very notion of tradition is a concoction of modernism; the attempt to validate African authenticity, or traditional identity, is a reaction to western domination and is betrayed by its dependence on western epistemological tools, western categories of knowledge" (Harrow 2007, 27). African cinema, then, has to become the fundamental tool for harmonizing the old with the new from the local, rightful perspective.

Sembène's last two films are subtle and subdued in their use of sound, which is in line with the rest of his aesthetic career. He preferred visual narrative fluidity, which meant frequent use of fixed shots and long takes. According to Françoise Pfaff, he "favors long shots, panoramic shots, and eye-level shots (in rural areas), while in urban settings he uses more close-ups, medium shots, and more sophisticated camera and lens movement, as well as contrasting shots with varied angles to delineate his protagonists' conflicts in unfamiliar territory" (1984, 50). These conflicts are exacerbated when the protagonists find themselves in the animated city—the camera in *Faat Kiné* breaks up the urban space into segments—but these are not necessarily defining traits only for Sembène's characters. Mambety's Badou, Mory, and Marigo face alienation in the urban environment, too. For both directors the individual takes shape in the middle of this fragmentation, in the public sphere. This idea closely follows Frantz Fanon's view that the individual, the postcolonial subject, has been forced to close himself or herself within his or her own subjectivity (1968, 47). To offset the negative effects of this limitation, the individual must contribute to the conception of a collective and public subjectivity, and fight an identity problem posed by colonialism: "Because it is a systematic negation of the other person and a furious determination to deny the other person all attributes of humanity, colonialism forces the people it dominates to ask themselves the question constantly: 'In reality, who am I?'" (Fanon 1968, 250).

Faat Kiné answers that question from the perspective of the modern Senegalese woman, whom Mambety never got a chance to investigate adequately (more precisely, he did not investigate "real" female characters, inasmuch as both of his later heroines, Ramatou and Sili, have an overriding allegorical bent). Aurally the film features a radio, and as in Varda's and Godard's films the characters are oblivious to the message coming from it. The voice on the radio discusses the elections of 1999 (the film came out in 2000 when President Abdoulaye Wade's term began, marking an important political shift followed by more disappointment). The radio plays a role in *Moolaadé*, too, although in this instance the women of the village are forced by the male leaders to gather all their radios in the middle of the village where they are burned. The shift from the expansive urban to the limiting rural is underlined because the burning of the radios means that the village will be cut off from the rest of the world. Yet in *Faat Kiné*, no one even listens to the news in Kiné's car, so people are cut off from reality in the city as well. The value of these two films lies more with the female postcolonial subject than it does with the larger idea of postcolonial (aural) space. Kiné is no longer the classical cinema trophy, the object of desire. Instead she is the one who makes all the decisions. She is a businesswoman who owns her own gas station, who is autonomous in her relationships with men (multiple men in fact), and who takes lavish lunches with her friends during which they talk freely about sex, HIV, condoms, and even Viagra. It is *Sex and the City*, the Dakar version. Like the characters of the famous

American series, Kiné represents the modern woman who is liberated and emancipated sexually and socially.

Moussa Touré follows in the footsteps of Sembène for whom he worked as an electrician (Diawara 2010, 316). Like Sembène, Touré seems much less interested in form than in content. His films, beginning with *Toubab Bi* (1991), which follows two young men's voyage in Europe, explore the social relations between France and its old colony. In *TGV* (1997), the filmmaker tracks those relations in the limiting space of a bus in which he places a heterogeneous group of people—a microcosm of society that mirrors Guy de Maupassant's short story *Boule de suif* (1880). The same logic and theme apply to *La pirogue* (2013), in which the microcosm of society is placed on a boat rather than a bus. Space is a constant theme and it is always diminished. Touré has been vocal about not desiring to be categorized or even included in a political conversation (Diawara 2010, 317). It is difficult to escape these links: during the 2013 Panafrican Film and Television Festival of Ouagadougou (FESPACO), he declared that his latest film is "a political film. I slap those who govern us, so that they will realize that they have given up"[5] (Forster 2013).

La pirogue follows a mixed group of Senegalese men and one woman who attempt to reach the coast of Spain in a large pirogue. Their attempt fails, but what is striking is that the ideas of escaping Senegal and searching for the elusive Eldorado are still alive and relevant more than fifty years after independence. The Spanish frontier police send the two main characters, who are brothers, home. Their return to the family, to the core values, hints subtly at a positive outlook. But it is just that, a hint. The pirogue is a vessel that is all too similar metaphorically to the boats that carried slaves to the Caribbean. Most people who attempt to cross over to Europe do not make it alive in the tumultuous waters of the Atlantic, just as they did not survive the Atlantic crossing during colonial times. Moreover, this boat harbors the passengers in its hold, its belly—"*la cale*" in French—which is the metaphorical place of birth for (contemporary) slaves and manufactured subjectivities. The creaking noises of the *Ancerville* from *Touki Bouki* echo this monstrous belly whose aural specter perhaps convinces Mory not to embark. It is slavery, but in a new form. This was the case in 1973 for Mambety, and it is the same for Touré and his characters who are still disillusioned by their quest in 2013.

It is surprising to discover to what extent the characters of Touré's film feel alienated from their original space, and more importantly from their projected space of freedom, the space of the pirogue. They all become aware of how badly they fit within that nauseating space and of the poisonous alienation that creeps into their consciousness. Ann Willey discusses alienation in terms of a binary relationship between tradition and modernity: "The form that alienation takes in Africa is marked specifically by the difference between 'tradition' and 'technology'; the West's technological and scientific modernity is 'other' to Africa's tradition" (Willey 2003, 74). Fanon, too, considers the recognition (and implicit acceptance) of alienation as a major step toward the cultural emancipation of a colonized country (1968, 226–227). Fanon continues his argument to claim that this step is marked by an "occult instability" (227), which returns us to the metaphor of the pirogue. The passengers on the boat are first of all unbalanced physically because they are not used to being at sea—they are literally sick—and later on because the boat itself drifts aimlessly. They are lost physically and emotionally. In Touré's vision, the dream of Eldorado is still alive in the African consciousness even in the twenty-first century. The postcolonial subject is still trying to find himself or herself, but suddenly it no longer seems a viable possibility. Identity is drifting aimlessly just like the boat.

Touré's space, already reduced, is even further restricted through cinematic artifice; the camera limits itself to close-ups during the last few episodes on the boat. This choice restricts what the audience can see and further imprisons the characters in an atrophying space. Yet the sound escapes the confines with which the visual complies. The audience can still hear the thoughts of all the characters in voice-over. The voice-over jumps from one character to another (according to classical rules, there should only be one narrative voice-over). In this important scene, Touré allows several characters to speak (in voice-over) and the result is that of a common subjectivity. It would be worth pursuing the metaphor of the voice-over in order to remark that changing the source of interior sound suggests the impossibility of a real subjectivity, one that is fixed and not fluid. In short, via the aural Touré presents the birth of a new version of postcolonial identity, a common one, impossible to control and increasingly adrift. The multiple voices on the soundtrack split from the bodies, their sources, and unite on the soundtrack to suggest, just as with Mambety's acousmatic panopticon, that there is one space inherently owned by the postcolonial subjects on the boat—it is not the boat itself, not the ocean, certainly not Europe, but simply the soundscape. The shifting, wobbly identity of the people on the boat is akin to that of African cinema: this instability may offer the beginning of an answer to one of the ongoing debates on African film that issues from the ever-necessary desire to catalog it historically and aesthetically.

Where does African cinema fit? In the last part of *Postcolonial African Cinema*, Harrow argues it is postmodern, using Mambety's documentary *Parlons grand-mère* as an example. This film follows the filming of Burkinabe director Idrissa Ouédraogo's second feature, *Yaaba* (1989). A wonderful play on the contrasts and similarities between the diegetic and the nondiegetic occurs in this film because the subject of the documentary, its diegesis, is in fact the diegesis of the fictional film. As Harrow explains, "The diegetic world is, in a sense, not the world of the *story* of *Yaaba*, but of the *film* of *Yaaba*, and the extradiegetic world is that of the *filming* of *Yaaba*" (2007, 219).[6] In the next couple of pages, Harrow shifts his attention to the role of the sound that facilitates the "dissolve of inside/outside boundaries" (2007, 221), and that then "can only be called postmodern" (ibid.). In addition to a postmodern tendency that "underlines the relationship between power and knowledge," Murphy and Williams also see modernist and oral traces in Mambety's work (2007, 97);[7] furthermore, his cinema "reflects both the utopian and the dystopian nature of modernity" (104). Given that the modern, the postmodern, and the postcolonial all relate to Mambety's cinema, Murphy and Williams have smartly proposed the term "humanism" as a hint of a solution to the never-ending conversation on the modern and the postmodern: "As the films of Djibril Diop Mambety illustrate, the cinematic exploration of what it means to be human in postcolonial Africa might just help us to break out of endless terminological debates about the modern, the postmodern and the postcolonial" (109).

Yet the common humanity of the characters in these films is challenged by the fact that African cinema offers all types of Other—a symptom of modernity—with an emphasis on the colonized as Other and on the woman as an Other of the Other to the colonizer and to the colonized male. Kenneth Harrow has recently proposed a new perspective on the idea of the Other. In a series of university-hosted talks, Harrow posits that the new Other in African cinema is actually African cinema itself. His conversation stems from Manthia Diawara's problematic use of the word "authentic." Harrow claims that African cinema no longer sets itself up as Other to the European auteurist tradition or to Hollywood. Instead, it opposes and attempts to remove itself from "Sembène's specter" (Harrow 2014). I believe the "specter" materializes in two ways: in Sembène's construction of the first paradigm of African cinema (content over form, linearity, etc.) and in his international fame, which will be difficult to match. However, the paradigm-shifting opposition to Sembène started contemporaneously with Mambety and his visual and aural experimentation. In fact, the issue of authenticity may take on new and important aspects when viewed from the perspective of sound. In the last four pages of *Postcolonial African Cinema*, Harrow begins to think about the role of sound. He hints at Chion's *acousmêtre* and at the fused aural space of the documentary by observing, and repeating three times, that "the music never stops" (2007, 223). But these thoughts remain at an exploratory stage, an open end to build on, which is hopefully part of what this study accomplishes.

By way of conclusion, I would like to look very briefly at the recent work of two new female Senegalese directors. *Deweneti* (2006) is a short film made by Dyana Gaye that encompasses several themes and motifs dear to Mambety in fifteen minutes. It centers on a little boy, Ousmane, who begs in the streets of Dakar. He convinces people to give him money because of his charm and because he promises to pray for them. The plot reveals that he is one of those children who beg for a "master," a marabout who teaches the Qur'an but who ultimately is only interested in his own comfort (this one wants to save enough to make his pilgrimage to Mecca). Ousmane also wants to write a letter to Santa Claus and eventually he dictates it to a notary. In it the young boy asks Santa for everything he had promised to the people who had given him money. As he leaves, the notary asks him if he wants anything. The boy smiles and says, "of course," but does not specify what. Like Mambety's Sili, Ousmane appears cut out of a fairy tale, a fantasy of altruism, and a hope for a better Senegal.

The short film begins with an establishing shot that sweeps from left to right, from the sea to the city where it exposes the *car rapide* station. On the soundtrack a song plays; a male voice repeats the lyrics, "My father has left me / The orphan is asking for charity / My mother has left me / The orphan is asking for charity." The voice of the nondiegetic singer and the voice of the main character double, as two stories converge in these lyrics. Once again, the feeble division between diegetic and nondiegetic collapses onto itself and creates a space of fantasy. And just to be certain that the spectator registers this overlap, when the boy traverses the street at the very end of the film, he comes across a man playing the accordion. At the same time, the sound of an accordion—but not the diegetic one that is swallowed up by the noise of the street—surfaces on the soundtrack. Ousmane—a character in the vein of Mambety's "little people" and concern with the societal role of money—walks by the beach, and behind him the island of Gorée reappears in the far background, reigniting the traumatic memory of colonization. The film looks unsurprisingly similar to *La petite vendeuse*, although it is more than just a homage to Mambety. For example, the very last scene takes place in front of the famous *Chambre de commerce* featured heavily in Sembène's *Xala*. And of course the name of the character, while a very popular first name in Senegal, cannot but remind us of Sembène who brought people's prayers to reality in his own way. Worryingly though, after ignoring the cuteness of the film, what is left behind is that Dakar in 2006 looks strikingly similar to the Dakar of the 1970s and the 1990s, to Sembène's Dakar and Mambety's Dakar.

No one may continue Mambety's legacy more poignantly than his own niece, Mati Diop, daughter of Wasis Diop. Akin Adesokan has suggested that "culture can be inherited: not genetically, but in the sense that cultural institutions are continually produced, replenished, repeated, and perpetuated" (2011, 181). The emergence of Mati Diop continues to build the "cultural institution" that is the Diop family, an institution whose local and international reach endures into the twenty-first century. The young filmmaker is the latest incarnation of the griot—

"a necessary symbol of cultural continuity" (Murphy and Williams 2007, 25)—and hopefully much more. Mati Diop has produced a few short films and has also completed a fiction-documentary short, *Mille soleils* (*A Thousand Suns*) (2013). The film follows Magaye Niang, the actor who played Mory in *Touki Bouki*, and stages a conversation with Myriam Niang, the actress who played Anta opposite him. One of the first shots of the film finds Magaye herding a troupe of beasts across the Dakar highway. Like Mory, Magaye has stayed behind, in Dakar. In an interview with *Cinema Scope*, Diop talks about her overall cinematic interests: "Yes, I talk about exile, identity, and desire like intimate experiences because that's what they are above all. In regards to the spaces, it's the notion of territory that is important to me, as they are interconnected to the interiority and trajectory of a character. My characters rarely find themselves where they want to be in the world: there is always somewhere to escape from, to return to, or to conquer by means of the imagination" (Picard 2013). The circularity of the visual narrative of *Touki Bouki* parallels a traditional soundtrack that always returns to a musical theme or chorus. The visual takes on the typical characteristics of sound, but the sound does not follow the same pattern. Instead, it emerges as capable of carrying a separate story. As the image continues to tell its own story, it is the various aural narrative planes and subsequent stories born out of sounds and noises that give Mambety's cinema its uniqueness. And on that note, Mati Diop's words are edifying:

> I cannot really explain my relationship to music. It is at the heart of my life since forever. I became interested in sound long before I was interested in images. In fact, I think my first script resembled a sonic work more than it did a film. I made music when I was younger, and I conceived soundtracks for friends' theatre pieces that literally consisted of writing through sound. When cinema took over, my approach remained very musical. I began thinking of the conception of a short film like that of a song. (Picard 2013)

It sounds like Mambetian cinema, the humanist cinema of emotions, of noises and voices, is in capable hands.

Notes

Introduction

1. Since language choice is a vital point of discussion in African cinema, the titles of African films will be kept in the original language (French or Wolof) and their meaning will be explored in subsequent chapters. All other non-English titles will appear in translation.
2. I will, however, also refer occasionally to the 1988 documentary *Parlons grand-mère*.
3. See Niang 2002, 16–20.
4. This is one of two French-language works on the director, along with Nar Sene's *Djibril Diop Mambety: la caméra au bout . . . du nez*, 2001. I will refer to Sene's book sporadically, inasmuch as it is more a hyperbolic hymn to the artist (perhaps because Sene was a friend, as Murphy and Williams note [2007, 91]) than a substantial analysis of his work.
5. Among the general writings on African cinema that also discuss Mambety (although the concentration of the commentary is on *Touki Bouki*, 1973), a few works stand out: Ukadike's *Black African Cinema* (1994: 170–175); Françoise Pfaff's *Twenty-five Black African Filmmakers* (1988, 218–228); Ann Willey's "Orality into Literacy" (2003); Charles Sugnet's "Wolof Orality, Senghorian Literacy, and the Status of Cinema in Djibril Diop Mambety's *La Petite Vendeuse de Soleil*" (2006); David Murphy and Patrick Williams's *Postcolonial African Cinema: Ten Directors* (2007, 91–109); and especially Kenneth Harrow's *Postcolonial African Cinemas* (2007), notably the chapters on *Hyènes* and on Žižek).
6. Considering Mambety's ample use of animals in *Hyènes* (1992) and the overall importance of animals to folk tales and fables, it may be worth noting, anecdotally, that this neighborhood draws its name from one of the largest African lizards that used to populate the area.
7. It must be mentioned that "First Cinema" also includes the extensive history of Western avant-garde cinema that has long experimented with sound and image. See the introduction to *Experimental Cinema, The Film Reader*, edited by Wheeler W. Dixon and Gwendolyn Audrey Foster (2002, 1–17). For reasons of length and efficiency, this study deliberately excludes these vast references.
8. One has to consider the possibility that Hollywood-style cinema had a positive influence, and the idea that Mambety may have made films simply to entertain. Anthony R. Guneratne warns of the essentialism that blights the breakdown of the three cinemas: "The seemingly hermetic division of cinemas into those represented by big-budget commercial films (First Cinema), independent, *auteur* films (Second Cinema) and films made by militant collectives (Third Cinema), led to various misinterpretations such as the automatic assumption that First Cinema was necessarily a cinema of entertainment, the Second one of intellect and interiority, and the Third one of political radicalism" (Guneratne and Dissanayake 2003, 10).

9. Clyde Taylor deemed the application of the term "postmodernism" to African contexts and cultures "absurd" (2000, 136) and an "alien-term," since these cultures were excluded from the theoretical framework of the postmodern and because they were so obviously and violently denied participation in modernism.

10. Kenneth Harrow describes *Touki Bouki* as "his masterpiece of realist political satire" (2013, 40).

11. All translations from French are mine: "Mambety se construisit un projet de langage cinématographique dès *Contras' City* . . . D'abord il y eut l'exploration de l'espace cinématographique, des possibilités de combinaisons, de juxtaposition, de narration et de description par l'entremise de l'image et du son."

12. In fact, Godard is of French-Swiss extraction.

13. Given the importance of this word to postcolonial studies, I choose to use it instead of the more appropriate "synthesis."

14. "Son cinéma n'est classable dans aucun tiroir."

15. "Un cinéphile n'est pas dans le même état d'esprit, quand il va voir un film de Godard, de Howard Hawks, de Kurosawa, ou de Satiajit Ray parce qu'ils sont 'épithètes' chacun dans son genre. Il en est de même pour Djibril."

16. This is Sembène's playful term for "putting together [bricolage] a film on the cheap like a cigarette pieced together [montage] using butts [mégot]" (Harrow 2007, 238n5).

17. "Celui où pour la première fois les images convergent pour illustrer un projet de société obliquement nationaliste."

18. Harrow 2007. See the preface, as well as 117–119.

19. Althusser's interpellation, which leads to an ideological identity, also important to contemporary theorists such as Kenneth Harrow and Mladen Dolar, will be discussed in the last chapter.

20. It must be signaled that the director rejects the use of this word: "Style is a word that I do not like. I have never pursued a single style. . . . I believe that each filmmaker goes his own way, but each person is constantly evolving." (quoted in Ukadike 2002, 126).

21. The tensions characteristic of the binary relations between colonizer and colonized are not the same as those between First (Hollywood)/Second Cinemas and Third Cinema, so the intent is not to make Third Cinema analogous to Bhabha's "third space." It is within the corpus of Third Cinema that similar spatial struggles and tensions arise.

22. Several theories have been advanced on disembodied sound (voice in particular), but not as much has been said about the body that is "left behind"; this is, essentially, a hollowed body. In other words, it is not just the sound that is disembodied, since a physical effect on the body itself can be traced; an aural dismemberment, as it were.

23. As in "have meaning."

24. For a more detailed perspective, see the chapter titled "Unstable Objects: The Making of Radio in Nigeria" (Larkin 2008, 48–72).

25. See Ibrahima Diallo's detailed account of current language use (including percentage of French in relation to regional languages) on the radio in Senegal (Diallo 2010, 145–153).

26. This basically amounts to a theory of global aesthetics; for more see Adesokan 2011, especially 13–19.

27. The book, *In Senghor's Shadow: Art, Politics, and the Avant-Garde in Senegal, 1960–1995* (Harney 2004), surveys an incredible range of Senegalese artists and artistic

forms. It is particularly effective in its depiction of the avant-garde and the post-avant-garde movements (105–216).

28. Even though Diawara's categories, like Gabriel's, have since been contested (for example, Alexie Tcheuyap calls for an "update" on the "dated system," 2011, 235), they are still an important reference point and a springboard into current conversations about African cinema production.

29. This developed two years later into a book-length project (Barber 2007). Of particular relevance are 67–102.

30. According to Paulla Ebron a similar process takes place in the world of music: "When non-Western music, especially African music, was cited in critical conversations about music, it was often invoked as antithetical to Western art music. African music was viewed as primitive, not-quite-music, noise" (2002, 39).

31. Sembène also insisted on keeping the titles of his films in Wolof. This choice may point to the filmmaker's general displeasure with president Léopold Sédar Senghor's educational policies in Senegal. Charles Sugnet suggests that Mambety considered Senghor's approach to widen the spectrum of the French language wrong (2006, 1226). Therefore, the use of Wolof becomes a resistance tool that reverses the noxious effects of the initial Western representations of Africa: "These movies inverted African values by imposing the language and culture of the colonizer on the colonized" (Ukadike 1994, 35). It also pushes back at "the notion that only European languages are universal and capable of a story across frontiers, ethnic and cultural boundaries" (Diawara 2010, 42).

32. In *Xala* (1975), besides the street noises and cars honking, there is a short dialogue between guests at a wedding who wonder how one says "weekend" in English. The apparent gratuitous departure from the main story should provide us with even more reason to assert that Sembène references Godard's famous tracking shot of highway traffic from *Weekend*. Murphy and Williams observe that *Xala* harbors "a strange confluence between European, modernist practice and 'popular,' African oral narrative devices" (2007, 22); while this is not the norm for Sembène, that confluence suffuses all of Mambety's films.

33. At the same time, *Contempt* is also a clear attack on Hollywood, producers, the dependency on stars and money, and the like (for more see Monaco 2004, 141–147).

34. Astruc precedes the structuralist thought of the 1970s, especially Christian Metz, who unveiled "the language of cinema" (1974, 31–91).

35. Ukadike identifies song and dance as "not just accessories to life, they are transmitters of culture, indispensable to African existence" (1994, 216).

36. Ukadike also points to the importance of rhythm: "The rhythm of African music and dance is inspiring in its sophisticated and intended form. It evokes and manifests the cadences of creation, life and death struggles" (1994, 216).

37. As will be discussed, Antonin Artaud also relies on the need for vibration in his ideas about theater of cruelty: such vibration is essential in theater and it is needed even before finding meanings for the sounds (1964, 125).

38. It should be noted that Brown's study is on sound in theater, but given my own study's connections with theater, the reference seems justified.

39. Altman seems to be missing a crucial distinction: both light and sound take time to travel, but light travels at the fastest possible speed in the universe while sound is relatively very slow. Ross Brown does touch on this distinction when quoting Richard

Thomas on the difference between how sound and light travel in order to prove that sound "depends greatly on the *mass* that conveys it; its speed varies according to the density of that *mass*" (2010, 180, my emphasis).

40. Chion repeats or revisits many of his earlier arguments from two distinct books (Chion 1985, 1994) in more recent works.

41. At this point in his writing, Gabriel favors the geographical notion of Third World cinema, as opposed to the ideological Third Cinema.

42. For more on this, internal/external place, and extension as the essence of the body, see *Principles of Philosophy* (1982), Part II, 37–79.

43. This notion of mental place is also part of Descartes's/Kant's definition (space is both an inside and an outside experience as both experiences relate to one's body).

44. This is quite different from the medieval "imaginary space" (spatium imaginarium) which referred to the extracosmic void. See Grant 1981, chapter 6.

45. Ideological space, according to Žižek, is "made of non-bound, non-tied elements, 'floating signifiers,' whose identity is very 'open,' overdetermined by their articulation in a chain with other elements—that is, their 'literal' signification depends on their metaphorical surplus-signification" (2008b, 95).

46. Brief vocabulary explanations are warranted here since these terms will be used throughout: diegetic sound occurs within the visual borders of the screen and has a clear source; nondiegetic sound comes from offscreen. Extradiegetic sound also comes from offscreen but it is connected to the diegetic, although it has no place being there; it is illogical. Intradiegetic is initially nondiegetic sound that eventually reveals a clear diegetic source.

47. Senghor, as quoted by Fanon: "It is the vital element par excellence. It is the essential condition and the hallmark of Art . . . Such is rhythm primordial in its purity; such it is in the masterpieces of Negro art, especially sculpture" (2008, 102).

48. Murphy and Williams oppose Mambety here with Sembène's known rejection of Negritude, which the latter saw as a "deliberate obfuscation of contemporary realities in favour of an essentialist vision turned towards the past" (2007, 94).

49. Diagne 2011 defends Senghor's legacy (as does Diawara, 2010, 148–151) and deals at length with his engagement with Bergson's philosophy. Diagne claims that Senghor's distinction between reason and emotion, reductively Hellenistic art and African art, does not mean that the two are conclusively opposed, which is in line with Ebron's comparative analysis of music, and with mine of cinema.

50. The auditorium may be compared with Plato's famed Allegory of the Cave (1985, 209–210).

1. Aural Space and the Sonic Rack Focus in *Touki Bouki*

A modified, much shorter version of this reading of the film appeared in Dima 2012a. I have used parts of the article throughout the book.

1. "Il est difficile de se souvenir d'un plan tourné en intérieur dans un film de Djibril. Mambety est clair. Il travaille en plein jour et devant tout le monde."

2. Another clear connection to Godard's film comes to life later in Mambety's career: Godard's Patricia is really a *petite vendeuse* herself, but in the Parisian context where she sells the *Herald Tribune*, not unlike Mambety's Sili.

3. "*Touki Bouki* nous fait vibrer de cette ambivalence: fascination pour l'ailleurs et intégration de l'origine. Certains ont voulu y voir une opposition entre tradition et modernité. Mambety a toujours échappé à ce manichéisme. Pour lui, la modernité était dans la marginalité, dans l'irrévérence et l'indiscipline, dans l'indocilité, dans la force de dire 'je' tout en intégrant le 'nous,' non pas le 'nous' des contraintes sociales mais celui des valeurs essentielles portées par l'origine, transmises par le conte et le mythe."

4. "Qui se traduirait par *un voyage qui a été hyénisé*."

5. Diawara offers a wonderful explication of *Sundiata* and its "key transitional moments in the life of the hero," and an extended explanation of the reasons why the griot remains a powerful figure in contemporary West Africa (1998, 88–99).

6. This appears most famously in Sergei Eisenstein's *Strike* (1925) but also, for example, in Georges Franju's *Le sang des bêtes* (1949).

7. Eisenstein was primarily a master of the socialist realism genre, which is more reminiscent of Sembène's work and not to be confused with Diawara's "social realism" category. However, the focus here is on the intellectual montage component of Eisenstein's formalist tendencies.

8. My terminology here follows in the footsteps of Michel Chion's audio dissolves, or auditory tracking shots (2009, 47–51). For the latter, the sound movement makes the camera move along, which suggests a reversal to me, sound again becoming the primary means to tell a story.

9. A quick parenthesis here should help explain this claim better. An object changes its meaning depending on its context. Take for example the mask from Sembène's *La noire de . . .* (1966). For those not familiar with the plot, Diouana leaves Senegal to work as a nanny in France, but once there, she is treated like a maid by her employers. This eventually leads to her suicide, and a lasting visual impression: the contrast between her inert black body and the white bathtub. The mask is a fetish object that she takes from her little brother and gives to Monsieur and Madame. The former returns the mask to Diouana's family at the end of the film. The mask changes its signified value depending on where and to whom it belongs: authentic African artifact for the French family, toy for the little boy, identity for Diouana, and so on. In essence, it is one of Žižek's three types of *objet petit a*, a remnant of the real. Similarly, sound in the postcolonial context of Senegal should vary its meanings depending on its source and context.

10. Niang claims that an amalgam of sounds is heard during this episode (among which he erroneously states are conversations), and that the prayer is called "*la fatiha*," but he offers no analysis of the actual sounds (2002, 97–98).

11. "Tous ses films se baignent dans ce contexte [de l'Islam] et affirment l'importance de ce facteur dans le quotidien des personnages."

12. "[Anta] ne veut être ni épouse ni mère, encore moins soumise à un mari qui ne pourra lui permettre d'accéder au confort convoité."

13. Really it could be considered a flash-forward, but regardless it is uncommon and consistent with countercinema aesthetics.

14. "C'est sur la terre entière le paradis."

15. At the end of Marc Allégret's *Zouzou* (1934), Baker appears "in a music hall performance as a feathered bird in a golden cage" (Tobing Rony 1996, 201). She is a singing bird in a cage, exhibited as an object, trapped literally (inside the cage) and metaphorically (or rather, ethnographically, as she is reduced to a stereotype).

16. "Finally, we have a third kind of object: the birds in *The Birds*, for example (we could also add, in *Marnie*, the body of the giant ship at the end of the street in which Marnie's mother lives). This object has a massive, oppressive material presence; it is not an indifferent void like the MacGuffin, but at the same time it does not circulate between the subjects, it is not an object of exchange, it is just a mute embodiment of an impossible *jouissance*" (Žižek 2008b, 208–209).

17. Césaire is referenced elsewhere, too, for example in Sissako's *La vie sur terre* (Mali, 1998), in which a DJ calls the writer "our brother from Martinique."

18. "L'affreuse inanité de notre raison d'être."

19. Murphy and Williams briefly discuss Mambety's "exploration of masculinity," which yields male characters who are "often cast as inept, disorganized and even slightly effeminate," "ineffectual," or "the antithesis of the strong male lead" (2007, 100–101).

20. According to Western feminism, these women/bodies are clearly still objectified, just not through the lens of African stereotypes.

21. "Le cinéma, c'est simple, il faut fermer les yeux . . . et voilà on a une histoire."

22. Homophobia at the state level in Senegal does not match that codified in Uganda's laws, for example, but it is present nonetheless. In an endnote, Murphy and Williams claim that in Africa homosexuality "still remains a largely taboo subject" (2007, 109). Adesokan attempts to complete their intervention by declaring, also in a footnote: "in *Charlie* . . . we are presented with a convincing (if brief) treatment of a homosexual underground in contemporary Senegal" (2011, 192). For a historical perspective on homophobia in Senegal, see M'Baye 2013. For a more sensationalist take, see Zimmerman (2013).

23. "Il se fait tour à tour parieur, cambrioleur, prostitué, homme macho, amateur de bistros clandestins, politicien véreux avant de retrouver son âme de berger."

24. "Mory, le premier personnage méticuleusement construit de Djibril Diop Mambety, s'exprime autant par le mouvement et la gestuelle que la parole, se déplace constamment, n'a ni famille, ni ami, et tentera jusqu'aux derniers moments du film de quitter le pays."

2. Flaneur, Geography, and *Caméra-Flâneur* in *Badou Boy* and *Contras' City*

1. An analogous relationship, according to Deleuze and Guattari, occurs between music and the voice, with the former deterritorializing the latter.

2. Or more accurately, the microphone—Claudia Gorbman actually proposes the term *caméra-magnéto*, camera as tape recorder, which would function in conjunction with or replace Astruc's caméra-stylo (2007: 156).

3. This 1968 version translates the original French "on" as "they." While technically not wrong, the translation misses the first person nuance of the French pronoun, "we," which includes the author in the squalor of the town.

4. This was likely an ad for cigarettes.

5. Of course, this issue can be complicated further in terms of spectatorship; consider spectators who sit in a theater or at home, not in the film, not in the subway station, not next to a map.

6. Conley mentions several other theorists who have dealt with maps and mapping as tools of appropriation, control, and power (2007: 5).

7. "Transgressent les limites spatiales manichéennes de la ville, embrassent et exposent la diversité culturelle de Dakar."

8. As a matter of fact, play or playing (as irony, pastiche, or artifice) can operate politically from an African subject position. For philosopher Johan Huizinga play or playing relies on the notion of freedom: to play is freedom and there are no boundaries. If cinema is a "game," then Mambety is a masterful player who is aware of stepping in and out of the boundaries of reality, or of the rules of "game" (Huizinga 1949, 8). The "game" of cinema and the powers of artifice for artifice's sake liberate Mambety.

9. Harvey observes, "It took more than one hundred years to complete the bourgeois conquest of central Paris" (2012, 17).

10. "L'observateur est un prince qui jouit partout de son incognito."

11. For more on the city as labyrinth see Wilson 2001, 80–88.

12. "Voir le monde, être au centre du monde et rester caché au monde."

13. "Le flâneur est un animal urbain . . . issu des transmutations sociales, économiques, techniques, politiques et psychologiques qui on fait de *homo sapiens* un être à la fois anonyme et public, plus intime and plus exhibé que jamais dans l'histoire."

14. "Celui qui en est le sujet, pour ne pas rester anachronique, peut et doit traverser la carte du monde à une vitesse plus grande que son ancêtre baudelairien."

15. "le monument témoigne toujours d'une force dominante enracinée et verticale."

16. In Sembène's *Guelwaar*, we witness a celebration of the Nord/Sud cooperation in the beginning of the film. But it is a cynical episode: through the main character of this film, Sembène forcefully suggests that Africans should no longer beg, no longer have their hands out waiting for help from the West.

17. This is a small instrument with three or four strings and tight skin head, held horizontally. It is called *ngoni* in Bambara and *hoddu* by the Toucouleurs along the Senegal River. The same instrument is heavily used in *Xala*, too.

18. The beginning of Jean-Luc Godard's *Contempt* is the classic example; during the credits we are shown a camera on tracks from a static point of view, and a few minutes later, we get a tracking shot from the camera previously filmed.

19. In the late 1960s and early 1970s, this was the only properly equipped theater in francophone Africa (for more on its importance, see Rubin, Diakhaté, and Eyoh [1997], 23–25, 242–248).

20. Similarly, Sembène's Diouana flips through *Elle* magazine but does so rather aloofly (one would imagine this is partly because she cannot read French). Interestingly, it is the boyfriend who had brought the magazine—he is the one under the "spell" of the influential fashion magazine. The African man does not have to move to France in order to be corrupted by the "white women with their diseases," as Anta's mother warns.

21. For a full list of the neighborhoods visited see Niang 2002, 49.

22. "Lepp looy wut rekk am na marsé Colobane."

23. In spite of its official status as a minority religion, Catholicism exerts considerable influence in Senegal (for more see Murphy's analysis of *Guelwaar* [Murphy 2001, 205–213]).

24. "La parole ne fait pas l'histoire, la parole ne fait pas la mémoire."

25. One of the first official French settlements in Senegal; a different kind of return to the source may be insinuated here.

26. While Sembène might not be an acoustic auteur, he certainly "qualifies" for auteurship: horizontal layering (as opposed to, for example, Hitchcock's verticality) and

the recurrence of diegetic posters stand out among several aesthetic choices that add up to a personal style. Moreover, even a tendency for which he has been occasionally criticized—slowness and linearity—could be construed as an authorial "signature."

27. Harrow astutely notes that the French word for repetition ("*repetition*") is also used for "rehearsal" (2007, 218).

28. Sada Niang dedicates a few pages (2002, 74–94) to treating the theme of solitude in *Badou Boy* in relation to the western, analyzes the visual connections with the same genre (such as the use of the low-angle shot), and provides a list of the western movies that may have influenced Mambety. Moreover, the filmmaker identifies the genre as his favorite during childhood (Givanni 1995, 30).

29. The disorienting playfulness of non- and extradiegetic sound (or the "fantastical gap" mentioned in the introduction) in this instance recalls the famous opening of John Schlesinger's *Midnight Cowboy* (1969). The film begins on a blank screen while whoops of Native Americans are heard on the soundtrack. As the camera backtracks, the audience realizes that the blank screen is a drive-in theater. The yells (extradiegetic sound) go quiet, and the voice of Joe Buck (Jon Voight) begins singing, but at this point it is nondiegetic music, music that could be part of the soundtrack. When the film cuts to the shower, the voice of the "cowboy" is finally anchored in the diegetic world and sound becomes intradiegetic. This opening sets up a deconstruction of the cowboy myth similar to the one proposed by Mambety. In fact, Schlesinger takes it even further; the first shot inside the shower follows the dropped soap, which, in Urban Dictionary terms (http://www.urbandictionary.com/define.php?term=drop+the+soap), puts the character in a vulnerable position. His power is further undermined by several hard cuts that take the audience away from Joe to the dishwashing room, his workplace, where people ask "Where is that Joe Buck?" So he is a fake cowboy, much like the sound of the scene.

30. This is a shot of the officer and his bicycle, which funnily enough he never actually rides. It is as if the bike actually impedes his movement about the city: he huffs and puffs when he lifts and carries the bike around.

31. Badou is also often seen in the little *car rapide*, a public transportation contraption very common in the streets of Dakar. At one point he even takes a break at what must be the *car rapide* terminal because there are stationary vehicles on both sides of the road. These cars further suggest, through their role as the city's public transportation, that Dakar is being remapped.

32. For a more detailed perspective, see Dima 2012b.

3. Trauma and Zombie Narratives in *Hyènes*

1. Her last name, Linguère, translates as "blood queen," according to Sene 2001, 31n1.

2. The same structure is repeated later in the film: the superimposition of slaves walking and sugarcane fields is matched up with sounds of whips, soft music, and a humming chorus (no actual words are sung).

3. Other etymological influences come from the Bonda language and from Gabon.

4. This term designates the part of the soul that gives the body personality.

5. For more on the psychoanalytical take, see Leys on Freud and trauma (2000, 19–40). For example: "Freud's rejections of the notion of trauma as direct cause and his emphasis on psychosexual meaning involved a tendency within psychoanalysis to interiorize trauma, as if the external trauma derived its force and efficacy entirely from

internal psychical processes of elaboration, processes that were understood to be fundamentally shaped by earlier psychosexual desires, fantasies, and conflicts" (21).

6. "Absence is transhistorical and signifies an existential lack whereas loss is always historically specific and tangible: something is taken away or let go" (LaCapra 2001, 47–48).

7. There is also something to be said about undermining the Western myth of the return, the hero who comes back home after an odyssey—Ulysses is the obvious reference—with the intention to rebuild his kingdom. Ramatou is not a traditional hero, and she wants to eradicate the kingdom.

8. Žižek also uses this example, which interestingly contains another connection with Shakespeare.

9. "*Draman Dramé*, avec ses 'D' lourds . . . qui sonnent comme deux ultimes signes de vie d'un éléphant. . . . Chez nous, le son 'D' signifie mort. *Draman Dramé* est mort deux fois: une première fois dans sa conscience, *Draman*. Une deuxième fois dans son 'évanescence,' *Dramé*."

10. In spite of Žižek's controversial status among academics, his sustained interest in finding the points of intersection between Hegel, Marx, and Lacan generates a radical theoretical synthesis that seems appropriate for the study of *Hyènes* in particular (as Harrow 2007 demonstrates)

11. In his book from 2007, Harrow writes that Ramatou goes down into a bunker common for the peninsula on which Dakar is built, but he also suggests that she may be on Gorée Island itself (2007, 181; see also 246–247n2 for a longer discussion of islands). The 2013 book revisits and corrects her placement.

12. Interestingly, Mona's photographer from Gerima's *Sankofa* diegetically refers to the "magic hour" that he is about to lose (because Mona disappears into the past), which rings hollow in comparison to the loss incurred by Shola and by slaves in general.

13. The same year, Sembène made *Guelwaar*, which begins with mourning for the main character's death. In the family's bedroom, there is an empty suit laid out on the bed. In both cases the empty fetish clothes emphasize the lack of the actual bodies.

14. I have already pointed to the connections between Mambety and Sembène when it comes to maps, but the latter is also notorious for his use of posters and images that depict remarkable historical figures of the colonial past or of the colonial confrontation. In *La noire de . . .* , we see a poster of Patrice Lumumba (the Congolese independence leader) and one that anticipates *Emitai* (1971) in its portrayal of the colonial army. In *Xala*, Rama (whose name also carries a homonymic resemblance to Ramatou's) has posters of Amilcar Cabral (of Guinea-Bissau) and Samori Touré (a Dyula, who operated in Guinea and then Ivory Coast). Rama also possesses a poster of Charlie Chaplin, who perhaps serves here as a subversive signifier, being a known sympathizer of the Communist Party. I will return to Chaplin in the last chapter. At the end of *Xala*, we also see clearly the poster for *La noire de. . . .* The "external" poster becomes intradiegetic. In *Faat Kiné* (2001), the title character's house is adorned with portraits of Nelson Mandela (South Africa), Thomas Sankara (Burkina Faso), Kwame Nkrumah (Ghana), and Amilcar Cabral again. All these posters constitute a running theme throughout Sembène's work that offers a narrative alternative; the posters on the walls are to be consumed by the viewers simultaneously with the main narrative of the film.

15. Or she is barbaric, because the two fake witnesses describe "a cruel people from the Far East."

16. The prop of the American newspaper may be a reference to Godard's Patricia from *Breathless* and her famous call for people to buy the newspaper as she walks the streets of Paris.

17. The setup of a mise en abyme audience [spectators and character-spectators] is also employed by Mambety in the beginning of *La petite vendeuse*.

18. Buck-Morss (1991, 185–187) discusses at length the subject of the prostitute as the only possible female flaneur. The gender dominance of the male over the flaneur character is the reason why I have opted for the term *caméra-flâneur*, as opposed to the more grammatically accurate *caméra-flâneuse*.

19. This is a rare instance in which Sembène appears to contradict himself. Generally he is regarded as a proponent of modern technology and industrial processes (see Genova 2013, 78; Murphy 2001, 33).

20. For more on the link between parapraxes and the object voice, see Dolar 2006, 139–141.

21. Zombies can no longer produce language, only grunts; this means they are pre-symbolic.

22. As already noted, Harrow (2007, 181) has a comment to the contrary, but even if the scene of Ramatou descending into the bunker was shot on Gorée it is not made clear by the surroundings.

23. Gerima's *Sankofa* accomplishes this with Cape Coast; in one telling sequence, Gerima's camera first tilts up from the waves to the castle/island, and in the next shot it tilts down from the sky to the castle/island. The result—the island being cinematically squeezed between the two shots moving in opposite directions—emphasizes the materiality of the island.

24. Although Joseph Gai Ramaka's film does reverse the gaze from the island toward the city, it does not insist on the role of Gorée as much as it does on the narrative value of song, dance, and performance.

25. "Ici la musique et l'histoire avancent dans une parfaite réputation, tant et si bien qu'on ne sait si c'est l'histoire qui engendre la musique, ou si l'homme a construit son film à partir de la musique. Cette version me paraîtrait plus sûre."

26. The bulldozers here also evoke the ending to Sembène's *Camp de Thiaroye* (1988), in which the French tanks level the camp of the tirrailleurs.

27. It is not polite in French and francophone cultures to use one's first name in a formal context. Therefore, with this personal touch Mambety echoes his own words that he sees himself as the playwright's equal.

28. A nonmusical example: in *Xala* the sound continues beyond the freeze-frame that ends the film and thus sound takes over as the primary narrative method of delivery—it literally outlasts the image.

29. For more on Marxism in African film, see Murphy 2001, 108–109, and Genova 2013, 11.

4. Voice(s) in *Le franc* and *La petite vendeuse de soleil*

1. Stilwell gives the following explanation for the term: "The phrase 'fantastical gap' seemed particularly apt for this liminal space because it captured both its magic and its danger, the sense of unreality that always obtains as we leap from one solid edge toward another at some unknown distance and some uncertain stability" (Stilwell 2007, 187).

2. There is also a veiled reference to Chaplin in *Badou Boy*. One businessman in the *car rapide* acts strikingly like Chaplin, and even wears a hat and cane, which Badou borrows in a later scene. At the very end of the film, Badou's friend takes a swing at him, but Badou ducks, and his friend ends up hitting the officer straight across the face in a classic physical comedy routine. Chaplin is a figure who comes back elsewhere in West African film. For example, Mahamat-Saleh Haroun's *Abouna* (Chad, 2002), abounds with references to Truffaut's *The 400 Blows* and intertextual posters, including one of Chaplin in *The Kid*.

3. Žižek's definition of spectral sound differs vastly from my interpretation of it in the previous chapter.

4. She is also a nameless character. So it is not the name that is relevant—who she is—but rather what she does—controlling and owning land.

5. Mary Ann Doane remarks that "as soon as the sound is detached from its source, no longer anchored by a represented body, its potential work as a signifier is revealed. There is always something uncanny about a voice which emanates from a source outside the frame" (1985, 167).

6. Varda suggests that she is like a singing bird in a cage. The initial resemblance between Cléo and a caged bird is supported by the moments she spends on the swing hanging from the ceiling in her apartment—a larger version of the miniature swings found in birdcages. Unlike the case of Josephine Baker, also trapped in a cage, Cléo's situation never appears dire.

7. "Le personnage de Marigo est burlesque, avec ses mouvements raides, ses gesticulations excessives, ses mimiques et ses expressions de visage cocasses."

8. "Il a rêvé d'une Afrique libre et grande où celui qui a faim ne serait pas piétiné."

9. In the same video interview, Mambety makes a reference to the third film he was going to shoot that would have completed the trilogy—*L'apprenti voleur* (The Thief Apprentice). He muses on the fact that what he finds fundamental in the trilogy is the increasing role that money plays in society, which has led to a radical change in the way people interact.

10. This is a peculiar choice that could refer to the five stages of the Tree of Life or to the five senses. Or perhaps it is one degree removed from the maleficent 666.

11. In French this action carries a double entendre: "prendre la porte" (to take the door) means to leave a room, or, more generally, to escape. Marigo does both; he escapes while literally taking the door with him.

12. The ticket is reminiscent of Hitchcock's plot device, the MacGuffin.

13. "Ce marché avait été à Dakar un merveilleux exemple d'art déco que l'on pouvait admirer dans *Contras' City*" ("This market had been a wonderful example of art deco in Dakar that we can admire in *Contras' City*" [Wynchank 2009]).

14. This is not to say that there are no examples of dominating male voices. Sissako's film also foregrounds a male voice-over—one of the key practices of Hollywood cinema according to Silverman (1988, 48).

15. There is a semantic similitude not to be missed here between the chora and the kora, the stringed instrument that is present visually and aurally throughout Mambety's films (most insistently in *Badou Boy*).

16. "*Le Franc*, comme les autres films de Mambety, est marqué par l'esthétique de la tradition orale . . . le fantastique et l'irrationnel que l'on rencontre dans les contes traditionnels, occupent une place prépondérante dans le film de Mambety. . . . Par ailleurs, on

pourrait considérer Marigo comme le Décepteur ou le Malin des contes oraux. Il réussit longtemps à déjouer les stratagèmes de sa logeuse qui le poursuit pour lui réclamer ses six mois de loyer. De plus, Mambety introduit dans son film un personnage des contes oraux, Kuus, qui, comme dans le conte transcrit par Birago Diop, *Les Calebasses de Kouss*, procure la richesse au héros."

17. He edited the former's *A Voice and Nothing More* (2006).

18. Sugnet identifies this as a *talif*, a Wolof poem that "everyone in Senegal would recognize as a request for alms" (2006, 1227).

19. "L'Afrique quitte la zone franc."

20. 1998 marked the sixth and last Chicago Bulls championship with Jordan.

21. He brings to mind Spike Lee's character Radio Raheem in *Do the Right Thing* (1989). Lee is a well-respected and influential figure for the West African directors particularly Bekolo.

22. This is the second time that Scotland features in a film by Mambety, following the quote from Duncan from *Macbeth*. The connection, to reiterate, is perhaps facilitated by Scotland's subaltern status to England.

23. For more on these formulas see Sugnet 2006, 1230–1231, in which he rightly insists that the film be read as a fable.

24. Sugnet covers at length the "shocking rate of illiteracy" among the Senegalese (2006, 1223).

25. The fear of being eaten by the black man circles us back to the motif of the zombie.

26. Žižek can be helpful here, too. If we follow an old imperialist myth, the businessman and the new Senegalese bourgeoisie are substituted for the upper class. That upper class replenishes its life energy by feeding off the poor, that is, through contact with the lower class (Sili). Once satisfied, the businessman returns to his secluded life, and in fact is never seen again. According to this reading, the act of giving money is not altruistic but selfish (a fact corroborated by the reference to the grandmother and the fact that he wants her to pray for him).

27. I discuss this concept further, as well as connections between Baroque architecture and the use of sound in Godard's cinema, in Dima 2012b. Here I am proposing an upgrade of previous thoughts and research.

28. During the silent-movie era, it was primarily the orchestra that provided the audience with a complementary source of sound, but it did not hold the aural monopoly in the least: "The sounds coming from the pit were often eclipsed by the sound coming from the audience" (Altman 2004, 53).

Conclusion

1. I limit myself here to the effects on Mambety's countrymen, while acknowledging the need for a larger project on other francophone countries. For example, Malian director Abderrahmane Sissako's *Bamako* (2006) uses voices and the radio to delineate the postcolonial space in Mali's capital—the law court, the street, and characters' lives are all ontologically linked to sound. The radio once again plays an important role in Sissako's *La vie sur terre* (1999) and in Cameroonian director Jean-Pierre Bekolo's *Aristotle's Plot* (1996).

2. A quick reminder of that history: the first documented film made by an African is considered to be a short by Chemam Chikly from Tunisia, titled *The Girl from Carthage*

(1924). There are records of films made in Egypt in the late 1920s, but it was only in the 1950s and 1960s that filmmaking started to emerge in Africa. Many consider Paulin Vieyra's *Afrique-sur-Seine* (1955), which was made in collaboration with a collective of sub-Saharan filmmakers, to be the first real African film ever made. However, the model for all of African cinema to pursue was set in 1963 by Sembène's short, *Borom Sarret*.

3. For a more detailed perspective on materialism, see Genova's introduction (especially 13–19) and assessment of "collaboration" with France (133–141).

4. For more on the politics of finances see Mermin (1999), especially the comments on Sembène's *Guelwaar* (209–217).

5. "C'est un film politique. Je donne une claque à ceux qui nous gouvernent, pour qu'ils se rendent compte qu'ils ont baissé les bras."

6. I prefer to use "nondiegetic" in the hope of lessening confusion with the terms concerning sound, which can be both nondiegetic and extradiegetic. Harrow refers here to the narrative.

7. The common thought seems to be that African cinema simply leapfrogs modernism. Put in basic terms, modernism is essentially order; rationality and rationalization create order out of chaos. To support the binary opposing relationship between order and disorder, a dichotomy that keeps fueling the notion of modernity, modern society has substituted "disorder" for forms of the Other, also defined in terms of binary oppositions: nonwhite, nonheterosexual, nonrational, and so on.

Bibliography

Adesokan, Akin. 2011. *Postcolonial Artists and Global Aesthetics*. Bloomington: Indiana University Press.
Althusser, Louis. 1971. *Lenin and Philosophy*. Translated by Ben Brewster. London: New Left Books.
Altman, Rick. 1992. "Sound Space." In *Sound Theory. Sound Practice*. Edited by Rick Altman. London: Routledge, 46–64.
———. 2004. *Silent Film Sound*. New York: Columbia University Press.
Appiah, Kwame. 1992. *In My Father's House: Africa in the Philosophy of Culture*. New York: Oxford University Press.
Artaud, Antonin. 1958. *Theater and Its Double*. Translated by Mary Caroline Richards. New York: Grove Press.
Balazs, Bela. 1985. "Theory of the Film: Sound." In *Film Sound*, edited by Elisabeth Weis and John Belton, 116–125. New York: Columbia University Press.
Barber, Karin. 2005. "Text and Performance in Africa." *Oral Tradition* 20, no. 2: 264–277.
———. 2007. *The Anthropology of Texts, Persons and Publics: Oral and Written Culture in Africa and Beyond*. Cambridge: Cambridge University Press.
Barlet. Olivier. 2000. *African Cinemas: Decolonizing the Gaze*. London: Zed Books.
Barthes, Roland. 2007. *Image, Music, Text*. New York: Hill and Wang.
———. 2010. *Camera Lucida: Reflections on Photography*. New York: Hill and Wang.
Baudelaire, Charles. 1976. "Le peintre de la vie moderne." In *Oeuvres complètes*. Vol. 2, edited by Claude Pichois, 684–695. Paris: Gallimard.
Baudry, Jean-Louis. 1974. "Ideological Effects of the Basic Cinematographic Apparatus." Translated by Alan Williams. *Film Quarterly* 28, no. 2: 39–47.
Bazin, André. 1967. *What is Cinema?* Berkeley: University of California Press.
Belton, John. 1985. "Technology and Aesthetics of Film Sound." In *Film Sound*, edited by Elisabeth Weis and John Belton, 63–72. New York: Columbia University Press.
Benjamin, Walter. 2002. *The Arcades Project*. Cambridge, MA: Belknap Press of Harvard University Press.
Bhabha, Homi. 2010. *The Location of Culture*. London: Routledge.
Bordwell, David and Kristin Thompson. 1985. "Fundamental Aesthetics of Sound in the Cinema." In *Film Sound*, edited by Elisabeth Weis and John Belton, 181–199. New York: Columbia University Press.
Brown, Ross. 2010. *Sound: A Reader in Theatre Practice*. London: Palgrave Macmillan.
Buck-Morss, Susan. 1991. *The Dialectics of Seeing: Walter Benjamin and the Arcades Project*. Cambridge, MA: MIT Press.
Caruth, Cathy, ed. 1995. "Introduction." In *Trauma: Explorations in Memory*, 3–12. Baltimore: Johns Hopkins University Press.
Cavalcanti, Alberto. 1985. "Sound in Films." In *Film Sound*, edited by Elisabeth Weis and John Belton, 98–111. New York: Columbia University Press.

Césaire, Aimé. 1955. *Discours sur le colonialisme*. Paris and Dakar: Présence Africaine.
———. 1983. *Cahier d'un retour au pays natal*. Paris and Dakar: Présence Africaine.
Cham, Mbye B. 1996. "Introduction." In *African Experiences of Cinema*," edited by Imruh Bakari and Mbye B. Cham, 1–14. London: British Film Institute.
Chamoiseau, Patrick. 1994. *Guyane: trace-mémoires du bagne*. Paris: Caisse Nationale des Monuments Historiques et des Sites.
Chanan, Michael. 1997. "The Changing Geography of Third Cinema." *Screen* 38:4 (December 2013). http://www.mchanan.com/wp-content/uploads/2013/12/third-cinema.pdf
Châteauvert, Jean & and André Gaudreault. 2001. "The Noises of Spectators, or the Spectator as Additive to the Spectacle." In *The Sounds of Early Cinema*, edited by Richard Abel and Rick Altman, 183–191. Bloomington: Indiana University Press.
Chion, Michel. 1985. *Le son au cinéma*. Paris: Cahiers du Cinéma.
———. 1994. *Audio-Vision. Sound on Screen*. New York: Columbia University Press.
———. 1999. *The Voice in Cinema*. New York: Columbia University Press.
———. 2009. *Film, A Sound Art*. New York: Columbia University Press.
Cooke, Mervyn. 2008. *A History of Film Music*. Cambridge: Cambridge University Press.
Conley, Tom. 2007. *Cartographic Cinema*. Minneapolis: University of Minnesota Press.
Coulthard, Lisa. 2012. "The Attractions of Repetition: Tarantino's Sonic Style." In *Music, Sound, and Filmmakers: Sonic Style in Cinema*, edited by James Wierzbicki, 165–174. London: Routledge.
Davis, Wade. 1988. *Passage of Darkness: The Ethnobiology of the Haitian Zombie*. Chapel Hill: University of North Carolina Press.
De Certeau, Michel. 1988. *The Practice of Everyday Life*. Berkeley: University of California Press.
Deleuze, Gilles. 1986. *Cinema 1: The Movement-Image*. Minneapolis: University of Minnesota Press.
———. 1989. *Cinema 2: The Time-Image*. Minneapolis: University of Minnesota Press.
———. 1992. *The Fold: Leibniz and the Baroque*. Minneapolis: University of Minnesota Press.
———. 2004. "Desert Islands." In *Desert Islands and Other Texts, 1953–1974*, edited by David Lapoujade, translated by Michael Taormina, 9–14. Los Angeles: Semiotext(e).
Deleuze, Gilles, and Félix Guattari. 1987. *A Thousand Plateaus*. Minneapolis: University of Minnesota Press.
Descartes, René. 1982. *Principles of Philosophy*. Translated by Valentine Rodger Miller and Reese P. Miller. Dordrecht: Kluwer Academic Publishers.
Diagne, Souleymane Bachir. 2011. *African Art as Philosophy: Senghor, Bergson, and the Idea of Negritude*. Translated by Chike Jeffers. London: Seagull Books.
Diallo, Ibrahima. 2010. *The Politics of National Languages in Postcolonial Senegal*. Amherst, NY: Cambria Press.
Diawara, Manthia. 1992. *African Cinema: Politics & Culture*. Bloomington: Indiana University Press.
———. 1996. "Popular Culture and Oral Traditions in African Film." In *African Experiences of Cinema*, edited by Imruh Bakary and Mbye Cham, 209–219. London: British Film Institute.

———. 1998. *In Search of Africa*. Cambridge, MA: Harvard University Press.
———. 2000. "The Iconography of West African Cinema." In *Symbolic Narratives/African Cinema: Audiences, Theory and the Moving Image*, edited by June Givanni, 81–89. London: British Film Institute.
———. 2010. *African Film: New Forms of Aesthetics and Politics*. Berlin: Prestel Verlag.
Dima, Vlad. 2012a. "Aural Narrative Planes in Djibril-Diop Mambety's Films." *The Journal for Film and Video* 64, no. 3 (Fall 2012): 38–52.
———. 2012b. "The Aural Fold and the Sonic Jump-Cut: Godard's Baroque Sound," *Quarterly Review of Film and Video* 29, no. 3 (Spring 2012): 237–251.
Dixon, Wheeler Winston and Gwendolyn Audrey Foster, eds. 2002. *Experimental Cinema: The Film Reader*. London: Routledge.
Doane, Mary Ann. 1985. "The Voice in the Cinema: The Articulation of Body and Space." In *Film Sound*, edited by Elisabeth Weis and John Belton, 162–176. New York: Columbia University Press.
Dolar, Mladen. 2006. *A Voice and Nothing More*. Cambridge, MA: MIT Press.
Downing, John. 1987. "Afterword." In *Film and Politics in the Third World*, edited by John Downing, 311–318. New York: Praeger.
Eagleton, Terry. 1985. *Literary Theory*. Minneapolis: University of Minnesota Press.
Ebong, Ima. 1999. "Negritude: Between Mask and Flag—Senegalese Cultural Ideology and the *Ecole de Dakar*." In *Reading the Contemporary: African Art from Theory to the Marketplace*, edited by Olu Oguibe and Okwui Enwezor, 128–143. Cambridge, MA: MIT Press.
Ebron, Paulla. 2002. *Performing Africa*. Princeton, NJ: Princeton University Press.
Eisenstein S. M., V. I. Pudovkin, and G. V. Alexandrov. 1985. "A Statement on Sound." In *Film Sound*, edited by Elisabeth Weis and John Belton. New York: Columbia University Press.
Elliott, Kamilla. 2003. *Rethinking the Novel/Film Debate*. Cambridge: Cambridge University Press.
Essar, Dennis. 1996. "Review of *Touki-Bouki*." *African Arts*, 29, no. 4: 78–96.
Fairweather, Elizabeth. 2012. "Andrey Tarkovski: The Refrain of the Sonic Fingerprint." In *Music, Sound, and Filmmakers: Sonic Style in Cinema*, edited by James Wierzbicki, 32–44. London: Routledge.
Fanon, Frantz. 1968. *The Wretched of the Earth*. New York: Grove Press.
———. 2008. *Black Skin, White Masks*. New York: Grove Press.
Faure, Élie. 2006. *Fonction du cinéma*. Paris: Denoel/Meditations.
Fischer, Lucy. 1985. "*Applause*: The Visual and Acoustic Landscape." In *Film Sound*, edited by Elisabeth Weis and John Belton, 232–246. New York: Columbia University Press.
Forster, Siegfried. 2013. "Moussa Touré: 'La Pirogue est une claque à ceux qui nous gouvernent." http://www.rfi.fr/afrique/20130225-moussa-toure-fespaco-la-pirogue-une-claque-ceux-nous-gouvernent
Foucault, Michel. 1995. *Discipline and Punish: The Birth of the Prison*. New York: Vintage.
Freud, Sigmund. 1952. *The Major Works*. London: Encyclopedia Britannica, William Benton Publisher.
———. 1958. "'A Child Is Being Beaten': A Contribution to the Study of the Origin of Sexual Perversions." In *The Standard Edition of the Complete Psychological Works*

of Sigmund Freud, edited by James Strachey, Vol. 17. London: The Hogarth Press and the Institute of Psychoanalysis.

Gabriel, Teshome. 1982. *Third Cinema in the Third World: The Dynamics of Style and Ideology.* Ann Arbor: University of Michigan Press.

———. 1989a. "Towards a critical theory of Third World Films." In *Questions of Third Cinema,* edited by Jim Pines and Paul Willemen, 30–52. London: British Film Institute.

———. 1989b. "Third Cinema as Guardian of Popular Memory: Towards a Third Aesthetics." In *Questions of Third Cinema,* edited by Jim Pines and Paul Willemen, 53–64. London: British Film Institute.

Gallagher, Michael. 2010. "Are Schools Panoptic?" In *Surveillance and Society* 7, no. 3/4: 262–272.

Gardies, Andrés. 1989. *Cinéma d'Afrique noire francophone: l'espace miroir.* Paris: L'Harmattan.

Genette, Gérard. 1980. *Narrative Discourse.* Translated by Jane E. Lewin. Ithaca, NY: Cornell University Press.

Genova, James. 2013. *Cinema and Development in West Africa.* Bloomington: University of Indiana Press.

Ghali, Nourredine. 2008. "Interview with Ousmane Sembene." In *Ousmane Sembene: Interviews,* edited by Annett Busch and Max Annas, 73–81. Jackson: University of Mississippi Press.

Givanni, June. 1995. "African Conversations: An Interview with Djibril Diop Mambety." *Sight and Sound* 5, no. 9, 30–31.

Givanni, June, ed. 2000. *Symbolic Narratives/African Cinema: Audiences, Theory and the Moving Image.* London: British Film Institute.

Gleber, Anke. 1999. *The Art of Taking a Walk: Flanerie, Literature, and Film in Weimar Culture.* Princeton, NJ: Princeton University Press.

Godard, Jean-Luc. 1972. *Godard on Godard.* New York: Viking Press.

Gorbman, Claudia. 1987. *Unheard Melodies: Narrative Film Music.* Bloomington: Indiana University Press.

———. 2007. "Auteur Music." In *Beyond the Soundtrack: Representing Music in Cinema,* edited by Daniel Goldmark, Lawrence Kramer, and Richard Leppert, 149–162. Berkeley: University of California Press.

Gould, Peter, and Rodney White. 1974. *Mental Maps.* New York: Penguin Books.

Grant, Edward. 1981. *Much Ado About Nothing: Theories of Space and Vacuum from the Middle Ages to the Scientific Revolution.* Cambridge: Cambridge University Press.

Greimas, Algirdas Julien. 1986. *Sémantique structurale: recherche de méthode.* Paris: Presses Universitaires de France.

Gugler, Josef. 2003. *African Film: Re-Imagining a Continent.* Bloomington: Indiana University Press.

Guneratne, Anthony R. 2003. "Introduction: Rethinking World Cinema." In *Rethinking World Cinema,* edited by Anthony R. Guneratne and Wimal Dissanayake, 1–28. New York: Routledge.

Hall, Stuart. 1989. "Cultural Identity and Cinematic Representation." *Framework* 36: 68–81.

———. 1996. "When Was the 'Post-Colonial'? Thinking at the Limit." In *The Postcolonial Question: Common Skies, Divided Horizons,* edited by Iain Chambers and Lidia Curti, 242–259. London: Routledge.
Harney, Elizabeth. 2004. *In Senghor's Shadow: Art, Politics, and the Avant-Garde in Senegal, 1960–1995.* Durham, NC: Duke University Press.
Harrow, Kenneth. 2007. *Postcolonial African Cinema: From Political Engagement to Postmodernism.* Bloomington: University of Indiana Press.
———. 2013. *Trash: African Cinema from Below.* Bloomington: University of Indiana Press.
———. 2014. "African Cinema: Troubling the (Cinematic World) Order." Paper Presented at "Africa at Noon," University of Wisconsin–Madison, March 2014.
Harvey, David. 2012. *Rebel Cities: From the Right to the City to the Urban Revolution.* London: Verso.
Hegarty, Paul. 2007. *Noise/Music: A History.* New York: Continuum.
Hondo, Med. 1986. "What Is Cinema for Us?" *Jump Cut* 31: 47–48. http://www.ejumpcut.org/archive/onlinessays/JC31folder/WhatisCinemaForus.html
Howard, David. 2010. "Cartographies and Visualization." In *A Concise Companion to Postcolonial Literature,* edited by Shirley Chew and David Richards, 141–162. Sussex, UK: Wiley-Blackwell.
Huggan, Graham. 2008. "Decolonizing the Map: Postcolonialism, Poststructuralism and the Cartographic Connection." In *Interdisciplinary Measures: Literature and the Future of Postcolonial Studies,* edited by Graham Huggan, 21–34. Liverpool, UK: University of Liverpool Press.
Hughes, Alex & Williams, James (eds). 2001. *Gender and French Cinema.* Oxford: Oxford University Press.
Huizinga, Johan. 1949. *Homo Ludens: A Study of the Play-Element in Culture.* London: Routledge and Kegan Paul.
Kant, Immanuel. 1781. *Critique of Pure Reason.* https://ebooks.adelaide.edu.au/k/kant/immanuel/k16p/
Kracauer, Siegfried. 1997. *Theory of Film.* Princeton, NJ: Princeton University Press.
Kristeva, Julia. 1984. *Revolution in Poetic Language.* Translated by Margaret Waller. New York: Columbia University Press.
Lacan, Jacques. 1978. *The Seminar of Jacques Lacan, Book XI: Four Fundamental Concepts of Psycho-Analysis.* Translated by Alan Sheridan. New York: Norton.
———. 1992. *The Seminar of Jacques Lacan, Book VII: The Ethics of Psychoanalysis, 1959–1960.* Translated by Dennis Porter. New York: Norton.
———. 1998. *The Seminar of Jacques Lacan, Book XX: On Feminine Sexuality, the Limits of Love and Knowledge.* Translated by Bruce Fink. New York: Norton.
LaCapra, Dominick. 2001. *Writing History, Writing Trauma.* Baltimore, MD: Johns Hopkins University Press.
Laplanche J. and J.-B. Pontalis. 1973. *The Language of Psychoanalysis.* Translated by Donald Nicholson Smith. New York: Norton.
Larkin, Brian. 2008. *Signal and Noise: Media, Infrastructure, and Urban Culture in Nigeria.* Durham, NC: Duke University Press.
Lawrence, Amy. 1991. *Echo and Narcissus: Women's Voices in Classical Hollywood Cinema.* Berkeley: University of California Press.

Lefebvre, Henri. 1991. *The Production of Space*. Oxford: Blackwell.
——. 2009. *State, Space, World: Selected Essays*. Minneapolis: University of Minnesota Press.
Lellis, Georges. 1982. *Bertolt Brecht, Cahiers du Cinéma and Contemporary Film Theory*. Ann Arbor: University of Michigan Research Press.
Leys, Ruth. 2000. *Trauma: A Genealogy*, Chicago: The University of Chicago Press.
Loshitzky, Yosefa. 1995. *The Radical Faces of Godard and Bertolucci*. Detroit: Wayne State University Press.
Lowenstein, Adam. 2005. *Shocking Representation: Historical Trauma, National Cinema, and the Modern Horror Film*. New York: Columbia University Press.
Lynch, Kevin. 1960. *The Image of the City*. Cambridge: MIT Press.
Lyotard, Jean-François. 1988. *The Inhuman*. Palo Alto, CA: Stanford University Press.
MacCabe, Colin. 1980. *Godard: Images, Sounds, Politics*. London: MacMillan Press Ltd.
Maciocco, Giovanni, ed. 2009. *The Territorial Future of the City*. Berlin: Springer e-book.
Marx, Karl. 1974. *The German Ideology*. London: Lawrence and Wishhart.
M'Baye, Babacar. 2013a. "The Origins of Senegalese Homophobia: Discourses on Homosexuals and Transgender People in Colonial and Postcolonial Senegal." *African Studies Review* 56, no. 2: 109–128.
——. 2013b. "In Search of Mahalia Jackson and Aminata Fall: A Comparative Study of Senegalese and African American Blues." In *Crossing Traditions: American Popular Music in Local and Global Contexts*, edited by Babacar M'Baye and Alexander Charles Oliver Hall. Lanham, MD: Scarecrow Press, 101–120.
Merleau-Ponty, Maurice. 2004. *The World of Perception*. London: Routledge.
Mermin, Elizabeth. 1999. "A Window on Whose Reality? The Emerging Industry of Senegalese Cinema." In *African Cinema: Postcolonial and Feminist Readings*. Ed. Kenneth Harrow. Treaton: Africa World Press.
Metz, Christian. 1974. *Film Language*. Translated by Michael Taylor. Chicago: University of Chicago Press.
——. 1980. "Aural Objects." *Yale French Studies* 60, no. 1: 24–32.
——.1982. *The Imaginary Signifier*. Bloomington: Indiana University Press.
Minh-ha, Trinh T. 1989. *Woman, Native, Other: Writing Postcoloniality and Feminism*. Bloomington and Indianapolis: Indiana University Press.
Mintz, Penny. 1985. "Orson Welles's Use of Sound." In *Film Sound*, edited by Elisabeth Weis and John Belton, 289–297. New York: Columbia University Press.
Monaco, James. 2004. *The New Wave: Truffaut, Godard, Chabrol, Rohmer, Rivette*. Sag Harbor, NY: Harbor Electronic Publishing.
Murphy, David. 2000. "Africans Filming Africa: Questioning Theories of an Authentic African Cinema." *Journal of African Cultural Studies* 13, no. 2: 239–249.
——. 2001. *Sembene: Imagining Alternatives in Film & Fiction*. Trenton, NJ: Africa World Press.
——, and Patrick Williams. 2007. *Postcolonial African Cinema: Ten Directors*. Manchester, UK: Manchester University Press.
Nelson, Steve. 2008. "A Tale of Two Cities." *Artforum*, Nov. 2008. http://missingimage.com/node/250692
Niang, Sada. 2002. *Djibril Diop Mambety: Un cinéaste à contre-courant*. Paris: L'Harmattan.
Nietzsche, Friedrich. 1937. *The Philosophy of Nietzsche*. New York: Modern Library.

———. 1969. *On the Genealogy of Morals*. Tramslated by Walter Kaufmann and R. J. Hollingdale. New York: Random House.
Oyěwùmí, Oyèrónké. 1997. *The Invention of Women*. Minneapolis: University of Minnesota Press.
Penley, Constance. 1989. *The Future of an Illusion*. Minneapolis: University of Minnesota Press.
Pfaff, Françoise. 1984. *The Cinema of Ousmane Sembene, A Pioneer of African Film*. Westport, CT: Greenwood Press.
———. 1988. *Twenty-Five Black African Filmmakers: A Critical Study with Filmography and Bio-Bibliography*. Westport, CT: Greenwood Press.
———. 2004. "African Cities as Cinematic Texts." In *Focus on African Films*, edited by Françoise Pfaff, 89–106. Bloomington: Indiana University Press.
Picard, Andréa. "In the Realm of the Senses: Mati Diop on Mille soleils." *Cinema/Scope* 2013. http://cinema-scope.com/columns/filmart-realm-senses-mati-diop-mille-soleils/
Plato. 1985. *The Republic*. Translated by Richard W. Sterling and William C. Scott. New York: Norton.
Rosolato, Guy. 1996. *Essais sur le symbolique*. Paris: Gallimard.
Ross, Andrew. 1994. "Tribalism in effect." In *On Fashion*, edited by Shari Benstock and Suzanne Ferriss, 284–299. New Brunswick, NJ: Rutgers University Press.
Rubin, Don, Ousmane Diakhaté, and Hansel Ndumbe Eyoh, eds. 1997. *The World Encyclopedia of Contemporary Theater: Africa*. London: Routledge.
Said, Edward. 1979. *Orientalism*. New York: Vintage Books.
———. 1993. *Culture and Imperialism*. New York: Vintage Books.
Scarry, Elaine. 1985. *The Body in Pain: The Making and Unmaking of the World*. Oxford: Oxford University Press.
Sellier, Geneviève. 2008. *Masculine Singular: French New Wave Cinema*. Durham, NC: Duke University Press.
Sembène, Ousmane. 1971. *Voltaïque*. Paris: Présence Africaine.
Sene, Nar. 2001. *Djibril Diop Mambety: la caméra au bout . . . du nez*. Paris: L'Harmattan.
Shiel, Mark. 2006. *Italian Neorealism: Rebuilding the Cinematic City*. London: Wallflower Press.
Shohat, Ella. 2006. *Taboo Memories, Diasporic Voices*. Durham, NC: Duke University Press.
Shohat, Ella, and Robert Stam. 2014. *Unthinking Eurocentrism. Multiculturalism and the Media*. London: Routledge.
Silverman, Kaja. 1983. *The Subject of Semiotics*. New York: Oxford University Press.
———. 1988. *The Acoustic Mirror: The Female Voice in Psychoanalysis and Cinema*. Indianapolis: Indiana University Press.
———. 1996. *The Threshold of the Visible World*. New York: Routledge.
Singer, Ben. 2001 *Melodrama and Modernity*. New York: Columbia University Press.
Smith, Jeff. 2009. "Bridging the Gap: Reconsidering the Border between Diegetic and Nondiegetic Music." *Music and the Moving Image* 2, no. 1: 1–25.
Solañas, Fernando, and Octavio Getino. 1976. "Towards a Third Cinema." In *Movies and Method*, edited by Bill Nichols, 44–64. Los Angeles: University of California Press.
Spaas, Lieve. 2000. *The Francophone Film: A Struggle for Identity*. Manchester, UK: Manchester University Press.

Stafford, Andy. 2009. "Senegal: May 1968, Africa's Revolt." In *Bulletin Supplement 6, 1968: Memories and Legacies of a Global Revolt*. German Historical Institute, Washington, DC. http://www.ghi-dc.org/files/publications/bu_supp/supp006/bus6_129.pdf

Stam, Robert. 1985. *Reflexivity in Film and Literature: From Don Quixote to Jean-Luc Godard*. Ann Arbor: University of Michigan Research Press.

———. 2003. "Beyond Third Cinema: The Aesthetics of Hybridity." In *Rethinking Third Cinema*, edited by Anthony Guneratne and Wimal Dissanayake, 31–48. New York: Routledge.

Sterritt, Dave. 1999. *The Films of Jean-Luc Godard: Seeing the Invisible*. Cambridge: Cambridge University Press.

Stilwell, Robynn J. 2007. "The Fantastical Gap between Diegetic and Nondiegetic." In *Beyond the Soundtrack: Representing Music in Cinema*, edited by Daniel Goldmark, Lawrence Kramer, and Richard Leppert, 184–202. Berkeley: University of California Press.

Sugnet, Charles. 2006. "Wolof Orality, Senghorian Literacy, and the Status of Cinema in Djibril Diop Mambety's *La Petite Vendeuse de Soleil*." *French Review* 79, no. 6: 1222–1238.

Swoboda, Tomasz. 2013. *Histoires de l'oeil*. New York: Rodopi.

Taylor, Clyde. 2000. "Searching for the Postmodern in African Cinema." In *Symbolic Narratives/African Cinema: Audiences, Theory and the Moving Image*, edited by June Givanni, 136–144. London: British Film Institute.

Tcheuyap, Alexie. 2011. *Postnationalist African Cinemas*. Manchester, UK: Manchester University Press.

Thackway, Melissa. 2003. *Africa Shoots Back: Alternative Perspectives in Sub-Saharan Francophone African Film*. Bloomington: Indiana University Press.

Tobing Rony, Fatimah. 1996. *The Third Eye: Race, Cinema, and Ethnographic Cinema*. Durham, NC: Duke University Press.

Truffaut, François. 1983. *Hitchcock*. New York: Simon and Schuster.

———. 1994. *The Films in My Life*. New York: Da Capo.

Ubersfeld, Anne. 1999. *Reading Theater*. Toronto: University of Toronto Press.

Ukadike, Nwachukwu Frank. 1994. *Black African Cinema*. Berkeley: University of California Press.

———. 2002. *Questioning African Cinema: Conversations with Filmmakers*. Minneapolis: University of Minnesota Press.

Urban Dictionary, s.v. "Drop the soap." http://www.urbandictionary.com/define.php?term=drop+the+soap

Willemen, Paul. 1989. "The Third Cinema Question: Notes and Reflections." In *Questions of Third Cinema*, edited by Jim Pines and Paul Willemen, 30–52. London: British Film Institute.

Willey, Ann Elizabeth. 2003. "Orality into Literacy: Modes of Modernity and History in Kouyate's Keita and Mambety's La Petite Vendeuse." In *The Creative Circle: Artist, Critic, and Translator in African Literature*, edited by Angelina Overvold, 72–89. Trenton, NJ: Africa World Publishing.

Wilson, Elizabeth. 2001. *The Contradictions of Culture*. London: Sage.

Wood, Denis. 1992. *The Power of Maps*. New York: Guilford Press.

Wynchank, Anny. 2009. "*Le Franc* de Djibril Diop Mambety, une ré-invention du cinema africain." http://www.erudit.org/revue/rum/2009/v40/n1/044605ar.html
Zacks, Stephen A. 1995. "The theoretical construction of African cinema." *Research in African Literatures* 26, no. 3 6–17.
Zimmerman, Jonathan. 2013. "An African Epidemic of Homophobia." *Los Angeles Times*, June 29. http://articles.latimes.com/2013/jun/29/opinion/la-oe-zimmerman-africa-gays-20130630.
Žižek, Slavoj. 1989. "Looking Awry." *October* 50 (Fall): 30–55.
———. 1992. *Looking Awry: An Introduction to Jacques Lacan through Popular Culture.* Cambridge: MIT Press.
———. 1996. "*I Hear You with my Eyes:* or, The Invincible Master." In *Gaze and Voice as Love Objects*, edited by Renata Salecl and Slavoj Žižek, 90–127. Durham, NC: Duke University Press.
———. 2002. *Welcome to the Desert of the Real.* London: Verso.
———. 2007. *How to Read Lacan.* New York: Norton.
———. 2008a. *The Plague of Fantasies.* London: Verso.
———. 2008b. *The Sublime Object of Ideology.* London: Verso.
———. 2008c. *The Ticklish Subject: The Absent Center of Political Ontology.* London: Verso.

Filmography

Allégret, Marc. 1934. *Zouzou*. Les Films H. Roussillon, France. VHS.
Allouache, Merzak. 1994. *Bab-El Oued City*. Flash Back Audiovisuel, Algeria. DVD.
Bekolo, Jean-Pierre. 1992. *Quartier Mozart*. Kola Case Production, Cameroon. VHS.
———. 1996. *Aristotle's Plot*. JBA Production, France/Zimbabwe. DVD.
Boughedir, Férid. 1983. *Caméra d'Afrique*. Kino International, Tunisia. Netflix.
Chikly, Chemam. 1924. *The Girl from Carthage*. Museum of Cinema, Tunisia. 16 mm.
Cissé, Souleymane. 1987. *Yeelen*. CNC, Mali. DVD.
Diop, Mati. 2013. *Mille soleils*. Anna Sanders Films, France/Senegal. 35mm.
Diop, Mambety Djibril. 1968. *Contras' City*. Studio Kankourama, Senegal. DVD.
———. 1970. *Badou Boy*. Studio Kankourama, Senegal. VHS.
———. 1973. *Touki Bouki*. Trigon Film, Senegal. DVD.
———. 1992. *Hyènes*. ADR Productions/Maag Daan, Senegal/France/Switzerland. DVD.
———. 1989. *Parlons grand-mère*. Matthias-Film, Burkina Faso. 16 mm.
———. 1994. *Le franc*. Waka Films, Senegal. DVD.
———. 1998. *La petite vendeuse de soleil*. Waka Films, Senegal. DVD.
Drabo, Adama. 1996. *Taafe Fanga*. Atriascop, Mali. VHS.
Eisenstein, Sergei. 1925. *Battleship Potemkin*. Goskino, USSR. DVD.
———. 1925. *Strike*. Goskino, USSR. DVD.
Faye, Safi. 1975. *Kaddu beykat*. Safi Films, Senegal. 16 mm.
———. 1979. *Fad'jal*. Safi Films, Senegal. 35 mm.
———. 1996. *Mossane*. Muss Cinématographie Dakar, Senegal/France. DVD.
Franju, Georges. 1949. *Le sang des bêtes*. Forces et Voix de la France, France. DVD.
Gaye, Dyana. 2006. *Deweneti*. Andolfi Production, Senegal. YouTube.
Gerima, Haile. 1993. *Sankofa*. Ghana National Commission, USA/Ghana. VHS.
Godard, Jean-Luc. 1960. *A bout de souffle*. Les Films Impéria, France. DVD.
———. 1963. *Le Mépris*. Les Films Concordia, France. DVD.
———. 1965. *Pierrot le fou*. SNC, France. DVD.
———. 1967. *Week-end*. Les Films Copernic, France. DVD.
———. 1967. *2 ou 3 choses que je sais d'elle*. Argos Films, France. DVD.
———. 1967. *La Chinoise*. Athos Films, France. DVD.
Hall, Stuart. 1997. *Race the Floating Signifier*. Media Education Foundation, USA, VHS.
Haroun, Mahamat-Saleh. 2002. *Abouna*. Arte France Cinéma, France/Chad. DVD.
Hitchcock, Alfred. 1960. *Psycho*. Shamley Productions, USA. DVD.
———. 1963. *The Birds*. Alfred J. Hitchcock Productions, USA. DVD.
———. 1964. *Marnie*. Alfred J. Hitchcock Productions, USA. DVD.
Kaboré, Gaston. 1982. *Wend Kuuni*. Direction du Cinéma de Haute Volta, Burkina Faso. VHS.
Lamorisse, Albert. 1956. *The Red Balloon*. Films Montsouris, France. DVD.
Lee, Spike. 1989. *Do the Right Thing*. 40 Acres & A Mule Filmworks, USA. DVD.

Ouédraogo, Idrissa. 1989. *Yaaba*. Arcadia Films, Burkina Faso. 35 mm.
——. 1990. *Tilai*. COF/BBC, Burkina Faso/UK. 35 mm.
Pontecorvo, Gillo. 1966. *La battaglia di Algeri*. Casbah Film, Italy/Algeria. 35 mm.
Ramaka, Joseph Gaï. 2001. *Karmen Geï*. Arte France Cinéma, France/Senegal. DVD.
Ruttmann, Walther. 1927. *Berlin: Symphony of a Great City*. Deutsche Vereins-Film, Germany. 35 mm.
Sauvage, André. 1928. *Etudes sur Paris*. Carlotta Films, France. DVD.
Schlesinger, John. 1969. *Midnight Cowboy*. Florin Productions, USA. DVD.
Sembène, Ousmane. 1963. *Borom Sarret*. Doomireew Films, Senegal. DVD.
——. 1966. *La noire de . . . .* Doomireew Films, France/Senegal. DVD.
——. 1968. *Mandabi*. Doomireew Films, France/Senegal. DVD.
——. 1971. *Emitai*. Doomireew Films, Senegal. 35 mm.
——. 1975. *Xala*. Doomireew Films, Senegal. DVD.
——. 1988. *Camp de Thiaroye*. Doomireew/ENAPROC, Senegal. DVD.
——. 1992. *Guelwaar*. Doomireew Films/France 3, Senegal. 35 mm.
——. 2001. *Faat Kiné*. Doomireew Films, Senegal. DVD.
——. 2004. *Moolaadé*. Doomireew Films, Senegal/Burkina Faso. DVD.
Sissako, Abderrahmane. 1998. *La vie sur terre*. Haut et court, Mali/France. DVD.
——. 2006. *Bamako*. Archipel 33, Mali. DVD.
Sissoko, Cheick Oumar. 1990. *Finzan*. Kora Films, Mali/Germany. 35 mm.
Touré, Moussa. 1991. *Toubab Bi*. Cinémathèque Afrique, Senegal/France. 35 mm.
——. 1997. *TGV*. Les Films du crocodile, Senegal. 35 mm.
——. 2012. *La Pirogue*. Arte France Cinéma, Senegal. DVD.
Truffaut, François. 1959. *Les 400 coups*. Films du Carosse, France. DVD.
——. 1968. *La mariée était en noir*. Films du Carosse, France. DVD.
Varda, Agnès. 1962. *Cléo de 5 à 7*. Ciné Tamaris, France. DVD.
Vertov, Dziga. 1929. *The Man With a Movie Camera*. VUFKU, USSR. 35 mm.
Vieyra, Paulin. 1955. *Afrique-sur-Seine*. Groupe Africain, France. 16 mm.
Welles, Orson. 1941. *Citizen Kane*. RKO Radio Pictures, USA. DVD.
——. 1942. *The Magnificent Ambersons*. Mercury Productions, USA. 35 mm.

Index

Page numbers in italics refer to figures.

acousmatic panopticon, 2, 34, 36, 38, 77, 171, *182*, 191; manifestations of, 52, 66, 94, 101, 103, 139, 148, 152; space and, 107, 142, 144–145, 177
acousmêtre, 87, 152, 156, 160, 164, 198; definition of, 35–37. *See also* voice
adaptation, 19, 39, 43, 106–107, 125–126. *See also* theater
Adesokan, Akin, 63, 199, 206n22
alienation, 85, 127–130, 153, 158, 195–196. *See also* distanciation; theater
Allegory of the Cave, 204n50
Althusser, Louis, 168–169, 173, 202n19
Altman, Rick, 21–22, 53–54, 139–140, 212n28
Artaud, Antonin, 106, 127, 129–130, 191, 203n37
Astruc, Alexandre, 18–19, 91, 203n34, 206n2
audience, fourth wall, 175–179
auteur, 2, 9, 85, 179, 190, 198, 201n8, 207n26; concept of, 18–20, 125; Mambety and, 4, 6–8, 17–18, 43–44, 97, 145, 152. *See also* French New Wave; Second Cinema
authenticity, African cinema, 8–9, 194, 198

Baker, Josephine, 24, 63–65, 67–68, 205n15, 211n6
Barber, Karin, 13
Barlet, Olivier, 13, 43, 154
Barthes, Roland, 51–52, 122, 126
Baudelaire, Charles, 26, 57, 75, 83, 85
Baudry, Jean-Louis, 140
Bazin, André, 2, 18–19, 23, 38, 46, 131, 140, 192
Bekolo, Jean-Pierre, 212n21
Bekolo, Jean-Pierre, works by: *Aristotle's Plot*, 212n1; *Quartier Mozart*, 14
Belton, John, 21
Benjamin, Walter, 53, 128; flaneur and, 84–87
Bhabha, Homi, 10, 32, 202n21
Boughedir, Férid, works by: *Caméra d'Afrique*, 192
Brecht, Bertolt, 6, 106, 191; theater and, 127–129. *See also* distanciation

caméra-flâneur, 26, 76, 84, 93, 99, 154, 171, 191, 210n18; definition of, 87–88. *See also* flaneur
capitalism, 29, 53, 193
Caruth, Cathy, 110
Catholicism, 207n23
Césaire, Aimé, 206n17
Césaire, Aimé, works by: *Cahier d'un retour au pays natal*, 67
Chabrol, Claude, 18
Cham, Mbye B., 8
Chamoiseau, Patrick, 88, 95, 109
Chanan, Michael, 10
Chaplin, Charlie, 144, 151, 209n14, 211n2
Chion, Michel, 41, 46, 52, 55–56, 75, 80, 140, 155–156, 159, 177; acousmêtre and, 35–36, 198; audiovisual counterpoint, 23–25, 54, 176; voice and, 161–164, 167
chora, 163–164, 211n15
cinéma-vérité, 40, 76–77, 92
Cissé, Souleymane, works by: *Yeleen*, 15
classical Hollywood cinema, 4, 16, 32, 58, 82. *See also* First Cinema
colonialism, 16, 26, 78, 83, 111, 113, 158; Fanon and, 134, 195; traces of, 11, 96, 108. *See also* neocolonialism; postcolonialism

Conley, Tom, 77–79, 93, 99, 101, 159, 161, 166, 206n6

Dakar, Senegal, 3, 11, 31, 35, 38–39, 42, 58, 89–93, 101, 115, 138, 177, 199–200; *Badou Boy* and, 26, 104, 208n31; *Contras' City* and, 40, 55, 76–78, 87, 91, 96; *Le franc*, 147, 152, 160; Gorée Island and, 38, 66, 108, 157; *Hyènes*, 122, 142; map of, 74–78; markets of, 57, 86, 94, 96; *La petite vendeuse de soleil* and, 164–166, 168–169; Sembène and, 66–67, 74, 91, 195, 199; *Touki Bouki* and, 50, 68; urban space of, 81–82, 84, 88, 95, 122
Davis, Wade, 108–110, 118
de-acousmatization, 36, 103, 155, 171. *See also* acousmêtre; voice
De Certeau, Michel, 25, 27, 56
Deleuze, Gilles, 20, 29–30, 37, 39, 175–178, 206n1; islands and, 138, 155; maps and, 75, 79
Descartes, René, 27–28, 117, 204n43
Diawara, Manthia, 9, 17, 35, 79, 94, 196, 198, 203n31, 204n49, 205n7; categories of, 12–14, 203n28, 205n5
distanciation, 128. *See also* alienation; theater
Diop, Mati, 199
Diop, Mati, works by: *Mille soleils*, 200
Diop, Wasis, 20, 115, 170, 199
Doane, Mary Ann, 15, 30, 33–34, 39, 211n5
Dolar, Mladen, 30, 36, 155, 162, 167, 171, 173, 210n20
Drabo, Adamo, works by: *Taafe Fanga*, 14

Ebron, Paulla, 20, 31–32, 43, 59, 203n30, 204n49
Eisenstein, Sergei, 4, 32, 45, 48, 50, 191, 205n7; sound and, 22–23
Eisenstein, Sergei, works by: *Battleship Potemkin*, 61; *Strike*, 44, 205n6
Elliott, Kamilla, 125–126

Fanon, Frantz, 8–10, 30–31, 45, 110–111, 118, 161–162, 173, 195, 197, 204n47; colonialism and, 76–77, 83, 100, 134

fantastical gap, 30, 146, 149, 157, 160, 167, 179, 208n29, 210n1. *See also* music; soundtrack; voice
fantasy, 20, 24, 30, 33, 48, 68, 72, 98–99, 105, 107, 114, 117, 126, 147, 152, 169, 199; postcolonial, 3, 50, 61, 63–64, 66, 137–139; psychoanalytical dimension of, 130–131, 133–139, 159, 163; space of, 34, 39, 104, 108, 144, 177. *See also* fetish; objet petit a; psychoanalysis
Faye, Safi, 18, 162, 192
Faye, Safi, works by: *Fad'jal*, 194; *Kaddu beykat*, 194; *Mossane*, 15, 191, 193–194
feminism, 15, 206n20
fetish, 12, 34, 50–51, 64, 96, 120, 134, 170, 205n9, 209n13; island as, 66–67; voice as, 36, 155, 161, 171. *See also* fantasy; objet petit a; psychoanalysis
First Cinema, 4, 32, 201n7, 201n8. *See also* classical Hollywood; Second Cinema; Third Cinema
flaneur, 26, 40, 57, 72, 74–75, 77, 98, 102–103, 105, 107, 135, 152, 154; definition of, 83–87. *See also* caméra-flâneur
Foucault, Michel, 38, 139, 191; panopticon of, 2, 35–37, 107, 137, 145
fragmentation, 47, 144, 192, 195; city and, 53, 57, 77; narrative, 5, 56, 107, 128
French New Wave, 4–5, 17–21, 43–44, 69, 85; radio and, 152. *See also* auteur; Second Cinema
Freud, Sigmund, 21, 34, 114, 134–135, 138, 162, 208n5; ego and, 30, 39; unconscious and, 131–133

Gabriel, Teshome, 9–10, 12, 14, 16, 25, 45, 79, 203n28, 204n41
Genette, Gérard, 53–54, 147
Genova, James, 11, 82, 193, 210n19, 210n29, 213n3
Gerima, Haile, works by: *Sankofa*, 108, 209n12, 210n2
Getino, Octavio, 7
Givanni, June, 38, 208n28
Godard, Jean-Luc, 4–6, 17–19, 48, 65, 70, 82, 90, 92–93, 96–97, 104, 145, 153, 175, 179, 191, 195, 202n12, 212n27

Godard, Jean-Luc, works by: *Breathless*, 32, 42, 69–71, 87, 204n2, 210n16; *La Chinoise*, 89; *Contempt*, 18, 83, 203n33, 207n18; *Pierrot le fou*, 94, 152; *Two or Three Things I Know About Her*, 17–18, 91, 93, 122, 152; *Weekend*, 17, 83, 203n32
Gorbman, Claudia, 97, 145, 147–148, 206n2
Gorée Island, 66–67, 107, 114, 117, 124, 136–138, 155, *181*, 199, 210n24; geographical position of, 38, 108, 119, 152, 157, 209n11, 210n22
griots, 43, 193
Guneratne, Anthony R., 10, 12, 201n8

Hall, Stuart, 16, 31
Harrow, Kenneth, 7, 17, 34, 114, 118–119, 137, 194, 201n5, 202n10, 202n16, 208n27, 209n10, 209n11, 210n22, 213n6; authenticity and, 9; postmodernism and, 197–198
Harvey, David, 84, 207n9
Hegarty, Paul, 178
Hitchcock, Alfred, 18–19, 22, 126, 156, 207n26, 211n12
Hitchcock, Alfred, works by: *The Birds*, 46; *Marnie*, 206n16; *Psycho*, 44
Hondo, Med, 192–193
hybridity, 6–7, 10, 12, 20, 135

ideology, 7, 9, 15, 18, 82, 164, 168, 174
Islam, 51–52, 55, 95; Muslims and, 17, 49, 55, 100

Kaboré, Gaston, works by: *Wend Kuuni*, 15
Kant, Immanuel, 24, 28, 204n43
kora, 1, 31–32, 99, 101–102, 104, 156, *183*, *184*, 211n15
Kouyaté, Dani, 170
Kracauer, Siegfried, 23–24, 53, 131
Kuleshov effect, 23–24, 54, 64
Kristeva, Julia, 163

Lacan, Jacques, 39, 67, 112–115, 133, 156, 159, 162, 191; fantasy and, 133–139; mirror stage and, 34, 132, 168
LaCapra, Dominick, 111, 209n6
Lang, Fritz, 18

Larkin, Brian, 11, 202n24
Lee, Spike, works by: *Do the Right Thing*, 212n21
Lefebvre, Henri, 28–29, 56, 75, 84
Leibniz, Wilhelm Gottfried, 27–28, 176–177
LGBTQ, 69, 206n22
Lyotard, Jean-François, 21

Mambety, Djibril Diop, 1–2, 9; auteur and, 18, 20, 44, 83, 97, 145; biography of, 3–4, 39, 155, 157–158, 208n28; filmmaking approach, 5–6, 10, 12, 16, 18–19, 21, 47, 49, 59, 61, 67, 71, 87, 140, 170, 191; music and, 31, 63, 65, 99–100, 115, 145, 147, 170; sound and, 7, 11, 13–14, 22, 26, 29, 33, 35, 37–39, 41, 46, 51, 77, 90, 113, 139, 193–194; space and, 30, 75, 82, 93, 159, 162; Wolof and, 17, 79, 203n31
Mambety, Djibril Diop, works by: *Badou Boy*, 3, 26, 39–40, 52, 74, 76, 82, 85, 92, 98–105, 153, 161, 171, *183*, *184*, 191, 208n28, 208n31, 211n2; *Contras' City*, 3, 5, 26, 39–40, 52, 55, 74, 76–77, 79, 82, 87–89, 91–92, 96–98, 101–102, 108, 122, 141, 154, 158, 160, *181*, *182*; *Le Franc*, 1, 40, 144, 147–148, 153–154, 158–159, 165–166, 171–173, *187*, *188*; *Hyènes*, 4, 39–40, 66, 72, 92, 98, 106–107, 110–112, 115, 117–118, 120, 128–131, 136–137, 141, 143, 166, *184*, *185*, *186*; *Parlons grand-mère*, 197; *La petite vendeuse de soleil*, 7, 31, 34–35, 40, 42, 50, 55, 68, 97–98, 101, 107, 144, 147, 153, 163–165, 170, 174, 179, *188*, *189*, 199, 210n17; *Touki Bouki*, 6–7, 24, 26, 33, 39–44, 46, 49–50, 52–53, 56, 62–63, 66–68, 70–71, 73, 78, 87, 93, 98, 100, 102, 104, 106, 115, 117, 123, 130–132, 134, 136, 138, 159, 163–164, *180*, *181*, 196, 200, 202n10
maps, 36, 51, 56, 75–78, 80–83, 86, 88, 93, 95, 101, 150, 154, 159, 166, *181*, 191, 206n5, 206n6, 209n14; aural, 26, 39, 102, 149; mental, 51, 53, 80–81, 102; *Xala* and, 78–79, 193
Marker, Chris, 18
Marxism, 3, 8, 106, 115, 142, 168, 210n29

Merleau-Ponty, Maurice, 28
Metz, Christian, 46, 140, 203n34
Murphy, David, 3, 31, 34, 42–43, 47, 49, 68, 198, 200, 201n5, 203n32, 204n48, 206n19, 206n22, 207n23, 210n19, 210n29
music, 13, 20–21, 23, 26, 30–32, 38, 49, 59–60, 63–65, 83, 127, 128–129, 144–148, 150–151, 157, 159, 164–165, 171–172, 174, 176, 178, 198, 200, 203n30, 203n35, 206n1, 208n2; anempathetic, 24, 65, 141; auteurism and, 97, 145; diegetic, 30, 107, 144, 146–148, 154; empathetic, 23–24, 63, 118, 141; jazz, 31, 59, 71, 148–149, 171; nondiegetic, 30, 35, 45, 47, 65, 72, 89–90, 96–100, 107, 113, 115, 123, 140–148, 162, 208n29. *See also* fantastical gap; radio; sound; voice

narrative, 1, 5–6, 9, 13–14, 22–23, 26–27, 35, 40, 42–43, 45–46, 48–49, 61, 68, 88, 104–109, 119, 123, 190; aural planes (sound) and, 1–2, 7, 11, 25, 30, 33, 38–39, 41, 51, 53, 73, 75–77, 101–102, 127, 132, 138, 146–147, 159, 191, 193, 200, 210n28; classic Hollywood, 34, 58, 62; folk stories and, 144, 203n32; fragmentation and, 5, 53, 149; Genette and, 53–54; music and, 31, 64, 141–143, 145, 148, 194; space and, 83, 99, 144; voice and, 15, 36, 91–92, 174–175, 197
Negritude, 8, 31, 79, 97, 204n48
neocolonialism, 11, 26, 70, 89, 91, 100, 134; postcolonialism and, 16. *See also* colonialism; postcolonialism
Niang, Sada, 3, 5, 55, 57, 67, 82, 89–90; *Badou Boy* and, 208n28; *Le franc* and, 158; *Hyènes* and, 106–107, 120, 124; *Touki Bouki* and, 7, 42–43, 48, 53, 57, 69, 72, 205n10
Nietzsche, Friedrich, 111, 121, 123–124

objet petit a, 66, 133–134, 136–138, 156, 159–160, 177, 205n9. *See also* fantasy; fetish; psychoanalysis
orality (oral), 13, 25, 38, 45, 88, 94–95, 99, 107, 144, 164, 168, 172–173, 190–191, 194, 198, 203n32; sound and, 13, 17, 33, 39; tales and, 1–2, 13, 37, 40, 42, 44, 165, 170
Ouédraogo, Idrissa, works by: *Tilai*, 15; *Yaaba*, 197
Oyěwùmí, Oyèrónké, 15

Penley, Constance, 133
Pfaff, Françoise, 3, 11, 26, 42, 49, 70, 78, 96–97, 195
Pontecorvo, Gillo, 17
Pontecorvo, Gillo, works by: *The Battle of Algiers*, 8
postcolonialism, 2, 4, 8–11, 14–17, 21, 67, 84, 89, 106–108, 133, 146, 160–161, 164, 190–193, 198, 212n1; city (Dakar) and, 39–40, 76, 81, 87–88, 105, 171; fantasy and, 3, 50, 61, 63–64, 66, 137–139; space and, 10–11, 34–38, 57, 77, 80–83, 107, 142, 145, 160, 192, 212n1; subject and, 26, 30, 34, 42, 48, 74–76, 83, 110, 112–113, 115, 117, 133, 137, 144, 153, 159, 195, 197. *See also* colonialism; neocolonialism
posters, 77, 83, 93, 96, 116, 122, 150, 154–155, 158–160, 173, 186, 211n2; Sembène and, 151, 207n26, 209n14
psychoanalysis, 30, 34, 39, 161, 208n5. *See also* fantasy; fetish; objet petit a

radio, 11–12, 103, 147, 171–172, 192, 195, 202n24, 202n25, 212n1; acousmatic panopticon as, 35, 152–154
Ramaka, Joseph Gai, works by: *Karmen Geï*, 114, 210n24
Resnais, Alain, 18
Rivette, Jacques, 18
Rohmer, Eric, 18
Rosolato, Guy, 162–163
Rossellini, Roberto, 6, 159
Rouch, Jean, 77, 194
Ruttmann, Walter, works by: *Berlin: Symphony of a Great City*, 26

Said, Edward, 10, 81–82, 96; orientalism and, 82, 100, 124, 191
Sauvage, André, works by: *Etudes sur Paris*, 26
Scarry, Elaine, 120–121

Second Cinema, 6–7, 16–18, 32, 82, 201n8, 202n21. *See also* auteur; French New Wave; First Cinema; Third Cinema
Sembène, Ousmane, 4, 9, 14, 17, 34, 47, 64, 75, 79, 94, 102, 122, 162, 191–193, 195–196, 198, 202n16, 203n31, 204n48, 205n17, 207n26, 210n19; sound and, 96–97, 194
Sembène, Ousmane, works of: *Borom Sarret*, 74, 91, 212n2; *Camp de Thiaroye*, 89, 210n26; *Emitai*, 96, 209n14; *Faat Kiné*, 67, 191, 195, 209n14; *Guelwaar*, 62, 207n16, 209n13, 213n4; *La noire de . . .* (film), 64, 74, 91, 93, 205n9, 207n20, 209n14; *La noire de . . .* (short story), 66; *Mandabi*, 49; *Moolaadé*, 14, 191; *Xala*, 50, 58, 67, 78–79, 97, 130, 199, 203n32, 207n20, 209n14
Sene, Nar, 6, 17, 41, 59, 113, 141, 155, 166, 201n4, 208n1
Senegal (Senegalese), 3–5, 8, 12, 35, 38, 40, 48–50, 58, 61–63, 66–71, 108, 130, 138, 142, 148, 157, 163–165, 168–170, 190, 192, 196, 199, 202n25, 202n27, 203n31, 205n9, 206n22, 207n23, 212n24; audience and, 178; France and, 17, 71, 78–79, 89, 117, 164; postcolonialism and, 2, 4, 11, 76, 153, 161
Senghor, Léopold Sédar, 12, 24, 59, 89, 93, 190, 204n47, 204n49; Negritude and, 31, 79, 97; Wolof/French and, 161, 172, 203n31
Shohat, Ella, 16
Silverman, Kaja, 5–6, 15, 30, 39, 44, 46, 128–129, 134, 161–163, 174, 194, 211n14
Sissako, Abderrahmane, works by: *Bamako*, 212n1; *La vie sur terre*, 15, 17, 62, 162, 206n17, 211n14
Sissoko, Cheick Oumar, works by: *Finzan*, 14
Smith, Jeff, 147–148
Solanas, Fernando, 7
Sonic jump cut, 104, 191
Sonic rack focus, 39, 46, 50–51, 60, 64, 100, 102, 149, 171, 191
Sonic space, 27–30, 32–33, 39, 48, 175

sound, 1–2, 4–5, 7, 14, 17, 26, 32–39, 41–65, 69–71, 80, 82–83, 95–97, 101, 128, 139–140, 145–148, 153–155, 160, 165, 171, 175–179, 190–191, 193–194, 197–200, 203n39, 212n28; asynchronous, 23, 29; diegetic, 27, 29–30, 35, 39, 48, 60, 103–104, 107, 113, 142, 144, 146–150, 171, 177, 204n46; extradiegetic, 1, 26, 30, 33, 48, 65, 99, 102–104, 146, 151, 204n46, 208n29; intradiegetic, 30, 65, 146, 148, 171, 204n46, 208n29; materiality (space) of, 13, 21, 27–30, 105, 127; nondiegetic, 29–30, 35, 39, 60, 65, 72, 100, 103–105, 107, 141–142, 144, 146–147, 150, 152, 157, 160, 162, 175, 194, 197, 199, 204n46, 208n29; postsynchronous, 66, 90, 99, 141; primary narrative, 1–2, 11, 73, 75, 77, 102, 205n8, 210n28; spectral, 40, 107, 113, 142–143, 151, 155–156, 211n3; synchronous, 29, 140; theory of, 21–25, 131–133, 140–141. *See also* music; soundtrack; voice
soundtrack, 1, 30, 33, 36, 47–52, 90–93, 95, 98–105, 113, 148, 150, 153, 155–156, 158, 161, 167, 171, 174, 179, 193–194, 197; music and, 77, 89, 91, 96–97, 101, 103, 123, 140–143, 145–146, 149, 151, 157, 170, 172, 177, 199–200, 208n29; theory of, 24–25; *Touki Bouki* and, 58–66, 69–71. *See also* fantastical gap; music; sound; voice
space. *See* acousmatic panopticon; Dakar, Senegal; fantasy; narrative; postcolonialism; sonic space
Stilwell, Robynn J., 146, 210n1
Sugnet, Charles, 13, 172, 201n5, 203n31, 212n18, 212n23

Taylor, Clyde, 4, 15, 202n9
theater, 3, 92–93, 106–107, 114, 125–130, 157, 203n37, 203n38. *See also* adaptation, alienation, distanciation
Third Cinema, 2–4, 6–10, 12, 14, 16, 21, 33, 201n8, 202n21, 204n41. *See also* First Cinema; Second Cinema
Touré, Moussa, works by: *La pirogue*, 192, 196–197; *TGV*, 192, 196; *Toubab bi*, 196

trauma, 39, 67, 106–115, 120–121, 123, 126, 132–134, 137–138, 141, 199, 208n5

Truffaut, François, 18–20, 22, 125–126

Truffaut, François, works by: *The Bride Wore Black*, 18; *The 400 Blows*, 17, 69–71, 211n2

Ukadike, Nwachukwu Frank, 2–4, 13, 17, 19, 40, 106, 201n5, 202n20, 203n31, 203n35, 203n36

Varda, Agnès, 18, 153, 195

Varda, Agnès, works by: *Cléo from 5 to 7*, 152, 211n6

Vertov, Dziga, 6

Vertov, Dziga, works by: *Man With a Movie Camera*, 26, 87

voice, 5, 17, 24–25, 30, 39–40, 63–65, 101–104, 118, 123, 140–141, 143–144, 148–160, 167, 171–175, 194, 202n22; directors', 90–91, 174; feminist theory and, 15, 34–36, 161, 164, 194, 211n5, 211n14. *See also* acousmêtre; de-acousmatization; fantastical gap; fetish; music; narrative; sound; soundtrack; voice-over

voice-over, 17, 30, 35, 39, 91, 108, 163, 179, 194, 197, 211n14; *Badou Boy* and, 101, 104; *Contras' City* and, 55, 79, 90–91, 96; *Le franc* and, 152; *La petite vendeuse desoleil*, 174–175; *Touki Bouki* and, 65. *See also* voice

Wade, Abdoulaye, 195

Welles, Orson, 18, 23, 29, 194

Welles, Orson, works by: *Citizen Kane*, 89–90; *The Magnificent Ambersons*, 91

Westerns (films), 98–99, 103, 116, 208n28

Willemen, Paul, 6–8, 12, 14, 16, 31, 81

Willey, Ann Elizabeth, 170, 172, 196–197, 201n5

Williams, Patrick, 3, 31, 43, 47, 68, 198, 200, 201n4, 201n5, 203n32, 204n48, 206n19, 206n22

Wolof, 17, 43, 79, 91, 167, 172, 192, 201n1, 203n31, 212n18

Wynchank, Anny, 153, 165

Zacks, Stephen, 8

Žižek, Slavoj, 34, 36, 54, 75, 90, 112–115, 129, 156, 167–169, 204n45, 209n8, 209n10, 211n3, 212n26; fantasy and, 133–137, 139; objet petit a and, 66, 136, 156, 205n9, 206n16; (spectral) sound and, 143, 147, 151, 156

zombie, 39–40, 106–110, 112–114, 116–117, 119, 124, 135, 210n21, 212n25

VLAD DIMA is Assistant Professor in French Studies with a specialty in African cinema at the University of Wisconsin–Madison. He received his doctorate in 2010 from the University of Minnesota–Twin Cities. He has published numerous articles on French and francophone cinemas, Hollywood, television studies, and literary studies.

www.ingramcontent.com/pod-product-compliance
Lightning Source LLC
Chambersburg PA
CBHW050441240426
43661CB00055B/2465